X Window System
User's Guide

Volume Three

X Window System
User's Guide

---

for Version 11 of the
X Window System

by Tim O'Reilly, Valerie Quercia, and Linda Lamb

O'Reilly & Associates, Inc.

Table of Contents

List of Figures

List of Tables

Preface

By convention, a preface describes the book itself, while the introduction describes the subject matter. You should read through the preface to get an idea of how the book is organized, the conventions it follows, and so on.

In This Chapter:

Preface

The *X Window System User's Guide* describes window system concepts and the application programs (clients) commonly distributed with Version 11, Release 2 of the X Window System.

Assumptions

This book assumes that X has already been installed on your system, and that all clients are available. In addition, although X runs on many different types of systems, this book assumes that you are running it on a UNIX system, and that you have basic familiarity with UNIX. If you are not using UNIX, you will still find the book useful—UNIX dependencies are not that widespread—but you may occasionally need to translate a command example into its equivalent on your system. The book also assumes that you are using a 3-button mouse, and that the operation of the window manager is controlled by the *default.uwmrc* file from the MIT X11 distribution (if this is not the case, the book provides information that will allow you to understand how *uwm* is configured on your system).

This book has been written for both first time and experienced users of the X Window System. First-time users should read the book in order, starting with Chapter 1.

Experienced users can use this book as a reference for the client programs detailed here. Since there is great flexibility with X, even frequent users need to check on the syntax and availability of options. Reference pages for each client detail command-line options, customization database (resource database) variables, and other detailed information.

Organization

The book contains the following parts:

Part One: Using X

Preface
Describes the book's assumptions, audience, and organization, and the conventions used in the book.

Chapter 1: An Introduction to the X Window System
Describes the basic terminology associated with the X Window System: server, client, window, etc. The clients described in the book and the chapters that describe them are listed.

Chapter 2: Getting Started
Shows the basics of using X: starting the server and creating the first terminal window; starting the window manager; adding additional windows; exiting. This chapter is tutorial in nature: you can follow along at a workstation as you read.

Chapter 3: Using the Window Manager
Describes how to use the *uwm* window manager. This client is used to manage multiple windows on the screen.

Chapter 4: The xterm Terminal Emulator
Describes how to use the *xterm* Terminal Emulator, the most frequently-used client. Certain aspects of *xterm* operation described in this chapter, such as scrolling and ''copy and paste,'' are common to other applications as well.

Chapter 5: Other Clients
Gives an overview of other clients available on X.

Part Two: Customizing X

Chapter 6: Command Line Options
Discusses some of the command line options that are common to most clients.

Chapter 7: Setting Application Defaults
Tells how to use the *Xdefaults* file to set defaults for client applications, and how to use *xrdb* (which saves you having to maintain multiple *Xdefaults* files if you run clients on multiple machines).

Chapter 8: Customizing the Window Manager
Describes the *.uwmrc* file by showing the default file shipped by MIT, and then examining the purpose and syntax of entries. A revised *.uwmrc* file is also offered for users to copy.

Chapter 9: Setup Clients
Describes how to set display and keyboard preferences using *xset* and how to set root window preferences using *xsetroot*. Demonstrates how to redefine the logical keynames recognized by X using *xmodmap*.

Part Three: Client Reference Manual

Extended reference pages for all clients.

Part Four: Appendices

Licensing Information

This manual has been designed for licensing and customization by manufacturers or distributors of systems supporting X11. As of this writing, it has been licensed by Masscomp, Graphic Software Systems, and Sony Microsystems. For information on licensing, call O'Reilly & Associates, Inc. at 617-527-4210, or send e-mail to tim@ora.UU.NET.

Acknowlegements

This manual is based in part on three previous X Window System user's guides, one from Masscomp, which was written by Jeff Graber, one from Sequent Computer Systems, Inc., and one from Graphic Software Systems, Inc., which were written by Candis Condo (supported by the UNIX development group). Some of Jeff's and Candis's material in turn was based on material developed under the auspices of Project Athena at MIT.

The reference pages in Part Three have been adapted from reference pages copyright © 1988 the Massachusetts Institute of Technology, or from reference pages produced by Graphic Software Systems. Refer to the **Authors** section at the end of each reference page for details.

Permission to use these materials is gratefully acknowledged.

Special thanks is given to Edie Freedman, whose cover design helped pull the X Window System Series together. Her advice and patience were invaluable.

We'd also like to thank others on the staff at O'Reilly & Associates who helped significantly with the book. Adrian Nye and Linda Mui helped to test the examples; Daniel Gilly, Kate Gibson, Sue Willing, and Tom Scanlon helped with the final production. Peter Mui indexed the book. We'd also like to thank Jim Fulton of the MIT X Consortium for his comments on the book.

Despite the efforts of these people, the standard authors' disclaimer applies: any errors that remain are our own.

Font and Character Conventions

The following typographic conventions are used in this book.

Italics   are used for:

  • new terms where they are defined.

  • file and directory names, and command and client names when they appear in the body of a paragraph.

`Courier`   is used within the body of the text to show:

  • command lines or options that should be typed verbatim on the screen.

  is used within examples to show:

  • computer-generated output.

  • the contents of files.

`Courier bold`   is used within examples to show command lines and options that should be typed verbatim on the screen.

`Courier italics`   are used within examples or explanations of command syntax to show a parameter to a command that requres context-dependent substitution (such as a variable). For example, *`filename`* means to use some appropriate filename; *`option(s)`* means to use some appropriate option(s) to the command.

Helvetica   is used to show menu titles and options.

The following symbols are used within the *X Window System User's Guide*:

[ ]   surround an optional field in a command line or file entry.

$ is the standard prompt from the Bourne shell, *sh*(1).

%   is the standard prompt from the C shell, *csh*(1).

name(1)   is a reference to a command called *name* in Section 1 of the *UNIX Reference Manual* (which may have a different name depending on which version of UNIX you use).

Part One:
Using X

Part One provides an overview of the X Window System and concepts, and describes how to use the most important programs available in the X environment.

An Introduction to the X Window System
Getting Started
Using the Window Manager
The xterm Terminal Emulator
Other Clients

1

An Introduction to the X Window System

This chapter provides an overview of the X Window System's client-server architecture, and briefly describes the most commonly used clients. It also defines some terms you are likely to encounter later in this book.

In This Chapter:

1
An Introduction
to the X Window System

The X Window System, called X for short, is a network-based graphics window system that was developed at MIT in 1984. Several versions of X have been developed, the most recent of which is X Version 11 (X11), first released in 1987.

X11 has been adopted as an industry-standard windowing system. X is supported by a consortium of industry leaders such as DEC, Hewlett-Packard, Sun, IBM, and AT&T that have united to direct, contribute to, and fund the continuing development of X. In addition to the system software development directed by the consortium, many independent developers are producing application software specifically for use with X. Because X11 is a relatively new standard, much of this application software has yet to be released.

X Architecture Overview

The X Window System architecture is divided into two distinct parts: *display servers* that provide display capabilities and keep track of user input, and *clients*, application programs that perform specific tasks.

This division within the X architecture allows the clients and the display server either to work together on the same system or to be separated over a network. For example, you might use a relatively low-powered PC or workstation as a display server to interact with clients that are running on a more powerful system. Even though the client program is actually runnning on the more powerful system, all user input and displayed output occur on the PC or workstation server and are communicated across the network using the X protocol. Figure 1-1 shows a diagram of such a network.

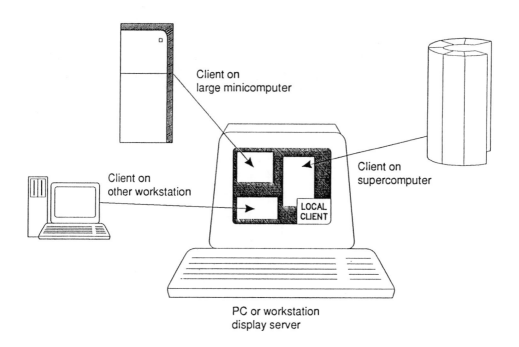

Figure 1-1. A sample X Window System configuration (Illustration courtesy of Sequent Computer Systems, Inc.)

The X Display Server

The X display server is a program that keeps track of all input coming from input devices such as the keyboard and mouse, and input from any other clients that are running. As the display server receives information from a client, it updates the appropriate window on your display. The display server may run on the same computer as a client or on an entirely different machine.

Servers are available for PCs, workstations, and even for special terminals, which may have the server partially in ROM.

Clients

X allows you to run many clients simultaneously. For example, you can run a database producing a pie-chart, display a menu of options, and run a text-editing session. While these programs may display their results and take input from a single display server, they may each be running on a different computer on the network. It is important to note that the same programs may not look and act the same on different servers since there is no standard user interface, since users can customize X clients differently on each server, and since the display hardware on each server may be different.

Several of the more frequently used client programs are discussed in the following paragraphs.

The Window Manager

A *window manager* is a client that allows you to specify the sizes and positions of windows on your display. The most popular window manager is *uwm* ("Universal Window Manager.") With *uwm* you can move and resize windows, rearrange the order of windows in the window stack, create additional windows, and convert windows into icons. *uwm* may also mandate a window layout policy. These functions are discussed in Chapter 2, *Getting Started*, and Chapter 3, *Using the Window Manager*.

In this book, we assume you are using *uwm*. If you are using a different window manager, or if the window manager has been customized at your site, many of the concepts should be the same. However, the actual procedures shown may well differ. See Chapter 8 for a discussion of how to customize *uwm*.

The xterm Terminal Emulator

X11 itself is designed to support only bitmapped graphics displays. For this reason, one of the most important clients is a terminal emulator. The terminal emulator brings up a window that allows you to log in to a multiuser system, and to run applications designed for use on a standard alphanumeric terminal. Anything you can do on a terminal, you can do in this window.

xterm is the most widely available terminal emulator. *xterm* emulates a DEC VT102 terminal or a Tektronix 4015 terminal. You can display both types of windows at the same time, but only one is active at a time.

Since you can bring up more than one *xterm* window at a time, you can run several programs at once. For example, you can have the system transfer files or process information while you focus your attention on a text-editing session. Multiple invocations of *xterm* provide the capability of displaying interactions in separate windows on your display. See Chapter 2, *Getting Started*, and Chapter 4, *The xterm Terminal Emulator*, for additional information.

Standalone Clients

The following is a brief list of some other clients commonly included with X.

xclock   displays the time of day continuously either in digital or analog form.

bitmap   allows you to change your pointers, icons, and background window pattern.

xcalc   provides a scientific calculator on your display.

xset   allows you to set various display and keyboard preferences, such as bell volume, cursor acceleration, screen saver operation, and so on.

xwd   dumps the contents of a window into a file.

xpr   translates an image file produced by *xwd* to PostScript®, suitable for printing on a PostScript laser printer.

xfd   displays the contents of a font on the screen.

For additional information on these and other clients, refer to Chapter 5, *Miscellaneous Clients*, and to the reference page for each client in Part Three of this manual. As more commercial and public-domain software is developed, many more specialized programs will become available.

Customizing Clients

Most X clients are designed to be customized by the user. A multitude of command-line options can be used to affect the operation of these clients. More conveniently, default values for each option can be stored in a file in your home directory called *Xdefaults*. If you are running clients on multiple machines, a program called *xrdb* (X resource database manager) allows you to store your defaults in the server so that you don't need to maintain an *Xdefaults* file on each machine.

There is a separate customization file for the window manager, called *.uwmrc*.

Client customization is described in Part Two of this manual.

Overview of Graphics Terminology

In the preceding discussion and throughout the rest of this manual, you will encounter terms that may not be familiar. The following list briefly discusses some of the most important terms. Many more terms are defined in Appendix G, *Glossary*.

windows   Rectangular regions on your display in which operations are performed. Windows often overlap each other much like sheets of paper on your desk or a stack of cards. This stack is often referred to as a stack of windows. Overlapping windows do not interfere with the process run in each window. You can reshuffle the windows, moving them to the front or the back of the other windows. The shaded area that fills the entire screen is called the *root* or *background* window. The window manager allows you to specify the sizes and positions of windows and icons on your display.

icons
Small symbols that represent windows but use little space on the display. Icons help keep your display uncluttered. You can label each icon to identify its content. The contents of the window are not visible when the window has been converted into an icon, but they are not lost. In fact, a client may continue to run whatever processes it was working on when you converted the window into an icon.

pointing device
A mouse or digitizer tablet with which you communicate information to the system. Most workstations use a 3-button mouse as the pointing device. When you slide the mouse around on your desktop, the pointer on the display follows or tracks the mouse movement. When you click a mouse button, the system performs an action.

cursor
The symbol on your display that tracks the position of the pointer and allows you to make selections in menus, size and position windows and icons, and select the window where you want to send your input. The cursor often changes shape as you move the pointer into different windows. A complete list is shown in Appendix B, *Standard Cursors*. Some of the most common cursor shapes are shown in Figure 1-2. Some applications allow you to select which cursor from this list to use.

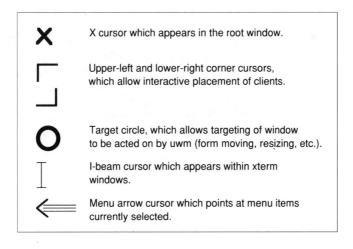

Figure 1-2. Some standard cursors

Even though the actual image on the screen is called a cursor, throughout this book we refer to "moving the pointer" to avoid confusion with the standard text cursor that can appear in an *xterm* window.

screen

In X, the terms *display* and *screen* are not equivalent. A display may consist of more than one screen. This feature might be implemented in several ways. There might be two physical monitors, linked to form a single display, as shown in Figure 1-3. Alternatively, two screens might be defined as different ways of using the same display. For example, on the Sun 3/110 color workstation, screen 0 is black and white, and screen 1 is color. By default, windows are always placed on screen 0, but you can "scroll" between the two screens with the mouse, or place a client window on screen 1 by specifying the screen number in the -display option when starting the client. (See Chapter 6 for more information on the -display option.)

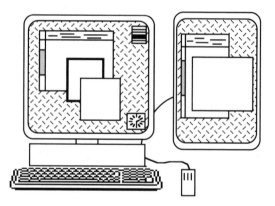

Figure 1-3. A display made up of two physical screens

2
Getting Started

This chapter provides a tutorial introduction to starting up the X server, the window manager, and the xterm *terminal emulator.*

In This Chapter:

2
Getting Started

This chapter shows the basics of using X: starting the server and creating the first terminal window; starting the window manager; adding additional windows; exiting. While it is written as a tutorial, you do not necessarily have to follow along at a workstation.

Before you can begin using the X Window System, you must do three things:

- Start the X server.

- Start at least one instance of the *xterm* terminal emulator.

- Start a window manager.

Depending on how X is installed, your workstation may automatically start the server and open up the first *xterm* window when the power is turned on. If this is the case, your screen should look something like Figure 2-1.

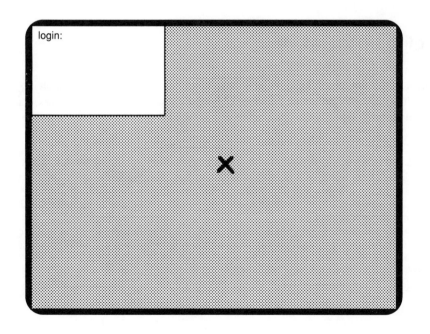

Figure 2-1. Workstation with xterm login window

Log in by typing your name and password at the prompts in the *xterm* window, just as if you were using a standard alphanumeric terminal. Skip to the section entitled *Bringing up the Window Manager*, later in this chapter.

If no windows are displayed on the workstation screen (i.e., if your login prompt appears on the full screen), log in, and read on. If another windowing system (such as SunWindows™) is running, first kill it, and then read on.

To start X manually, (using the standard X distribution from MIT), you must run a separate program for each of the three steps listed above:

% **xinit**   *Start the X server and create the first terminal window.*

% **uwm &**   *Start the window manager.*

% **xterm &**   *Start additional terminal windows.*

In many commercial distributions, these steps may be combined into one, and provided by a single program—called perhaps *xstart* or *startx*. (See your documentation for details.)

In the following discussion, we'll assume that you are bringing up the X Window System manually. In Appendix A, we'll show you how to set things up yourself so that it comes up automatically.

Note that X is very easy to customize. There are countless command options as well as startup files that control the way the screen looks or even what menus a program displays. If you are "trying out" X using someone else's system or login account, things may not work as described here. (See Chapters 6 through 9 for information on customizing the X environment.)

Bringing Up xterm

First, make sure that the X11 directory containing executable programs is in your search path*. If not, add the pathname */usr/bin/X11* to the path set in your *.profile* or *.login* file. Then, at the prompt type:

% **xinit**

xinit starts the X server, and creates the first *xterm* window in the upper-left corner of your display.† This *xterm* window is 80 columns across and 24 rows down in size and is called the

---

* For more information on how to set your search path, see Appendix A. Note that the appropriate pathname to add may be different in vendor distributions.

† If *xinit* produces a blank background, with no terminal window, software installation was not completed correctly. Reboot your workstation and try again. Before invoking *xinit*, look in the directory */usr/bin/X11* for a file whose name begins with a capital X, but otherwise has a similar name to your workstation (e.g. Xsun). When you find one that seems a likely possibility, try the following command:

% **xinit − −X***name*

If that works, link X*name* to X, and *xinit* will thereafter work correctly. For example:

% **cd /usr/bin/X11**
% **ln Xsun X**

login xterm window. The *xterm* window is surrounded by a background window called the *root window.* See Figure 2-2 below.

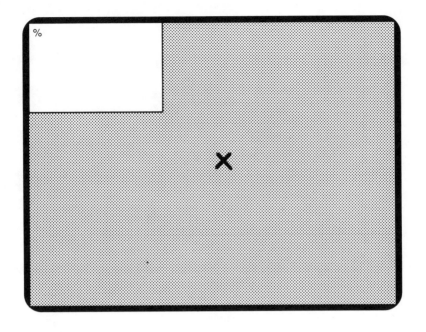

Figure 2-2. Login xterm window on the root window

Try moving the mouse. The pointer on your screen tracks or follows the mouse's movement. Notice what happens to the pointer and to the window borders as you move the pointer across the windows on your screen. If the pointer is in the root window, it looks like an "X". If the pointer is in the *xterm* window, it looks like an "I", and is commonly called an *I-beam cursor.* See Figure 2-3.

Notice that you can't type in the *xterm* window unless you place the pointer in that window. This is called *focusing.* Be sure that the pointer rests in the desired window before you begin typing. Note that the window border (if present) and text cursor are also highlighted when the pointer is in that window. This is a characteristic of *xterm:* other applications may not highlight display features.

The most important thing to recognize is that the position of the pointer is very important to most X clients. If something doesn't work the way you expect, make sure that the pointer is in the right place. After you use X for a while, awareness of pointer position will come naturally.

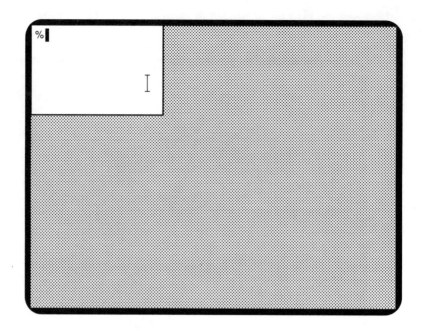

Figure 2-3. Focus on the console xterm window

Bringing Up the Window Manager

Make sure that the pointer is in the *xterm* window, so that the I-beam cursor is displayed. Start the *uwm* window manager by typing:

```
% uwm &
```

You should hear a beep, but nothing else should change visibly. However, the window manager is now running, and will allow you to move, resize and otherwise manipulate windows on the screen.

Note that it is important to run *uwm* in the background by placing an & at the end of the command line, so that you can continue to enter additional commands into the *xterm* window. If you neglected to do this on a system that supports job control, type Control-Z to suspend *uwm*, then use the *bg* command (see *csh*(1)) to place it in the background.

If the system you're on doesn't support job control, move the pointer to the root window and press the middle mouse button. Select New Window to create a new *xterm* window. Within the new window, use *ps*(1) to find the process id of *uwm*, kill it, and start over. (See the following section for information on placing the window. See Chapter 3 for more information on making menu selections.)

Starting a Second xterm Window

If you want to open a second *xterm* window, type the following command at the prompt in the first *xterm* window:

```
% xterm &
```

After a few moments, an upper-left corner cursor (⌐) appears on your screen, as shown in Figure 2-4.

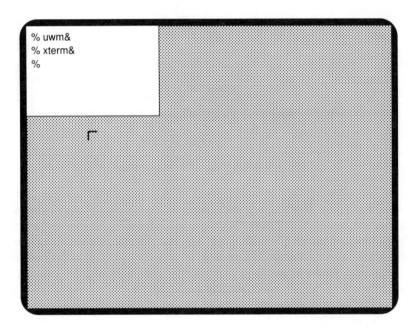

```
% uwm&
% xterm&
%
```

Figure 2-4. Placing a second xterm window

This corner cursor tracks pointer movement as you move the pointer across your screen.

Move the corner cursor to the desired position on your screen and *click* the left mouse button. (A click is defined as pressing the mouse button down and releasing it.) A new *xterm* window appears on your screen, with a prompt from whatever shell you are using. Figure 2-5 shows how your screen might look now. You can switch back and forth between windows simply by moving the pointer from one to the other.

If you have inadvertently positioned the second *xterm* window in front of the first one, don't be concerned. Just use the front window for now. Chapter 3 provides information on resizing and moving windows.

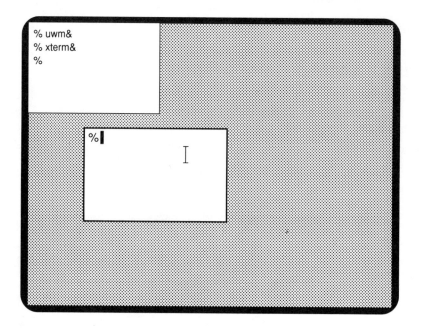

Figure 2-5. Two xterm windows

Notice how the text cursor and border in each *xterm* window are highlighted when you move the pointer into that window. Whatever you type will appear in the window with the filled cursor. Try starting a command in both windows. For example, start up *vi* or another text editor in the second *xterm* window. Notice how you can switch back to the first window to type a new command, simply by moving the pointer — even if you leave *vi* in insert mode, or some other command in the process of sending output to the screen. Whatever process was running in the window you left will continue to run, unless it needs input from you to continue.

Exiting from an xterm Window

When you are through using an *xterm* window, you can remove it by typing whatever command you usually use to log off your system. Typically, this might be `exit`, `logout`, or Control-D. You can also terminate an *xterm* window by selecting kill from the xterm menu, discussed in Chapter 4.

Be aware that terminating the *xterm* login window (the first *xterm* to appear) kills the X server and all associated clients. Be sure to terminate all other *xterm* windows before terminating the *xterm* login window. Also, be sure that if you are in an editor such as *vi* that you save your data before you terminate the window.

In fact, it may be wise to *iconify* the console window (shrink it into a small symbol, or *icon*, on the screen) and use other *xterm* windows instead, so that you don't inadvertently terminate it. See Chapter 3 for a discussion of how to do this.

Alternatively, you can type

```
% set ignoreeof
```

in the console window. This will limit the number of ways you can terminate the window to typing `exit`.

Special Keys

Most workstations have a number of "modifier" keys, so called because they modify the action of other keys.

Three of these modifier keys should be familiar to any user of a standard ASCII terminal or personal computer—Shift, Caps Lock, and Control. However, many workstations have additional modifier keys as well. A PC has an "Alt" key, a Macintosh a "fan" key—and a Sun workstation has no less than three additional modifier keys, labeled "Alternate," "Right," and "Left."

Because X clients are designed to run on many different workstations, with different keyboards, it is difficult to assign functions to special keys on the keyboard. A developer can't count on the same key always being present!

For this reason, many X clients make use of "logical" modifier keynames, which can be mapped by the user to any actual key on the keyboard.

Up to eight separate modifier keys can be defined. The most commonly used (after Shift, Caps Lock, and Control) has the logical keyname "meta."

We'll talk at length about this subject in Chapter 9, but we wanted to warn you here. When we talk later in this book about pressing the "meta" key, you should be aware that there is not likely to be a physical key on the keyboard with that name. For example, on one workstation, the meta key might be labeled "Alt," and on another, "Funct." And as we'll show in Chapter 9, you can choose any key you want to act as the meta key.

Unfortunately, X provides no easy way to find out which key on your keyboard has been assigned to be the meta key. You don't need to know this right away ... but when you do, please turn to the discussion of key mapping in Chapter 9 for information on how you can find out.

Starting Other Clients

You can start other X clients just like you can start another instance of *xterm*. At the command-line prompt in any *xterm* window, type the name of the client followed by an ampersand to make the client run in the background. For example, by typing:

```
% xclock &
```

you can cause a window displaying a clock to be placed on the screen. First a upper-left corner cursor will appear, just as it did when you created a second *xterm* window. Move the corner cursor to the position you would like the clock to appear, and then click the left mouse button. Figure 2-6 shows the *xclock* display, placed in the upper-right corner of the screen.

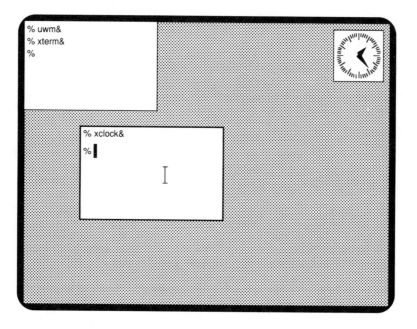

Figure 2-6. The xclock display

Unfortunately, the designers of *xclock* neglected to provide an easy way to make it go away. To remove the *xclock* display, you must identify and kill the process using the standard UNIX process control mechanisms. To find the process id for *xclock*, go to an *xterm* window and type:

```
% ps -ax | grep xclock
```

at a system prompt. Under System V, type:

```
% ps -e | grep xclock
```

at a system prompt. The resulting display should look something like this:

```
128   p0   0:00   xclock
142   p0   0:00   grep xclock
```

The number in the first column is the process id. Type:

```
% kill process_id
```

The *xclock* display will be removed and you will get the message:

```
Terminated    xclock
```

Where to Go From Here

There are many useful client programs supplied with the X Window System. Details of how to use the two most important of these clients, the *uwm* window manager and the *xterm* terminal emulator, are provided in the next two chapters. An overview and tutorial for other clients is provided in Chapter 5. All clients are described in detail in a reference page format in Part Three of this manual.

You should read at least the chapter on *uwm* before starting up any other clients. You can then go on to read more about *xterm* in Chapter 4, or about other clients in Chapter 5.

3
Using the Window Manager

This chapter describes uwm, *the "universal window manager" distributed with X.
Additional information on customizing the operation of* uwm *is provided in Chapter 8.*

In This Chapter:

Using the
Window Manager

3
Using the Window Manager

The *uwm* window manager is a client that allows you to:

- move windows around your screen;
- change the size of windows;
- raise windows (bring them to the front of others);
- lower windows (send them to the back of others);
- convert windows to icons and icons to windows;
- refresh your screen;
- create additional *xterm* terminal windows.

As described in Chapter 2, you start *uwm* by typing

```
% uwm &
```

in an *xterm* window. Nothing visible will happen, but your terminal will beep when *uwm* is running on the current screen.

Note also that you can run *xterm* or other X clients without running a window manager. Command line options could be used to place each new client window at the desired location on the screen. However, there is no way to change the size or location of windows on the screen without a window manager.

The *uwm* window manipulation functions can be invoked in three ways:

- using the WindowOps menu;
- by combinations of keyboard and mouse buttons;
- automatically, whenever a client is started.

The window manager also has a second menu, the Preferences menu, that allows you to set various keyboard and mouse preferences.

The following sections describe each of these subjects in detail.

The WindowOps Menu

The *uwm* WindowOps menu gives you access to many of the most frequently used functions. In the version of *uwm* shipped by MIT, you bring up this menu by moving the pointer to the root window and holding down the middle mouse button. The WindowOps menu and the menu pointer appear as shown in Figure 3-1.

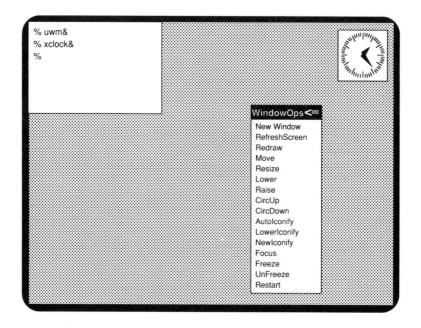

Figure 3-1. WindowOps menu

The following pages explain the functions of the *uwm* WindowOps menu. Remember that all of the window manager functions are customizable. Items can be added to or deleted from this menu by modifying the *.uwmrc* window manager startup file. Customizing the window manager is described in Chapter 8. This chapter describes the window manager as it is shipped with the MIT X Window System.

To bring up the WindowOps menu, move the pointer to the root window and hold down the middle button on the mouse. To *select* a menu item, continue to hold down the middle button and move the pointer to the desired menu item. A horizontal band, or *highlighting bar*, follows the pointer. When you've highlighted the desired menu item, release the button. The selected function will be executed. Note that you must keep the pointer within the menu as you drag down to make a choice, or the menu will disappear and you'll have to start over.

Some of the functions on the menus can be invoked simply by pressing a combination of mouse buttons and keyboard keys. We'll discuss these "keyboard shortcuts" as appropriate when discussing each menu function. These shortcuts all make use of the "meta" modifier key. See Chapter 9 for a discussion of how to determine which key on your keyboard serves as the meta key. (For the Sun-3 keyboard, meta is either of the keys labeled "Left" or "Right.")

Creating New Terminal Windows

You can create new *xterm* terminal windows from the WindowOps menu. To create a terminal window:

1. Bring up the WindowOps menu.

2. Select New Window with the menu pointer and release the mouse button. An upper-left corner cursor appears on your screen. This corner cursor tracks mouse movement. You now have three options:

   - **Making a Default-Size Window.** Move the corner cursor to the position desired for the upper-left corner of the window and click the left mouse button. A default-size (80 x 24) window appears on your screen. See Figure 3-2.

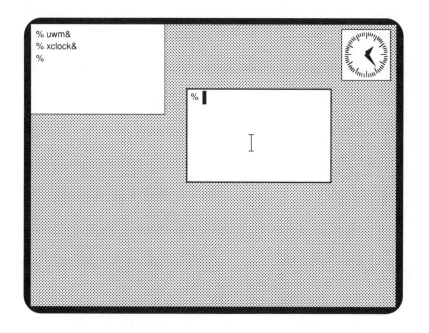

Figure 3-2. A default-size xterm window

   - **Making a Custom-Size Window.** Move the corner cursor to the desired position for the upper-left corner of the new window. Press and hold down the middle mouse button. Notice that the upper-left corner cursor is now fixed at that position and that a lower-right corner cursor appears.

     While holding down the middle button, move the corner cursor to the desired position for the lower-right corner of the window. The window size, as you change it, appears in the upper-left corner of your screen. Release the button. A window of the width and height you specified with the pointer appears. See Figure 3-3.

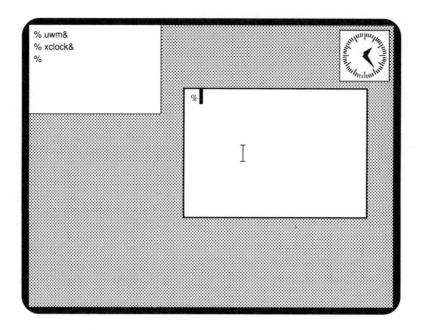

Figure 3-3. A custom-size xterm window

- **Making a Maximum-Height Window.** Move the corner to the desired position and click the right button. A default-width by maximum-height (to the bottom of the screen) window appears. See Figure 3-4.

Refreshing the Screen

Refreshing your screen means redrawing its contents. This is useful if system messages from outside the X window system appear on the screen, overlaying its contents, or if some ill-behaved client draws outside its window. To refresh your screen:

1. Bring up the WindowOps menu.

2. Select RefreshScreen with the menu pointer. The screen redraws itself. You can use the *xrefresh* client to achieve the same effect. Simply type xrefresh at the prompt in any *xterm* window.

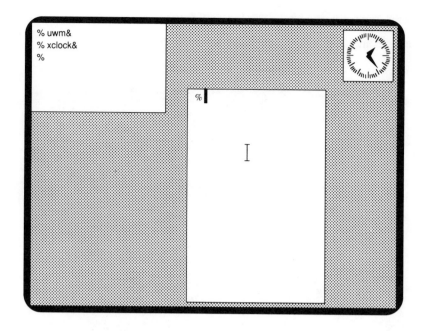

Figure 3-4. A maximum-height xterm window

Redrawing a Window

The Redraw option redraws (or refreshes) an individual window. To redraw a window:

1. Bring up the WindowOps menu.

2. Select Redraw with the menu pointer. The pointer changes to the target circle pointer.

3. Move the target circle pointer to the window you want to redraw.

4. Click the left or middle button to redraw the window.

Moving Windows and Icons

The Move option moves a window or icon to a new location. When you use this function, an outline, not the entire window or icon, tracks the mouse movement to the new location. See Figure 3-5. To move a window:

1. Bring up the WindowOps menu.

2. Select Move with the menu pointer. The pointer changes to the target circle pointer.

3. Move the target circle pointer to the desired window or icon. Hold down the middle button. The pointer changes to the cross pointer and a window outline appears. This outline tracks the pointer movement.

4. Move the cross pointer with the window outline to the desired location on your screen.

5. Release the middle button. The window will move to the new location.

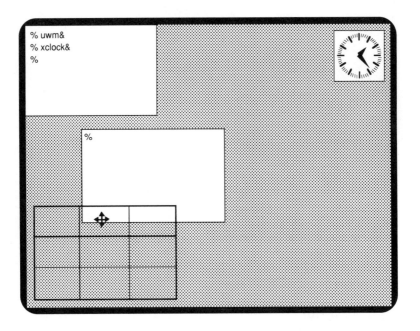

Figure 3-5. Moving windows or icons

You can also move a window or icon simply by moving the pointer to the window or icon you want to move, then pressing the right mouse button while holding down the meta key. The pointer at first changes to a small image of an icon. You can now let go of the meta key. Then, as you drag the mouse while holding down the button, the pointer changes to a cross, while the window or icon changes to outline form. Drag the outline to the new location, and let go of the right button. The window will be redrawn in the new location.

Resizing Windows

The Resize option resizes an existing window. See Figure 3-6. To resize a window:

1. Bring up the WindowOps menu.

2. Select Resize with the menu pointer. The pointer changes to the target circle pointer.

3. Move the target circle pointer to the window you want to resize. Place it near the border you want to move. The opposite border remains in its current position.

4. Hold down the middle button. The pointer changes to the cross pointer.

5. Move the window's border to obtain the desired window size. As you resize the window, a digital readout appears opposite the pointer showing the window size in pixels. (For the *xterm* client, size is in characters and lines.) Release the middle button.

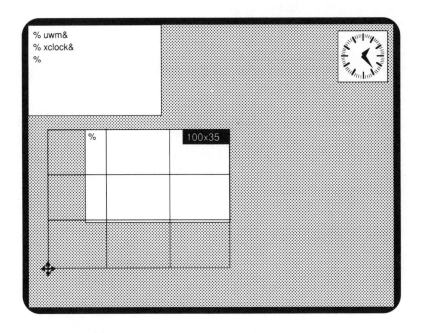

Figure 3-6. Resizing a window

Resizing a window will not change the dimensions of the text in the window. The terminal emulator itself will automatically know its new size (and will place the correct values into the TERMCAP environment variable), so that when you start an editing session the program will use the entire window. However, if you resize during an editing session, the editor may not know about the new size, and may operate incorrectly.

You can also resize a window without using the menu. Move the mouse so that the pointer is within the window you want to resize, placing the pointer near the window border you want to change. With one hand press and hold down the meta key on the keyboard. With the other hand, press and hold down the middle mouse button. The pointer starts as an icon pointer, but as you drag the pointer, it changes to a cross and a window outline appears. Move the mouse to resize the window. When the window is the proper size, release the middle button and the meta key.

Stacking of Windows

Under the X Window System, windows can overlap each other. When windows overlap, one or more windows may be fully or partially hidden behind other windows. You can think of these windows as being stacked on top of each other much the way papers are stacked on a desk. *uwm* can control the stacking order of the windows. Stacking functions include: raising a window to the top of the stack, making all of it visible; lowering a window to the bottom of the stack (possibly obscuring it by other windows); cycling up the bottom window to the top and lowering every other window one level; or cycling the top window to the bottom and raising every other window one level.

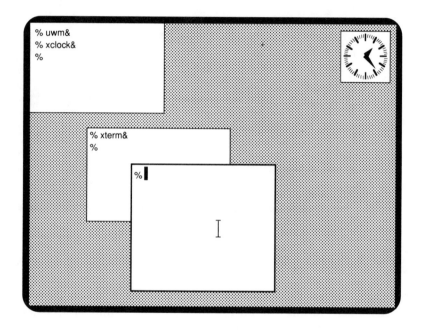

% uwm&
% xclock&
%

% xterm&
%

%

Figure 3-7. One xterm window overlapping another

Raising Windows (bringing in front of others)

Raise places a window at the top of a window stack. See Figure 3-8. To bring a window to the front:

1. Bring up the WindowOps menu.

2. Select Raise with the menu pointer. The pointer changes to the target circle pointer.

3. Move the target circle pointer to the desired window.

4. Click the left or middle button. The window is raised to the top of the stack.

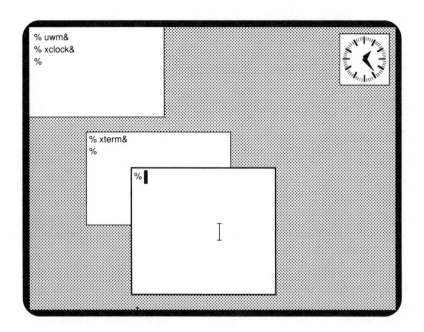

Figure 3-8. Raising a window

Lowering Windows (sending behind others)

Lower places a window at the bottom of a window stack. To place a window at the bottom:

1. Bring up the WindowOps menu.
2. Select Lower with the menu pointer. The pointer changes to the target circle pointer.
3. Move the target circle pointer to the appropriate window.
4. Click the left or middle button. The desired window is placed behind all windows except the root window.

Circulating Windows

CircUp and CircDown circulate the windows in a stack. CircUp raises the bottom window to the top and lowers every other one by one level. CircDown lowers the top window to the bottom and raises every other window by one level. CircUp and CircDown only affect over-lapping windows.

To circulate the windows in a stack:

1. Bring up the WindowOps menu.

2. Select CircUp or CircDown.

Note that both CircUp and CircDown circulate *every* window stack if there is more than one stack of windows on the screen.

Here's how to change stacking order using keyboard shortcuts:

- To raise a window, move the mouse so that the cursor is within the window you want to raise. With your other hand, hold down the meta key on the keyboard. Then click the right mouse button. The window is raised.

- To lower a window, move the mouse so that the cursor is within the window you want to lower. With your other hand, hold down the meta key on the keyboard. Then click the left mouse button. The window is lowered.

- To circulate all windows, you can use any of the above key and mouse button combinations with the pointer in the root widow. However, you do not place the cursor within any particular window (e.g., leave the cursor in the root window). The windows cycle through the stack, raising the bottom window to the top and lowering every other window one level.

Displaying Windows as Icons

If you want to make more space available on your screen, you can convert a window into an icon. An *icon* is a small symbol that represents the window. You also can convert the icon back into a window.

There are three commands to iconify and deiconify on the default WindowOps menu: AutoIconify, LowerIconify, and NewIconify. All three iconify a window or deiconify an icon. In addition, LowerIconify and NewIconify interactively move the icon or window to a new location. See Figures 3-9 and 3-10.

The sample *.uwmrc* file at the end of Chapter 8 recommends a WindowOps menu with the single general-purpose command (De)Iconify and Move. This corresponds to the NewIconify choice on the standard *uwm* menu. To convert a window to an icon or an icon to a window:

1. Bring up the WindowOps menu.

2. Select NewIconify with the menu pointer. The pointer changes to the target circle pointer.

3. Move the target circle pointer to the desired window or icon.

4. Hold down the left button and move the pointer to the desired location. The window or icon tracks the pointer to the new location.

5. Release the left button. The window is converted to an icon or the icon to a window in the new location.

While the pointer rests in the icon, you can edit the icon name by typing in the appropriate name or characters. Use the Delete key to delete unwanted characters.

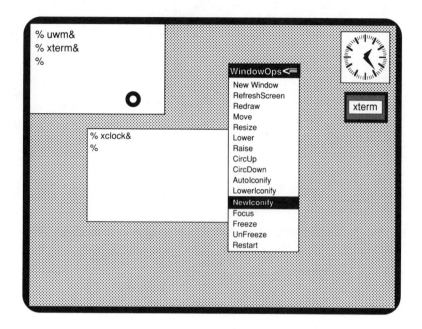

Figure 3-9. The login window is about to become an icon

NewIconify can also be used to display an icon as its orginal window. Follow the same procedure as to iconify a window, but start with an icon, and turn it into a window.

To iconify or deiconify a window using keyboard shortcuts, move the mouse so that the cursor is within the window you want to iconify. With one hand press and hold down the meta key on the keyboard. With the other hand press and hold the left mouse button and drag the window. The window converts to an icon-sized outline. Drag the outline to the desired position, and then release the mouse button and the meta key. The full icon appears in the specified position.

To bring back the window (deiconify it), move the mouse so that the cursor is within the icon. Then hold down the meta key and click the middle mouse button. Or hold down the meta key and use the left mouse button while dragging the window outline to a new location, just as you did to iconify the window in the first place.

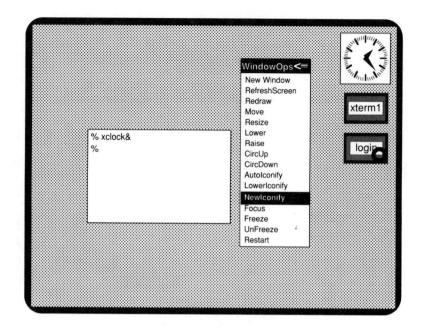

Figure 3-10. The login window is about to be deiconified

Changing Keyboard Focus

Normally, keyboard input goes to whichever window the pointer is currently in. The Focus option causes keyboard input to go only to a selected window (the *focus* window) regardless of the position of the pointer.

Focusing can be useful if you are working in one window for an extended period of time, and want to move the pointer out of the way. It also prevents the annoying situation in which you inadvertently knock the pointer out of the window while typing. (This can be very important for touch typists who look infrequently at the screen while typing!)

To choose a focus window:

1. Bring up the WindowOps menu.

2. Select Focus with the menu pointer. The pointer changes to the target circle pointer.

3. Move the target circle pointer to the window you want to choose as the focus window.

4. Click the middle button to choose the window.

The focus window becomes highlighted with a dark border.

In order to take the focus away from the selected window, you must give it back to the root window. To do this, choose focus again, and click anywhere on the root window. The keyboard focus will once again follow the pointer into any window.

Freezing and UnFreezing the Server

The X server normally responds to requests from clients in a first-come first-served order. There are times when you want one client (such as the window manager) to get priority treatment. For example, if there are many active X clients, or if you are running X across a slow network, you may find that *uwm* responds sluggishly while performing tasks such as moving or resizing a window. If you select Freeze, the window manager "grabs the server," so that no other clients have access. All events and requests to display to the screen by other clients are queued, or "saved up," and will be performed when the server is unfrozen.

To freeze the server:

1. Bring up the WindowOps menu.

2. Select Freeze with the menu pointer.

Since only the window manager has access to the server, window manager operations will go much more quickly. When you are finished moving or resizing windows (or whatever it was you wanted the window manager to do more quickly), select Unfreeze to resume normal operation.

Restarting the Window Manager

The Restart option restarts the window manager. This may occasionally become necessary if the window manager functions improperly. To restart the window manager:

1. Bring up the WindowOps menu.

2. Select Restart with the menu pointer.

Button Control of Window Manager Functions

Table 3-1 summarizes the keyboard shortcuts for window management functions. The first column lists the desired function; the second, the required location for the pointer; and the third, the button-key combination. In this column, "click" means to press and immediately release the specified mouse button; "down" means to press and hold the mouse button, and "drag" means to move the pointer while holding down the mouse button. In all cases, you can let go of the keyboard key as soon as you have pressed the appropriate mouse button.

Note that these key "bindings" can be changed in your *.uwmrc* file as described in Chapter 8. The combinations described in the table work for the *default.uwmrc* file.

Table 3-1. Keyboard Shortcuts for Window Manager Functions

Function	Pointer Location	Keyboard Shortcut
move	window or icon	meta right and drag
resize	window	meta middle and drag
raise	window or icon	meta right click
lower	window or icon	meta left click
circulate up	root	meta right click
circulate down	root	meta left click
circulate down	anywhere	meta-shift left click
iconify and move	window or icon	meta left and drag
deiconify and move	icon	meta middle click
Window Ops Menu	root	meta middle down
Window Ops Menu	anywhere	meta-shift middle down
Preferences Menu	anywhere	meta-shift right down

The Preferences Menu

The Preferences menu is generally included in the version of *uwm* provided with most systems. To display the Preferences menu, position the pointer on the root window and click the left mouse button. (Another button or combination might be used at your site.) If you cannot access the Preferences menu, this menu is included in the sample *.uwmrc* file at the end of Chapter 8.

The Preferences menu lists options for setting bell volume, keyclick volume, whether or not the Caps Lock key works, and the mouse tracking speed.* See Figure 3-11.

To make selections on the Preferences menu, bring up the menu and select a setting with the menu pointer. There is no visible change to the menu, but the new setting is made.

Placing Other Clients

As described in Chapter 2, you can start another client simply by typing its name at the command-line prompt in an *xterm* window. Some clients have a default size and/or location. A preferred size and location can also be specified in your *Xdefaults* file, as described in Chapter 7.

---

* The mouse tracking speed controls how much the pointer moves on the screen when you move the mouse. Experiment with each setting and see which you are most comfortable with.

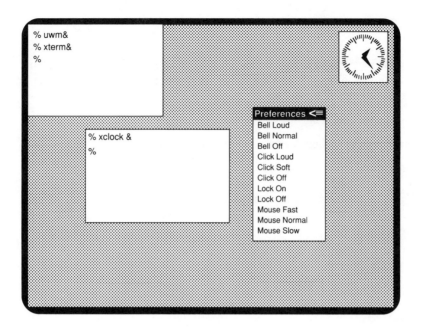

Figure 3-11. Preferences menu

When you start a client, you can also use the *-geometry* command-line option described in Chapter 6 to size and locate the window, overriding any defaults that the client has.

If none of these geometry specifications has been provided, *uwm* steps in and requires you to interactively size and locate the windows. You have already seen the process of interactively sizing and locating a window in Chapter 2, when we discussed how to start a second *xterm* or an *xclock* window.

First, the pointer turns into a corner shape (⌐), and the name of the client appears in the upper-left corner of the screen followed by the digital size readout 0x0.

To place the default-size client, move the pointer to the desired upper-left corner position for the new client. Click the left mouse button.

To both size and place the client, move the pointer to the desired upper-left corner position; press and hold down the middle mouse button. The pointer changes to a lower-right corner shape. Move the pointer to the desired window size. Release the mouse button.

Customizing uwm

The *uwm* window manager is a powerful tool that can perform many more functions than are described in this chapter. You can customize *uwm* using the *.uwmrc* file in your home directory. Customizing this file, you can:

- Define your own *uwm* menus.

- Bind functions to keyboard/mouse button combinations.

- Issue command strings to the shell.

For details on customizing, and an example of *.uwmrc*, see Chapter 8.

4

The xterm Terminal Emulator

This chapter describes how to use xterm, *the terminal emulator. You use this client to create multiple terminal windows, each of which can run any programs available on the underlying operating system.*

In This Chapter:

4
The xterm Terminal Emulator

xterm provides you with a terminal within a window. Anything you can do using a standard terminal, you can do in your *xterm* window. Once you have an *xterm* window on your screen, you can use it to run other clients.

You can bring up more than one *xterm* window at a time. For example, you might want to list the contents of a directory in one window while you edit a file in another window. Although you can display output simultaneously in several windows, you can type into only one window at a time.

Basic operation of *xterm* should be obvious to anyone familiar with a terminal. You should be able to work productively immediately. However, *xterm* has many additional features, such as scrollbars and a "copy and paste" facility, as well as many standard terminal setup options that are controlled through three menus.

Let's look first at the menus, before discussing scrolling and copy and paste.

xterm Menus

xterm has three different menus:

- xterm
- Modes
- Tektronix

As shown in Figure 4-1, the menus are divided into two sections, separated by a horizontal line. The top portion contains various modes that can be toggled. A check mark appears next to a mode that is currently active. Selecting one of these modes toggles its state. The bottom portion of the menu has command entries. Selecting one of these commands performs the indicated function. All mode entries can also be set by command line options when invoking *xterm*, or by entries in the *Xdefaults* startup file described in Chapter 7.

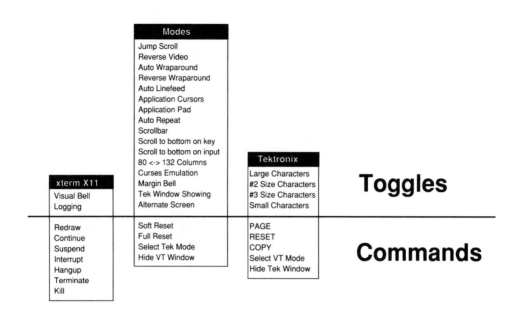

Modes		Tektronix	Toggles
Modes		**Tektronix**	
Jump Scroll		Large Characters	
Reverse Video		#2 Size Characters	
Auto Wraparound		#3 Size Characters	
Reverse Wraparound		Small Characters	
Auto Linefeed			
Application Cursors			
Application Pad			
Auto Repeat			
Scrollbar			
Scroll to bottom on key			
Scroll to bottom on input			
80 <-> 132 Columns			
Curses Emulation			
Margin Bell			
Tek Window Showing			
Alternate Screen			

xterm X11
Visual Bell
Logging

Redraw · Soft Reset · PAGE · **Commands**
Continue · Full Reset · RESET
Suspend · Select Tek Mode · COPY
Interrupt · Hide VT Window · Select VT Mode
Hangup · · Hide Tek Window
Terminate
Kill

Figure 4-1. Each menu is divided into two sections

Menus are displayed by a combination of keyboard keys and mouse buttons. The combination is described below with each menu. If you decide not to select a menu item after the menu has appeared, move the pointer off the menu and release the button. The menu disappears and no action is taken. Note that this menu works differently than *uwm*'s menu, in that you can move outside it without it disappearing, as long as you continue to hold down the pointer button.

The xterm Menu

The xterm menu controls characteristics of an *xterm* window.

To bring up the xterm menu, move the pointer to the *xterm* window you wish to effect changes on, hold down the Control key, and press the left mouse button. The pointer changes to the menu pointer and the following menu of two modes and five commands appears. (You can release the Control key but must continue to press the left button to hold the xterm menu in the window.) The menu title gives you the version number of *xterm*.

Note that xterm menu options apply only to the *xterm* window the pointer is in when you display the menu. To effect changes in another *xterm*, you must move the pointer to that window, display the menu and specify the options you want.

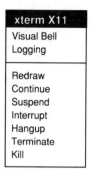

Figure 4-2. The xterm menu

To select a menu item, move the menu pointer to that item and release the left button. After you have selected a mode (Visual Bell or Logging), a check mark appears before the items to remind you that it is active. The following list describes each xterm menu mode and command.

Toggles (On/Off)

Visual Bell   causes your terminal window to flash whenever an event occurs that would ordinarily cause your terminal bell to ring.

Logging   logs *xterm* input/output into a file in your home directory called XtermLog.*xxxxx* where *xxxxx* represents the process ID number of the *xterm* window. Logging allows you to keep track of the sequence of data and, therefore, is particularly helpful while debugging code.

To display the data contained in the log file, at the *xterm* window prompt, type:

`more XtermLog.`*xxxxx*

The output file is sent to your *xterm* window.

To find out the exact name of the log file, list the contents of your home directory, looking for a log file with an appropriate time and date. Note that if you turn logging on in multiple *xterm* windows, there will be multiple log files.

Be sure to turn Logging off before displaying the log file in the *xterm* window. When Logging is on, anything in the window is appended to the end of the log file. If you display the log file while

xterm Terminal Emulator

logging is on, you will get into a continuous loop, much as if you typed cat * > *file*.

Commands

Redraw	redraws the contents of the window.
Continue	continues a process that has been suspended (technically speaking, this menu item sends the SIGCONT signal to the process group of the process running under *xterm*, usually the shell). The Continue function is especially useful on systems with job control if you accidentally type Control-Z, and suspend a process.
Suspend	suspends a process (sends the SIGTSTP signal to the process group of the process running under *xterm*, usually the shell).
Interrupt	interrupts a process (sends the SIGINT signal to the process group of the process running under *xterm*, usually the shell).
Hangup	hangs up the process (sends the SIGHUP signal to the process group of the process running under *xterm*, usually the shell). This ends up killing the *xterm* process. The window disappears from the screen.
Terminate	terminates the process (sends the SIGTERM signal to the process group of the process running under *xterm*, usually the shell).
Kill	kills the process (sends the SIGKILL signal to the process group of the process running under *xterm*, usually the shell). This ends up killing the *xterm* process. The window disappears from the screen.

See *signal*(3C) in the *UNIX Programmer's Manual* for more information on what each signal does.

Modes Menu

The Modes menu provides many VT102 setup functions. Some of these mode settings are analogous to those available in a real VT102's setup mode; others, such as *scrollbar*, are *xterm*-only modes.

To bring up the Modes menu, move the pointer to the *xterm* window, hold down the Control key, and press the middle button. (You can release the Control key but must continue to press the left button to keep the Modes menu in the window.) The menu shown in Figure 4-3 appears.

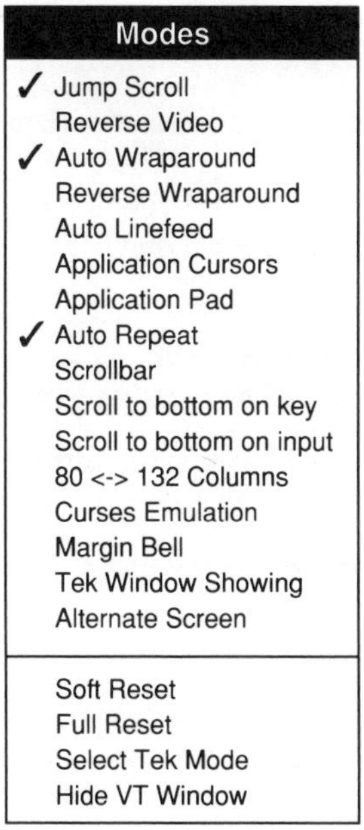

```
┌─────────────────────────────┐
│           Modes             │
├─────────────────────────────┤
│ ✓  Jump Scroll              │
│    Reverse Video            │
│ ✓  Auto Wraparound          │
│    Reverse Wraparound       │
│    Auto Linefeed            │
│    Application Cursors       │
│    Application Pad           │
│ ✓  Auto Repeat              │
│    Scrollbar                │
│    Scroll to bottom on key  │
│    Scroll to bottom on input│
│    80 <-> 132 Columns       │
│    Curses Emulation         │
│    Margin Bell              │
│    Tek Window Showing       │
│    Alternate Screen         │
├─────────────────────────────┤
│    Soft Reset               │
│    Full Reset               │
│    Select Tek Mode          │
│    Hide VT Window           │
└─────────────────────────────┘
```

Figure 4-3. The Modes menu

Check marks indicate the active modes. (For example, Jump Scroll, Auto Wraparound, and Auto Repeat are active in the Modes menu displayed above.) To turn off one of these modes, move the menu pointer to that mode and release the middle button.

The following list describes each mode and command of the Modes menu. (Many of these modes, Jump Scroll, for example, can be enabled as a command-line option or as an *Xdefaults* variable.)

Toggles (On/Off)

Jump Scroll	causes the window to move text several lines at a time rather than line by line. On by default.
Reverse Video	reverses the foreground color from black to white and the background color from white to black. Off by default.
Auto Wraparound	wraps the text or data to the next line automatically when the cursor reaches the window border. On by default.
Reverse Wraparound	allows the cursor to wraparound from the leftmost column to the rightmost column of the previous line. Allows you to

xterm Terminal Emulator

backspace to the previous line and overstrike data or erase data with the spacebar. Off by default.

Auto Linefeed
generates a linefeed automatically. Useful if you are using a program that generates a carriage return without dropping down a line on your screen. Off by default. (This option is not usually needed on UNIX systems.)

Application Cursors
generates ANSI escape sequences rather than standard cursor movement when you use the arrow keys. This option may be useful when working with certain applications. Off by default.

The following table lists the characters generated.

Table 4-1. ANSI characters generated by application cursors

Cursor Key (Arrow)	Reset (Cursor)	Set (Application)
Down	ESC [B	ESC O B
Right	ESC [C	ESC O C
Left	ESC [D	ESC O D

Application Pad
generates a control function rather than a numeric character when you use the numeric keypad. Off by default.

Auto Repeat
causes a keystroke to be repeated when the key is held down. On by default.

Scrollbar
causes a scrollbar to appear on the left-hand side of the *xterm* window. Off by default.

Scroll to bottom on key
repositions the cursor at the end of the text in the *xterm* window when a typewriter key is pressed. For example, if you have scrolled up the window to see past history, as soon as you begin typing your next command the cursor jumps to the bottom of the screen. Off by default.

Scroll to bottom on input
repositions the cursor at the end of the text in the *xterm* window when a typewriter key is pressed, or upon new output from a process in the *xterm* window. Off by default.

80 <-> 132 Columns
allows *xterm* to recognize the DECCOLM escape sequence, which switches the terminal between 80 and 132-column mode. The DECCOLM escape sequence can be included in a program (such as a spreadsheet) to allow the program to display in 132-column format. See Appendix D, *xterm Control Sequences*, for more information. Off by default.

Curses Emulation	enables the *curses* fix. Several programs that use the *curses* cursor motion package have some difficulties with VT102-compatible terminals. The bug occurs when you run the *more* program on a file which contains a line that is exactly the width of the window and which is followed by a line beginning with a tab. The leading tabs may disappear. This mode causes the tabs to be displayed correctly. Off by default.
Margin Bell	turns on the margin bell. Off by default.
Tek Window Showing	shows the current contents of the Tektronix window; you cannot input to that window until you choose Select Tek Mode. Off by default.
Alternate Screen	informs you that you are looking at the alternate screen. You cannot select this mode from the menu. If a check mark appears beside this mode, you are viewing the alternate screen. Off by default.

Commands

Soft Reset	resets the terminal scroll region from partial scroll (a portion of the window) to full scroll (the entire window). Use this command when a program has left the scroll region set incorrectly.
Full Reset	clears the window, resets tabs to every eight columns, and resets the terminal modes such as Auto Wraparound and Jump Scroll to their initial states.
Select Tek Mode	brings up a Tektronix window. You can input to this window.

Tektronix Mode Menu

Use Select Tek Mode to display a Tektronix window. Press and hold down the Control key on the keyboard. Move the mouse inside the Tektronix window and press the middle mouse button. The Tektronix mode menu appears. With this menu, you set the size of the text in the Tektronix window and select some commands.

A Tektronix window is not generally used for general-purpose terminal emulation, but for displaying the output of graphics or typesetting programs.

xterm Terminal
Emulator

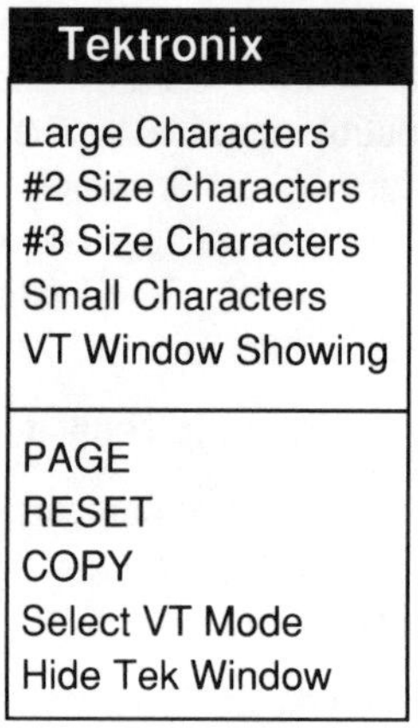

```
┌─────────────────────────┐
│  Tektronix              │
├─────────────────────────┤
│  Large Characters       │
│  #2 Size Characters     │
│  #3 Size Characters     │
│  Small Characters       │
│  VT Window Showing      │
│                         │
│  PAGE                   │
│  RESET                  │
│  COPY                   │
│  Select VT Mode         │
│  Hide Tek Window        │
└─────────────────────────┘
```

Figure 4-4. The Tektronix mode menu

Mode Settings

Large Characters
#2 Size Characters
#3 Size Characters
Small Characters

selecting one of these four options sets the point size of text displaying in the Tektronix window.

VT Window Showing

shows the current contents of the VT102 window; you cannot input to that window until you choose Select VT Mode.

Commands

PAGE   clears the Tektronix window.

RESET   closes down the Tektronix window.

COPY   writes a file of the Tektronix text and graphics commands.

Select VT Mode   makes the associated VT102 window active for input.

Hide Tek Window   removes the Tektronix window but does not destroy it. It can be brought back by choosing Select Tek Mode from the Modes menu.

Using the Scrollbar

When using *xterm*, you are not limited to the 24 lines shown in the display. By default, *xterm* actually remembers the last 64 lines that have appeared in the window. If the window was created with a scrollbar, you can scoll up and down through the saved text. You can add a scrollbar to the current window with the Scrollbar option on the Modes menu.

To create a single *xterm* window with a scrollbar, use the -sb command line option:

```
% xterm -sb &
```

To display all *xterm* windows with a scrollbar by default, set scrollBar in your *Xdefaults* file as described in Chapter 7:

```
xterm*scrollBar: on
```

Figure 4-5 shows an *xterm* window with a scrollbar.

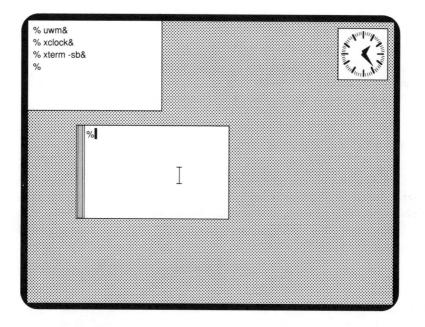

Figure 4-5. An xterm window with a scrollbar

The thumb (the highlighted area within the scrollbar) moves within the scroll region. The thumb displays the position and amount of text currently showing in the window relative to the amount saved. When an *xterm* window with a scrollbar is first created, the thumb fills the entire scrollbar. As more text is saved, the size of the thumb decreases. The number of lines saved is 64 by default, but can be changed with either the -sl command line option or the saveLines value in the *Xdefaults* file.

xterm Terminal Emulator

When the mouse is positioned in the scrollbar, the cursor changes to a two headed arrow. Clicking the left mouse button in the scrollbar causes the window to scroll toward the end of information in the window.

Clicking the right mouse button in the scrollbar causes the window to scroll toward the beginning of information in the window.

Clicking the middle mouse button moves the display to a position in the saved text that corresponds to the mouse's position in the scroll region. For example, if you move the pointer to the very top of the scroll region and click the middle mouse button, the display is positioned very near the beginning of the saved area.

If you hold down the middle button, you can drag the thumb up and down. When you release the button, the window displays the text at that location. This makes it easy to get to the top of the data by pressing the middle button, dragging it off the top of the scrollbar, and releasing it.

Copying and Pasting Text

Once your *xterm* window is created, you can select text to copy and paste within the same or other *xterm* windows using the mouse. You don't need to be in a text editor to use copy and paste. You can also copy or paste text to and from the command line.

Selecting Text to Copy

To select text, move the pointer to the beginning of the text you want to select. Hold down the left button while moving the pointer to the end of the desired text, then release the button. The selected text is highlighted and is saved in a memory area common to all terminal windows. (We could call this area the *clipboard*, by analogy with that feature in the Macintosh operating system.)

Note that with the current implementation of the copy and paste feature, tabs are saved as spaces.

Note that you can select a single word or line simply by clicking. To select a single word, place the pointer on the word and double-click the left mouse button. To select a single line, place the pointer on the line and triple-click the left mouse button.

The following table describes the button combinations and the resulting selection. Begin by placing the pointer on your desired selection.

Table 4-2. Button combinations to select text for copying

To select	Do this
words	double-click the left button
lines	triple-click the left button
passage	hold down the left button and move the mouse

Each selection replaces the previous selection in the clipboard. You can make only one selection at a time.

Once you have made a selection with the left button, you can extend that selection with the right button. The following example shows how this works:

1. Bring up *vi* (or any other text editor you are familiar with) in an *xterm* window, and type in this sample sentence:

   ```
   The X Window System is a network-based graphics window system that
   was developed at MIT in 1984.
   ```

2. Place the pointer on the word *graphics* in the sample sentence and select it with two clicks of the left button.

3. Press and hold the right mouse button. Move the pointer away from the word *graphics*, to the left or right. A new selection now extends from the last selection (*graphics*) to the mouse pointer's location looking like the following:

   ```
   The X Window System is a network-based graphics window system that
   was developed at MIT in 1984.
   ```

   or

   ```
   The X Window System is a network-based graphics window system that
   was developed at MIT in 1984.
   ```

Remember that your extension always begins from your last selection. By moving the mouse pointer up or down, right or left of the last selection, you can use this technique to select part of one line or add or subtract several lines of text.

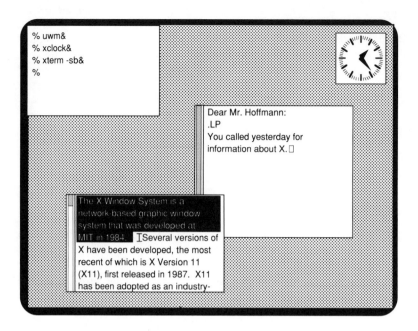

Figure 4-6. Highlighted text saved in the clipboard

To "unselect" text, move the pointer off the selection and click anywhere with the left button.

Pasting Text

The middle button inserts the text from the clipboard as if it were keyboard input. You can move data from one *xterm* window to another by selecting the data in one window with the left button, moving the pointer to another window, and clicking the middle button.

You can paste text either into an open file or at a command line prompt. To paste text into an open file, click the middle button within the window containing the file. The text from the memory area will be inserted where the text editor cursor is. (Of course, the file must be in a mode where it is expecting text input, such as the insert mode of an editor.) You can paste the same text as often as you like. It stays in the clipboard until you make another selection.

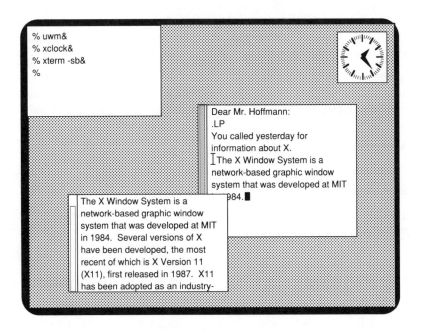

Figure 4-7. Pasting text into an open file

To paste text at a command line prompt, you must first close any open file within the window. Then clicking the middle button anywhere within the window automatically places the text on a command line at the bottom of the window (note that the window will scroll to the bottom on input).

You can make multiple insertions by repeatedly clicking the middle button.

The latest text selection replaces the previous text selected.

Users familiar with the Macintosh selection mechanism will find they can't paste *over* existing text in *vi*. However, if the editor you are using has an overwrite mode, you can.

The resize Client

xterm sets the TERMCAP environment variable for the dimensions of the window you create. Clients (including *xterm*) use this TERMCAP information to determine the physical dimensions of input and output to the window.

If you resize an *xterm* window, programs running within the window must be notified so they can adjust the dimensions of input and output to the window. If the underlying operating system supports terminal resizing capabilities (for example, the SIGWINCH signal in systems derived from BSD 4.3), *xterm* will use these facilities to notify programs running in the window whenever it is resized. However, if your operating system does not support terminal resizing capabilities, you may need to request explicitly that TERMCAP be updated to reflect the resized window.

The *resize* client sends a special escape sequence to the *xterm* window and *xterm* sends back the current size of the window. The results of *resize* can be redirected to a file that can then be sourced to update TERMCAP. To resize TERMCAP to match a window's changed dimensions, enter:

```
% resize > filename
```

and then *source* the resulting `filename`:

```
% source filename
```

TERMCAP will be updated and the dimensions of the text within the window will be adjusted accordingly.

Running a Program in a Temporary xterm Window

Normally, when you start up an *xterm* window, it automatically runs another instance of the UNIX Bourne or C shell (depending on which is set in your *.Xdefaults* file). If you want to create an *xterm* window that runs some other program, and goes away when that program terminates, you can do so with the *xterm* −e option.

```
% xterm -e [command] [arguments]
```

For example, if you wanted to look at the file *temp* in a window that would disappear when you quit out of the file, you could use the UNIX *more* program as follows:

```
% xterm -e more temp &
```

This option must appear last on the *xterm* command line. This is because everything after the −e option is read as a command.

5
Other Clients

This chapter describes how to run clients included in the standard MIT distribution. Additional information on each client is provided in Part Three.

In This Chapter:

5
Other Clients

In addition to *uwm* and *xterm*, the MIT distribution includes many other clients. This chapter describes these clients in general terms. Commercial X distributions may include other clients as well. In addition, as X becomes more widely available, there will doubtless be many applications available from third parties, just as there are in the PC world.

The discussion in this chapter is designed mainly to acquaint you with the major features of each of the available clients. Additional detailed information is provided on the reference pages for each client in Part Three of this book.

The one exception is *bitmap*, for which this chapter includes a detailed tutorial.

Desk Accessories

The clients *xclock*, *xcalc*, *xload*, *xlsfonts* and *xfd* can be thought of as *desk accessories*. (Desk accessories is a term we've borrowed from the Macintosh environment, meaning small applications available — and useful — at any time.)

You can start these clients from the command line in any *xterm* window, or, if you like, you can add them to a *uwm* menu (see Chapter 8).

xclock

xclock continuously displays the time, either in analog or digital form. The analog *xclock* shows a round 12-hour clock face. The digital *xclock* shows the 24-hour time (14:30 would be 2:30 PM) as well as the day, month and year. You can run more than one clock at a time. The analog clock is the default. Figure 5-1 shows two *xclock* applications being run (an analog clock above a digital clock).

Figure 5-1. Two xclock displays: analog clock above digital clock

Usually when you invoke *xclock* you will leave the clock running. However, if you experiment with *xclock* to test size, location, or color, you will notice that there is no obvious way to delete an unwanted clock. (Moving the cursor to the clock and pressing Control-C, Control-D, q, or Q doesn't work with *xclock*.) To kill the clock process, display the current X processes with the command:

```
% ps -ax | grep xclock
```

For System V, use the command:

```
% ps -e  | grep xclock
```

and then kill the process number for the clock as described in Chapter Two. The time displayed on the clock is the standard UNIX system time set with the *date*(1) command.

xcalc

xcalc is a scientific calculator that can emulate a TI-30, an HP-10C, and a slide rule. The calculator can be operated with the pointer by pressing any button on the calculator display, or with the keyboard by typing the same symbols shown on the calculator face. Figure 5-2 shows *xcalc* on the screen.

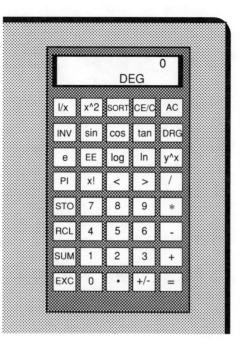

Figure 5-2. The xcalc application on the screen

The long horizontal window along the top of the calculator is the display, in which the values punched on the calculator and results are displayed. You can enter values either by clicking on the keys with the mouse, or by pressing equivalent keys on the keyboard.

By default, *xcalc* works like a Texas Instruments *TI-30* calculator. To interactively place *xcalc* in this mode, type:

% **xcalc &**

You can also operate the calculator in Reverse Polish Notation (like a Hewlett-Packard *HP-10C* calculator), by typing.

% **xcalc -rpn &**

In Reverse Polish Notation the operands are entered first, then the operator. For example 5 *
4 = would be entered as 5 Enter 4 *. This entry sequence is designed to minimize keystrokes for complex calculations.

To operate *xcalc* as a slide rule, type:

% **xcalc -analog &**

The resulting slide rule is shown in Figure 5-3. Drag the slide using the left mouse button. (We're told that the slide rule doesn't work very well— but we've included a picture just for fun.)

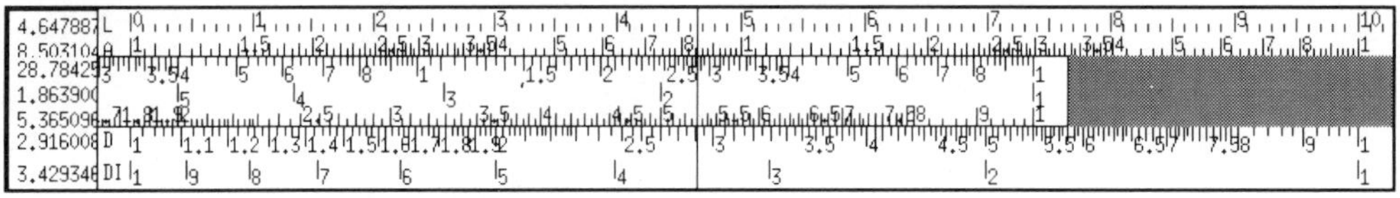

Figure 5-3. xcalc as a slide rule

For more information on the function of each of the calculator keys, see the *xcalc* reference page in Part Three of this manual.

Terminating the calculator

Terminate the calculator by either:

- clicking on the calculator's AC key with the right mouse button; or

- positioning the pointer on the calculator and typing q, Q, or Control-C.

Unfortunately, neither of these techniques work with the slide rule. You must terminate it with *kill* (1), as described above for *xclock*.

xbiff

xbiff is a simple title program that notifies you when you have mail. It puts up a window showing the keyboard picture of a mailbox. When you receive new mail, the keyboard beeps, the flag on the mailbox goes up, and the image changes to inverse video. When you read your mail, the image changes back to its original state. Figure 5-4 shows the *xbiff* mailbox before and after mail is received.

No mail   New mail has arrived

Figure 5-4. xbiff before and after mail is received

xload

By default, *xload* polls the system every 5 seconds. You can change this frequency with the update option. For example if you type at an *xterm* window

```
% xload -update 3 &
```

you can interactively place an *xload* window polling every 3 seconds.

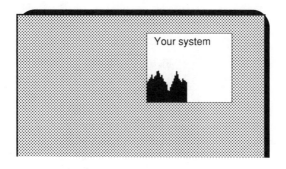

Your system

Figure 5-5. A sample xload window

xload periodically polls the system for the load average, and graphically displays that load using a simple histogram. If you are using two or more systems (either by remote login, or by using the `-display` option described in Chapter 6 to run an X client on a remote server), you can display loads for both systems and do your processing on the system that is fastest at that time. *xload* is only available for BSD-based UNIX systems.

xlsfonts and xfd

The X Window System supports many different display fonts, with different sizes and type styles. For example, you can choose the font used in *uwm* menus or for the text in *xterm* windows.

You can find out which fonts are available by doing a directory listing of */usr/lib/X11/fonts*, or by using the *xlsfonts* client.

If you use *ls*, you will see various other files in the directory; the font files themselves have an *.snf* extension appended to each name. (This extension is used by *make* when compiling the fonts.) *xlsfonts* lists only the font names. For example, you see *fg-16* rather than *fg-16.snf*.

In any event, the font names are not overly descriptive. For this reason, we've included a picture of each font in Appendix C. The characters in each font can also be displayed using the *xfd* (font displayer) client. To display the default font, which is named *fixed*, and is a 6x13 pixel mono-spaced font, type:

```
% xfd &
```

The result is shown in Figure 5-6.

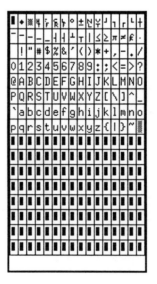

Figure 5-6. Default font, fixed

If you want to display a different font, use *xlsfonts* to display the available font names, then type the appropriate fontname as an argument to *xfd*. For example:

```
% xfd grk-s30 &
```

displays one of the two Greek fonts available.

Figure 5-7. Greek font

Each *xfd* window displays the first character of the font at the upper left of the window. This character is character number 0. To see a character's number, move the pointer to the desired character and click the middle button. That character's number is displayed in both decimal and hexadecimal at the bottom of the window, e.g.:

```
85.(0x55):
```

If you run *xfd* with the -start option, the first character of the font that appears at the upper left of the window is the one with that character number. For example, if you type the following on your command line

```
% xfd -start 15 grk-s25 &
```

the *xfd* window begins with Greek character number 15.

Every character in the font may not fit in the window at once. To see additional characters, move the pointer to the *xfd* window and click the right mouse button. The next window full of characters is displayed. To see the previous window of characters, click the left mouse button. *xfd* beeps if an attempt is made to go back past the first (0) character.

The characters are displayed in a grid of boxes, each large enough to hold any character of the font. If you have specified the -gray option, the characters are displayed using the foreground and background colors on a gray background. If you have not specified -gray, the characters are drawn using the foreground color on the background color.

To see information on a character's width, left bearing, right bearing, ascent and descent,

select the −verbose option, for verbose mode; then move the pointer to the desired character and click the middle button. To display the minimum or maximum values taken by each
of these fields over the entire font, move the pointer to the desired character and type < to
display the minimum values or > to display the maximum. The following information
appears at the bottom of the *xfd* window.

```
maximum bounds:
left bearing=n, right bearing=n
ascent=n, descent=n
```

To delete an *xfd* window, you can move the pointer to the window and type (one of) q, Q, or
Control-C.

Printing Utilities: xwd, xpr, xdpr

xwd stores window images in a formatted window dump file. This file can be read by various
other X utilities for redisplay, printing, editing, formatting, archiving, image processing, etc.

To create a window dump file, type

```
% xwd > file
```

The pointer will change to a small crosshair. Move the crosshair pointer to the desired window and click any button. The keyboard bell will ring three times in rapid succession to indicate that the dump is done.

To redisplay a file created with *xwd* in a window on the screen, use *xwud*.

xpr takes as input an X Window System dump file produced by *xwd* and converts it to a
printer-specific format that can be printed on the DEC LN03 or LA100 printer, a PostScript
printer such as the Apple LaserWriter, on the IBM PP3812 page printer. By default, output is
formatted for the DEC LN03 printer. Use the −device option to format for another printer.
For example, to format a window dump file for a PostScript printer, you'd type:

```
% xpr -device ps file > file.ps
```

Other options allow you to change the size, add headers or footers, and so on. See the reference page in Part Three for details.

You can use *xwd* and *xpr* together, using the standard UNIX pipe mechanism. For example:

```
% xwd | xpr -device ps | lpr
```

(Some installations have a command called *xdpr*, which rolls these three separate commands
into one.)

Note that when you start piping together the output of X clients, you run into some ambigui-
ties. For example, if you pipe the output of *xwd* to *xpr*, and for some reason, the *xpr* command fails, *xwd* will still be there waiting for mouse input. The original UNIX pipe mechanism doesn't have the concept of data dependent on mouse input! The integration of the UNIX
model of computing (in which standard input and output are always recognized), and the window model, is not always complete, leading to sometimes unexpected behavior.

As an even more flagrant example, you can create a pipe between two programs the first of which doesn't produce standard output, and the second of which doesn't recognize standard input. The shell doesn't know any better, and the programs themselves go on their merry way with mouse and windows.

However, it is nice to know that you can pipe together output of programs, even when some of those programs may not produce output until you intervene with the pointer.

Even without pipes, you should start thinking about how these programs could work together. For example, the pictures of fonts in Appendix C were created by the steps:

1. Display a font with *xfd*.

2. Use the *uwm* menu (click on the middle button while the pointer is in the root window) and select Resize to resize the window to a standard (5'' wide) size.

3. Create a PostScript file from the dump with the command `xpr -device ps`.

4. Print the PostScript file on an Apple LaserWriter with the standard print command *lpr*(1).

Even though the UNIX shell will accept a pipe between *xfd*, *xwd*, and *xpr*, what actually happens is that *xwd* starts up faster than *xfd*, and is ready to dump a window before the *xwd* window appears.

Creating Icons and Other Bitmaps

The *bitmap* program allows you to create and edit small bitmaps. A bitmap is a grid of pixels, or picture elements, each of which is white, black, or, in the case of color displays, a color. You can use *bitmap* to create backgrounds, icons, and pointers.

At this point in X Window System development, *bitmap* is a primarily a programming tool for application developers. However, several applications allow you to design your own icon or background pattern with *bitmap*, save it in a bitmap file, and specify that filename on the command line.* For example, *xsetroot* (described in Chapter 9) allows you to specify a bitmap that will be used as the background pattern for the root window.

To invoke *bitmap*, type:

```
% bitmap filename &
```

An upper-left corner cursor ($\ulcorner$) appears on the screen for you to interactively place the default-size 16x16 *bitmap* window.

---

*There are many bitmaps included in the X distribution. These can be found in the directory */usr/include/X11/bitmaps*. Samples are shown in Appendix E.

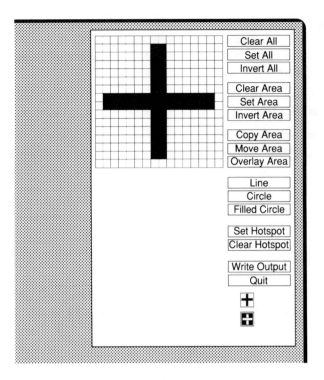

Figure 5-8. Bitmap Window

The window that *bitmap* creates has three sections:

1. The largest section is the checkerboard grid, which is a magnified version of the bitmap you are editing. If this grid isn't large enough for comfortable editing, resize the window.

2. On the right-hand side of the window is a list of commands in command boxes that you can invoke with any mouse button.

3. Beneath the commands is an actual size picture of the bitmap you are editing; below this is an inverted version of the same bitmap. Each time the grid changes, the same change occurs in the actual-size bitmap and its inverse.

Pointer Commands

When the pointer is in the checkerboard grid, each mouse button has a different effect upon the single square under the pointer.

left button   changes a grid square to the foreground color and sets the corresponding bitmap bit to 1. (On a monochrome display, background color means white and foreground color means black.)

middle button   inverts a grid square, changing its color and inverting its bitmap bit.

right button   changes a grid square to the background color and sets the corresponding
                  bitmap bit to 0.

Bitmap Command Boxes

To invoke any *bitmap* command, move the pointer to the appropriate command box and click
any button. *bitmap* does not have an Undo command. Once you have made a change, you
cannot retrieve the original.

Acting on the Entire Grid: Clear All, Set All, Invert All

To Clear All, Set All, or Invert All click on the appropriate command box.

Clear All   changes all the grid squares to the background color and sets all bit-
                   map bits to 0.

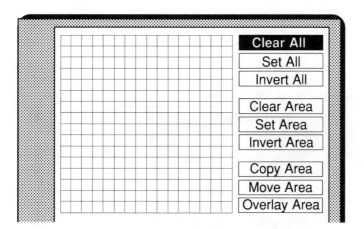

Figure 5-9. Clearing All

Set All   changes all the grid squares to the foreground color and sets all bit-
                   map bits to 1.

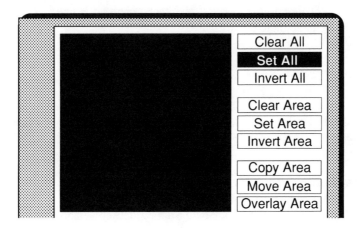

Figure 5-10. Setting All

Invert All

inverts all the grid squares and bitmap bits, as if you had pressed the
middle button over each square.

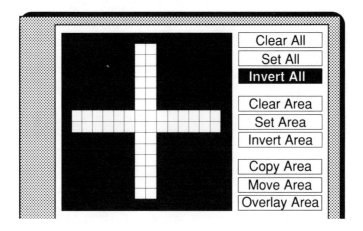

Figure 5-11. Inverting All

Acting on an Area: Clear Area, Set Area, Invert Area

Clear Area   clears a rectangular area of the grid, changes it to the background color, and sets the corresponding bitmap bits to 0.

Set Area   changes a rectangular area of the grid to the foreground color and sets the corresponding bitmap bits to 1.

Invert Area   changes a rectangular area of the grid from the background color to the foreground color or the foreground color to the background color.

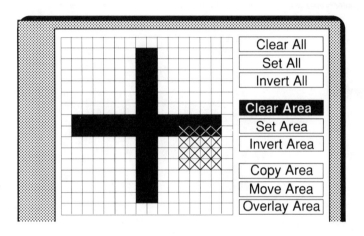

Figure 5-12. Selecting an area to clear, set, or invert

The procedure to act on an area is as follows:

1. Click the pointer over the command (Clear Area, Set Area, or Invert Area). The pointer turns into an upper-left corner.

2. Move the pointer over the upper-left corner of the area you want to clear, set, or invert. Press and hold any button. The pointer changes to a lower-right corner.

3. Move the pointer to the lower-right corner of the area you want to act on. X's cover the rectangular area as you move the pointer. Release the button.

   If the pointer has changed to a lower-right corner and you wish to abort the command without inverting an area, either click another button, move the pointer outside the grid (or move the pointer above or to the left of the upper-left corner).

Copy Area, Move Area, Overlay Area

Copy Area   copies a rectangular area from one part of the grid to another.

Move Area   moves a rectangular area from one part of the grid to another.

Overlay Area   lays a rectangular area from one part of the grid over a rectangular area in another part of the grid. Overlay is not a pixel for pixel copy, but those pixels which are clear (bitmap bits set to 0) allow those pixels that are set (bitmap bits set to 1) to show through the overlay.

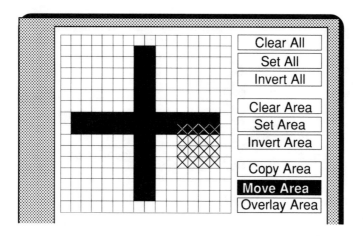

Figure 5-13. Selecting an area to copy, move, or overlay

The procedure to Copy Area, Move Area, or Overlay Area is as follows:

1. Click the pointer over the command (Copy Area, Move Area, or Overlay Area). The pointer turns into an upper-left corner.

2. Move the pointer over the upper-left corner of the area you want to copy, move, or overlay. Press and hold any button. The pointer changes to a lower-right corner.

3. Move the pointer to the lower-right corner of the area you want to act on. X's cover the rectangular area as you move the pointer. Release the button. The pointer changes to an upper-left corner.

4. Move the pointer to the desired location and click any button.

    OR

    Press and hold any button to see the outline of the destination rectangle, move the pointer to the desired location, then release the button.

5. To cancel an overlay, move the pointer outside the grid and release the button.

Drawing: Line, Circle, Filled Circle

When you use a drawing command, the drawing is always done in the foreground color.

Line   draws a line between any two points you select.

Circle   draws a circle. You specify the center and the radius.

Filled Circle   draws a filled circle. You specify the center and the radius.

To draw a line or circle:

1. Click the pointer over the command Line, Circle, or Filled Circle. The pointer turns into a •.

2. Move the pointer to the first point of the line or to the center of the circle. Click any button. An X fills the square which is the starting point of the line or center of the circle.

3. Move the pointer to the end point of the line or to the outside circumference of the circle. Click any button. The graphic is drawn.

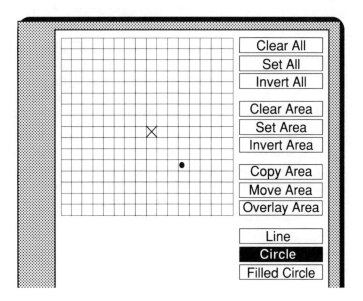

Figure 5-14. Selecting center and radius of circle

Hot Spots: Set Hotspot, Clear Hotspot

Set HotSpot   designates a point on the bitmap as the hotspot. If a program is using your bitmap as a pointer, the hotspot indicates which point on the bit- map will track the actual location of the pointer. For instance, if your pointer is an arrow, the hotspot should be the tip of the arrow; if your pointer is a cross, the hotspot should be that point at which the perpendicular lines intersect.

Clear HotSpot   removes a hotspot defined on this bitmap.

To set or clear a hotspot:

1. Click the pointer over Set Hotspot or Clear Hotspot.

2. Move the pointer to the location of the hotspot. Click any button. When a hotspot is active a ◊ appears.

Saving and Quitting: Write Output, Quit

Write Output   writes the current bitmap value to the file specified in the command line. If the file already exists, the original file is first renamed to *filename~*.

                         If either the renaming or the writing cause an error (e.g., Permission denied) a dialog box appears, asking if you want to write the file */tmp/filename* instead. If you click Yes, all future Write Output com- mands write to */tmp/filename*. See the *bitmap* reference page in Part Three of this book for information on the format of the output file.

Quit   terminates *bitmap*. If you have edited the bitmap and have not invoked Write Output, or you have edited it since the last time you invoked Write Output, a dialog box appears, asking if you want to save changes before quitting. Yes does a Write Output before ter- minating; No just terminates, losing the edits; Cancel means you decided not to terminate after all.

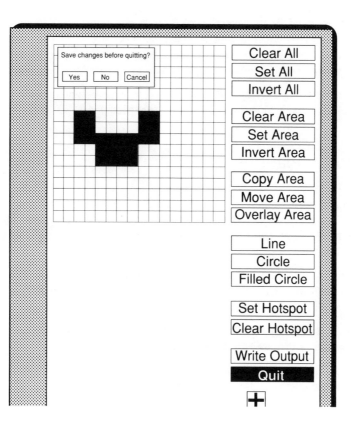

Figure 5-15. Quit Dialog Box

Other Clients

In addition to the clients in the standard MIT X distribution, there are many public domain clients distributed over Usenet (and perhaps with various commercial distributions). If you have access to Usenet, read the newsgroup *comp.windows.x* for sources and voluminous discussions of X programming.

In particular, you can expect to see many new window managers. Two window managers that are currently growing in popularity are:

awm   another window manager

twm   "the window manager"

Even though these window managers implement some additional features, they are not sufficiently advanced over *uwm* to represent the last word. X clients are designed to leave many user interface features to the window manager, so you can expect to see manufacturers vying to develop value-added window managers with many ease-of-use features.

Commercial products (such as spreadsheets, word processors and graphics or publishing applications) based on the X Window System can be expected in 1989.

X Toolkit Applications

Many clients have been written (or rewritten) with a programming library called the X Toolkit. The X Toolkit provides a number of predefined components called *widgets*. Widgets make it easier to create complex applications; they also ensure a consistent user interface between applications.

Most of the clients described in this book were written before the X Toolkit was fully developed. Although in Release 2 they have been rewritten to use the X Toolkit, they don't necessarily make full use of all its features.

However, between them, they do use enough of these features that you can see what to expect from future applications that are based more fully on the X Toolkit.

This section briefly reviews some features of X Toolkit applications, with reference to where they are implemented in the current crop of clients.

Dialog Boxes

A dialog box is used when an application requires a small piece of information from the user, such as a filename. A dialog box typically has three elements; it always has the first element, it may or may not have the second and/or third elements:

- A prompt that identifies the purpose of the widget. This might be as simple as the string "Filename:"

- An area in which you can type your response

- Buttons that allow you to confirm or cancel the dialog input.

A dialog box is usually a pop-up window, which goes away after the required information is provided.

The X client *bitmap* is the only current application that uses a dialog box. It displays the dialog displayed in Figure 2-7 when you quit the application. Future X applications can be expected to make far heavier use of dialogs like this.

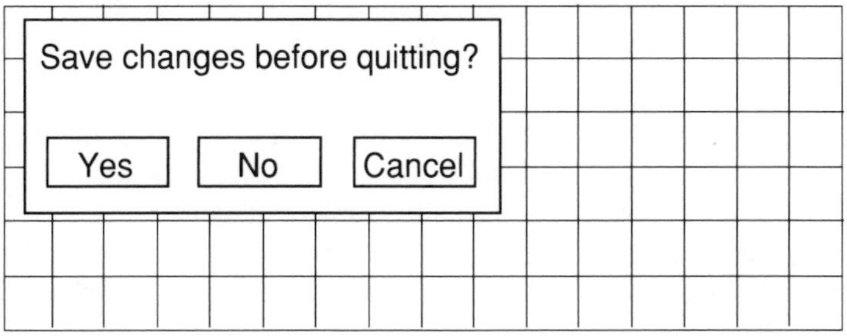

Figure 5-16. A dialog box with Yes, No, and Cancel command buttons

The command button is itself a widget rectangle that contains a text label. When the pointer is on the button, its border is highlighted to indicate that the button is available for selection. When a pointer button is clicked, some action (presumably indicated by the label) is performed by the program.

Some applications use the following convention for command buttons:

Whenever you press a button that may cause you to lose some work or is otherwise dangerous, a dialog box will appear asking you to confirm the action. This dialog box will contain an Abort button and a Confirm button. Pressing the Abort button cancels the operation, and pressing the Confirm button will proceed with the operation.

(A very handy shortcut exists in some applications: if you press the original button again, it will be interpreted as a Confirm. If you press any other command button, it will be interpreted as an Abort.)

Scrollbars

As described in the discussion of *xterm* in Chapter 4, applications can use a scrollbar to move up and down through data that is too large to fit in a window. The scrollbar consists of a sliding bar (often called the *thumb*) within a columnar slide region. The position of the thumb within the scrollbar corresponds to the position of the data displayed within the visible portion of the window with respect to the entire body of data. If no data has yet been displayed in the window, the thumb fills the entire scrolling region, as shown in Figure 2-8.

xterm uses a vertical scrollbar; other applications may use a horizontal scrollbar, or both. One type of widget with both horizontal and vertical scrollbars is called a *viewport*.

When the pointer is moved into the scrollbar, the cursor appears as an arrow that points in the direction that scrolling can occur. If scrolling can occur in either direction, the cursor appears as a two-headed arrow.

When the middle pointer button is clicked at any point in the scrollbar, the thumb moves to that point, and the data in the window scrolls to the corresponding position. When the middle pointer button is pressed and held down, the thumb can be "dragged" to a desired position in the scrollbar. If you click the left button in the scrollbar, the data in the window scrolls up, one line for each click. If you click the right button, the data in the window scrolls down, one line for each click.

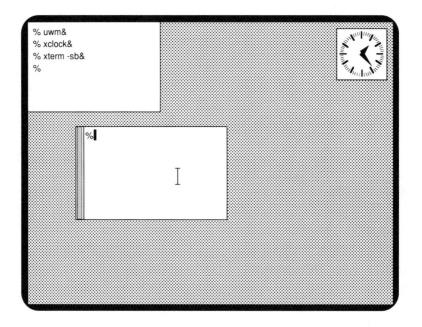

Figure 5-17. An xterm window with scrollbar

Selecting for Copying and Pasting

As described in the discussion of *xterm* in Chapter 4, when you select contents from one file, those contents are copied to a memory buffer that is available to other clients. (This buffer is known as a *clipboard* in other environments.) For example, right now you can select text in one *xterm* window and paste the text into any other *xterm* window. Selecting and copying graphic data between clients will be possible with future clients.

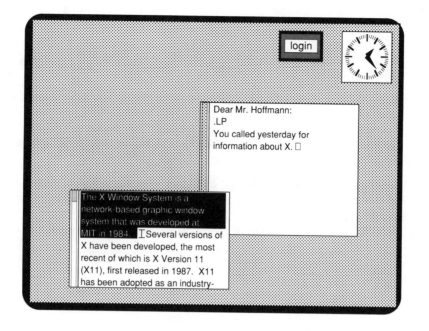

Figure 5-18. Selecting text to be copied

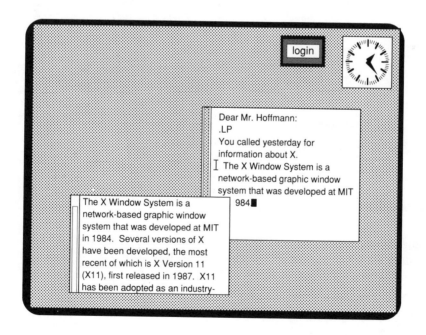

Figure 5-19. Pasting the selected text to another window

Vertical Panes

A VPaned widget arranges a series of windows one above the other without overlapping (i.e., they are *vertically tiled*).

A small region, called a *grip*, appears on the border between each subwindow. When the pointer is positioned on the grip and a button pressed, an arrow is displayed that indicates the direction in which the border between the two windows can be moved. If you move the pointer in the direction of the arrow (while keeping the button depressed), one subwindow will grow, while the other will shrink.

The individual panes can be any other type of widget. For example, the *xmh* mail handler includes dialog boxes with buttons, viewports containing text widgets and so on, as shown in Figure 2-10. (We refer to the *xmh* client solely to illustrate vertical panes that can be used by other X clients. The current *xmh* client is not discussed in this book because it is not widely used.)

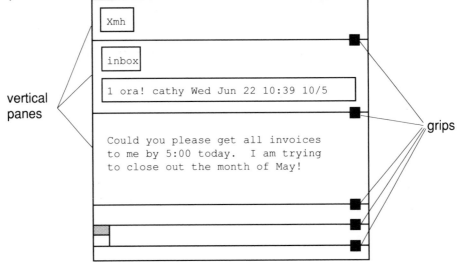

Figure 5-20. Vertical panes and grips in the xmh client

Text Editing Widget

Many applications include one or more areas in which you can enter text. All such text entry areas support the same set of editing commands. At this point, *xedit* is the only application that uses a text widget.

Various Control and Meta keystroke combinations are bound to a set of commands similar to those provided by the *emacs* text editor.* In addition, the mouse buttons may be used to

*The commands may be bound to keys different from the defaults described below through the standard X Toolkit key rebinding mechanisms.

select a portion of text or to move the insertion point in the text. Pressing the left mouse button (button 1) causes the insertion point to move to the pointer. Double-clicking the left button selects a word, triple-clicking selects a paragraph, and quadruple-clicking selects everything. Any selection may be extended in either direction by using the right mouse button (button 3).

In the following list of commands, a *line* refers to one displayed row of characters in the window. A *paragraph* refers to the text between carriage returns. Text within a paragraph is broken into lines based on the current width of the window.

The following keystroke combinations are defined as indicated. (Note that "Control" and "Meta" are two of the "soft" key names X recognizes. They are mapped to particular physical keys which may vary from keyboard to keyboard. See the *xmodmap* section in Chapter 9 for a discussion of modifier key mapping.)

Control-A	Move to the beginning of the current line.
Control-B, or Control-H	Move backward one character.
Control-D	Delete the next character.
Control-E	Move to the end of the current line.
Control-F	Move forward one character.
Control-J, or LineFeed	Create a new paragraph with the same indentation as the previous one.
Control-K	Kill the rest of this line.
Control-L	Repaint this window.
Control-M, or Return	New paragraph.
Control-N	Move down to the next line.
Control-O	Break this paragraph into two.
Control-P	Move up to the previous line.
Control-V	Move down to the next screenful of text.
Control-W	Kill the selected text.
Control-Y	Insert the last killed text.
Control-Z	Scroll the text one line up.
Meta-<	Move to the beginning of the file.
Meta->	Move to the end of the file.
Meta-[	Move backward one paragraph.

Meta-]	Move forward one paragraph.
Meta-B	Move backward one word.
Meta-D	Kill the next word.
Meta-F	Move forward one word.
Meta-H, or Meta-Delete	Kill the previous word.
Meta-I	Insert a file. If any text is selected, use the selected text as the filename. Otherwise, a dialog box will appear in which you can type the desired filename.
Meta-V	Move up to the previous screenful of text.
Meta-Y	Stuff the last selected text here. Note that this can be text selected in some other text subwindow. Also, if you select some text in an *xterm* window, it may be inserted in an *xmh* window with this command. Pressing pointer button 2 is equivalent to this command.
Meta-Z	Scroll the text one line down.
Delete	Delete the previous character.

Part Two:

Customizing X

X has been designed to put the user in the driver's seat. Everything from the colors of windows to the contents of the uwm *menu displays is customizable by the user. This part of the book tells you how to reshape X to your liking.*

6
Command Line Options

This chapter describes command-line options that are common to all (or most) clients. Some of this information is also used in writing the resource files described in Chapter 7. For example, the format of a geometry string or a color specification is the same whether it is specified as an argument to an option or as the value of a resource definition.

In This Chapter:

6
Command Line Options

X is highly customizable. Each user can:

- Specify numerous (very numerous!) command line options when starting most clients.
- Specify default values for options in a startup file called *Xdefaults*, or use *xrdb* to set defaults for clients running on remote machines. These default values will be referred to in this book as "resource manager defaults," since clients use a facility called the resource manager to combine their own default values with user preferences set in *Xdefaults* or with *xrdb*.
- Customize the operation of the window manager using a startup file called *.uwmrc* to change the contents of the menus or the keys used to invoke particular functions.
- Use special setup clients to specify preferences for features such as pointer acceleration, use of a screen saver (to prevent screen burnout when a workstation is left unattended for a long period of time), and so on.

This chapter discusses some of the command line options that are common to most clients. The *Xdefaults* and *.uwmrc* files are discussed in Chapters 7 and 8, respectively. Various setup clients are described in Chapter 9.

General Syntax of Command Line Options

Most X programs can take a variety of command line options. Command line options are detailed on the man pages for each client contained in Part Three of this book.

Notice that some examples show options preceded with a minus sign, while others do not. Whether the minus sign is required depends on both the option and the client program. See the reference page for each client in Part Three of this book for syntax of all options.

All options can be shortened to the shortest unique abbreviation. For example, `-display` can be shortened to `-d` if there is no other option beginning with "d." (Note that while this is true for all the standard MIT clients, it may not be true of any random client taken off the net.)

Table 6-1 lists the standard options that are recognized by X Toolkit applications. The first column gives the option name, the second the resource name to which it corresponds (see Chapter 7), and the third a brief description. Subsequent sections provide additional detail on the most important of these options.

Table 6-1. Standard X Toolkit Options

Option	Resource	Description
-background	background	Background color of window
-bd	borderColor	Border color of window
-bg	background	Background color of window
-borderwidth	borderWidth	Border width of window in pixels
-bordercolor	borderColor	Color of window border
-bw	borderWidth	Border width of window in pixels
-display	display	Display for client to run on
-fg	foreground	Foreground (drawing or text) color of window
-fn	font	Font for text display
-font	font	Font for text display
-foreground	foreground	Foreground (drawing or text) color of window
-geometry	geometry	Geometry string for window size and placement
-iconic		Start the application in iconified form
-name	name	Name of application
-reverse	reverseVideo	Reverse foreground and background colors
-rv	reverseVideo	Reverse foreground and background colors
+rv	reverseVideo	Don't reverse foreground and background
-synchronize	synchronize	Synchronous mode (used for debugging)
-title	title	Window title (not necessarily displayed)
-xrm	value of next arg	Next argument is a quoted string containing a resource manager specification as described in Chapter 7.

Which Display to Run On

Generally, the results of a client program are displayed on the system where the client is running. However, if you are running a client on a remote system, you probably want to display the results on your local server.

An option of the form:

```
-display host:server.screen
```

can be used to tell a client which server to display results on and take input from.

The *host* argument specifies which machine to create the window on, the *:server* argument specifies the server number, and the *.screen* argument specifies the screen number. Note that the *server* argument always begins with a colon (a double colon on DECnet nodes), and that the *screen* argument always begins with a period. If the *host* is specified as *unix*, the local node is used.

xterm and other X clients normally get the host, server and screen to use from the environment variable DISPLAY, which is set automatically by *xinit*. (By default, DISPLAY specifies screen 0 on the current host and server.) However, you may want to specify the host, server and screen explicitly. You can do this for all clients by resetting the value of the DISPLAY variable, or for a single invocation of a client by using the −display option.

For example:

% xterm −display *your_node:0.1* **&**

creates an *xterm* window on screen 1 of server 0 on the machine named *your_node*.

Although much of the current X Window System documentation suggests that any of the parameters to the −display option can be omitted and will default to the local node, server and screen 0, respectively, we have not found this to be true. In our experience, only the *host* and *screen* parameters (and the period preceding *screen*) can be omitted. The colon and *server* are necessary in all circumstances.

We've also found that if you create an *xterm* window using −display with incomplete parameters, the DISPLAY environment variable does not get set in the new *xterm* window. Therefore, any client started from that window won't work unless the display option is specified.

For example, say you create an *xterm* window using a command line with an incomplete display specification such as the following:

% xterm −display :0 &

If you then try to start another client (such as *xcalc*) from this *xterm* window, you will get the error message:

```
Can't Open Display
```

This is clearly a bug, and may not be true with all implementations. However, we thought you should be warned. If you think you are having this problem, type *printenv* (*env* in System V) to check environment variable settings. You can set the DISPLAY environment variable from the command line in the new window (setenv DISPLAY=*host:server.screen*). But it seems far simpler to type an *xterm* command line with a complete −display option in the first place.

The −display option can be abbreviated as −d. Prior to Release 2, no option flag was necessary at all. Instead, any argument containing a colon was assumed to be a display specification.

Name and Title

The name of the program (as known to the server) and the title of the window can be changed by the user. If your application has a titlebar, or if the window manager you are using puts titlebars on windows, the string specified by the −title option will appear in the titlebar. This can be useful for distinguishing multiple instances of the same application.

Why you would want to change the name of the application itself is an arcane piece of business, having to do with the way applications interpret resource files. This option is discussed further in Chapter 7.

Window Geometry

As of Release 2, all clients take a geometry option (-geometry =geometry) that specifies the size and location of the client window.

The -geometry option can be (and often is) abbreviated to -g, unless there is a conflicting option that begins with "g."

The argument to the geometry option (geometry) is referred to as a "standard geometry string," and has the form widthxheight±xoff±yoff. The variables, width, height, xoff, and yoff are values in pixels for many clients. However, application developers are encouraged to use units that are meaningful to the application. For example, xterm uses columns and rows in the xterm window as width and height values.

You can specify any or all elements of the geometry string. Incomplete geometry specifications are compared to the resource manager defaults and missing elements are supplied by the values specified there. If no default is specified there, and uwm is running, the window manager will require you to place the window interactively.

The symbols for the offsets have these effects:

- A positive x offset (+xoff) specifies the distance the left edge of the window is offset from the left side of the display.
- A positive y offset (+yoff) specifies the distance the top edge of the window is offset from the top of the display.
- For some clients, a negative x offset (-xoff) specifies the distance the right edge of the window is offset from the right side of the display.
- For some clients, a negative y offset (-yoff) specifies the distance the bottom edge of the window is offset from the bottom of the display.

For example, the command line:

```
% xclock -g =125x125-10+10 &
```

places a clock 125x125 pixels in the upper-right corner of the display, 10 pixels from both the top and right edge of the screen.

For xterm, the size of the window is measured in characters and lines. (80 characters wide by 24 lines long is the default terminal size.) If you wanted to use the vt100 window in 132-column mode, with 40 lines displayed at a time, you could use the following geometry options:

```
% xterm -g =132x40-10+350 &
```

This will place an xterm window 132 characters wide by 40 lines long in the lower-right corner, 10 pixels from the right edge of the screen and 350 pixels from the top of the screen. Figure 6-1 illustrates window offsets.

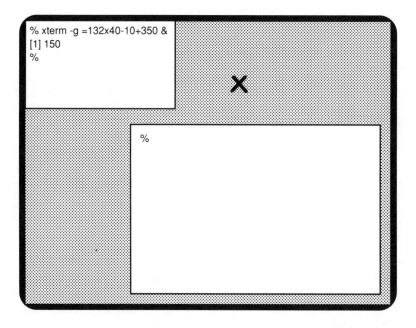

```
% xterm -g =132x40-10+350 &
[1] 150
%
```

```
%
```

Figure 6-1. Window offsets

Some clients may allow you to specify geometry strings for the size of the icon or an alternate window. For example, *xterm* takes a geometry string beginning with % rather than = as the geometry for the Tektronix window, and one beginning with # as the geometry for the icon. Neither of these options requires a preceding -g. Check each client's man page for details such as this. (Note also that prior to Release 2, any argument beginning with an equals sign was taken to be a geometry string. No -geometry flag was needed. This may still work with some clients.)

You should be aware that, as with all user preferences, you may not always get exactly what you ask for. Clients are designed to work with a window manager, which may have its own rules for window or icon size and placement. However, priority is always given to specific user requests, so you won't often be surprised.

Border Width

Many clients also allow you to specify the width of the border to be placed around the window. The border width is specified in pixels. For example:

```
% xterm -bw 10 &
```

sets a border of 10 pixels around the *xterm* window.

You will have to experiment to get a feeling for the translation between the number of pixels and actual sizes and distances. It will vary, depending on the type of workstation you are using.

If you are experimenting with geometry measurements, use the *xwininfo* client to display information about windows on the screen.

Type xwininfo -int & at the command line prompt in an *xterm* window and then click on the window for which you want to display information. You should see a display something like this:

```
Upper left X: 392
Upper left Y: 407
Width: 499
Height: 316
Depth: 1
Border width: 1
Window class: InputOutput
Window Map State: IsViewable
```

which gives various characteristics of the window in question. All numerical information is in pixels, except depth, which is in bits per pixel. (See the discussion of color later in this chapter for the significance of window depth.) The upper left X and Y coordinates are particularly useful for setting the location of a window using the geometry option. Upper left X corresponds to the positive x offset (+*xoff*) and upper left Y corresponds to the positive y offset (+*yoff*).

The width and height in pixels are somewhat less useful, since the geometry option to *xterm* requires that these figures be specified in characters and lines. (Using the *fixed* font, a character is approximately 6 pixels wide and a line approximately 13 high.) However, you will undoubtedly become accustomed to thinking in terms of pixels by specifying the geometry of other clients. (See the *xwininfo* reference page in Part Three for more details.)

You can determine the number of pixels in each dimension of the entire screen by invoking xwininfo and clicking on the root window.

Color Specification

Many clients have options that allow you to specify the color of the window background, foreground (the color text or graphic elements will be drawn in), or window border. These options often have the form:

-bg *color*   sets the background color.

-fg *color*   sets the foreground color.

-bd *color*   sets the border color.

Some clients allow additional options to specify color for other elements, such as the cursor, highlighting and so on. See the appropriate reference pages in Part Three of this book for details.

By default, the background is usually white and the foreground black, even on color workstations. You can specify a new color using either the names in the X Window System's *rgb.txt* file or hexadecimal values.

Color Names

The *rgb.txt* file, usually located in */usr/lib/X11*, is supplied with X and consists of predefined colors assigned to specific text names.*

The following are the default color names that come with the X Window System. (See Appendix A for information on customizing color name definitions.)

aquamarine	mediumaquamarine	black	blue
cadetblue	cornflowerblue	darkslateblue	lightblue
lightsteelblue	mediumblue	mediumslateblue	midnightblue
navyblue	navy	skyblue	slateblue
steelblue	coral	cyan	firebrick
gold	goldenrod	mediumgoldenrod	green
darkgreen	darkolivegreen	forestgreen	limegreen
mediumforestgreen	mediumseagreen	mediumspringgreen	palegreen
seagreen	springgreen	yellowgreen	darkslategrey
darkslategray	dimgrey	dimgray	lightgrey
lightgray	khaki	magenta	maroon
orange	orchid	darkorchid	mediumorchid
pink	plum	red	indianred
mediumvioletred	orangered	violetred	salmon
sienna	tan	thistle	turquoise
darkturquoise	mediumturquoise	violet	blueviolet
wheat	white	yellow	greenyellow

These names can be used directly when the specific color is wanted.

For example, the command line:

```
% xterm -bg lightblue -fg darkslategrey -bd plum &
```

creates an *xterm* window with a background of light blue, foreground of dark slate grey, and border of plum.

At the command line, a color name should be typed as a single word (for example, `darkslategrey`). However, you can type the words comprising a color name separately if you enclose them in quotes, as in the following command line:

```
% xterm -bg "light blue" -fg "dark slate grey" -bd plum &
```

---

*A corresponding compiled file called simply *rgb* contains the definitions used by the server; the *rgb.txt* file is the human-readable equivalent.

Hexadecimal Color Specification

You can also specify colors more exactly using a hexadecimal color string. You probably won't use this method unless you require a color not available by using a color name. In order to understand how this works, you may need a little background on how color is implemented on most workstations.

The RGB Color Model

Most color displays on the market today are based on the RGB color model. Each pixel on the screen is actually made up of three phosphors: one red, one green, and one blue. Each of these three phosphors is excited by a separate electron beam. When all three phosphors are fully illuminated, the pixel appears white to the human eye. When all three are dark, the pixel appears black. When the illumination of each primary color varies, the three phosphors generate a subtractive color. For example, equal portions of red and green, with no admixture of blue, makes yellow.

As you might guess, the intensity of each primary color is controlled by a three-part digital value—and it is the exact makeup of this value that the hexadecimal specification allows you to set.

Depending on the underlying hardware, different servers may use a larger or smaller number of bits (from 4 to 16 bits) to describe the intensity of each primary. To insulate you from this variation, most clients are designed to take color values containing anywhere from 4 to 16 bits (1 to 4 hex digits), and the server then scales them to the hardware. As a result, you can specify hexadecimal values in any one of the following formats:

```
#RGB
#RRGGBB
#RRRGGGBBB
#RRRRGGGGBBBB
```

where R, G, and B represent single hexadecimal digits and determine the intensity of the red, green, and blue primaries that make up each color.

When fewer than four digits are used, they represent the most significant bits of the value. For example, #3a6 is the same as #3000a0006000.*

What this means concretely is perhaps best illustrated by looking at the values that correspond to some colors in the color name database. We'll use 8-bit values (two hexadecimal digits for each primary) because that is the way they are defined in the *rgb.txt* file:

```
#000000      black
#FCFCFC      white
#FF0000      red
#00FF00      green
#0000FF      blue
#FFFF00      yellow
```

---

*If you are unfamiliar with hexadecimal numbering, see the Glossary for a brief explanation, or a basic computer textbook for a more extended discussion.

```
#00FFFF          cyan
#FF00FF          magenta
#5F9F9F          cadet blue
#42426F          cornflower blue
#BFD8D8          light blue
#8F8FBC          light steel blue
#3232CC          medium blue
#23238E          navy blue
#3299CC          sky blue
#007FFF          slate blue
#236B8E          steel blue
```

As you can see from the colors given above, pure red, green and blue result from the corresponding bits being turned full on. All primaries off yields black, while all nearly full on gives white. Yellow, cyan and magenta can be created by pairing two of the other primaries at full intensity. The various shades of blue shown above are created by varying the intensity of each primary—sometimes in unexpected ways.

The bottom line here is that if you don't intimately know the physics of color, the best you can do is to look up existing colors from the color name database and experiment with them by varying one or more of the primaries till you find a color you like. Unless you need precise colors, you are probably better off using color names.

How Many Colors are Available?

The number of distinct colors available on the screen at any one time depends on the amount of memory available for color specification.

A color display uses multiple bits per pixel (also referred to as multiple planes or the *depth* of the display) to select colors. Programs that draw in color use the value of these bits as a pointer to a lookup table called a *colormap*, in which each entry (or *colorcell*) contains the RGB values for a particular color.* As shown in Figure 6-2, any given pixel value is used as an index into this table—for example, a pixel value of 16 will select the sixteenth colorcell.

Why is this technical detail important? Because it explains several issues that you might encounter in working with color displays.

First, the range of colors possible on the display is a function of the number of bits available in the colormap for RGB specification. If eight bits is available for each primary, then the range of possible colors is 256^3 (somewhere over 16 million colors). This means that you can create incredibly precise differences between colors.

However, the number of different colors that can be displayed on the screen at any one time is a function of the number of planes. A four-plane system can index 2^4 colorcells (16 distinct colors); an eight-plane system can index 2^8 colorcells (256 distinct colors); and a 24-plane system can index 2^{24} colorcells (over 16 million distinct colors).

---

*There is a type of high-end display in which pixel values are used directly to control the illumination of the red, green and blue phosphors, but far more commonly, the bits per pixel are used indirectly, with the actual color values specified independently, as described here.

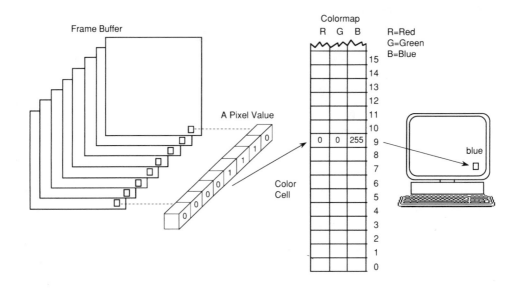

Figure 6-2. Multiple Planes Used to Index a Colormap

If you are using a four-plane workstation, the fact that you can precisely define hundreds of different shades of blue is far less significant than the fact that you can't use them all at the same time. There isn't space for all of them to be stored into the colormap at one time, or any mechanism for them to be selected even if they could be stored.

This limitation is made more significant by the fact that X is a multi-client environment. When X starts up, usually no colors are loaded into the colormap. As clients are invoked, certain of these cells are allocated. But when all of the free colorcells are used up, it is no longer possible to request new colors. When this happens, you will usually be given the closest possible color from those that have already been allocated. However, you may instead be given an error message and told that there are no free colorcells.

In order to minimize the chance of running out of colorcells, many programs used "shared" colorcells. Shared colorcells can be used by any number of applications, but they can't be changed by any of them. They can only be deallocated by each application that uses them, and when all applications have deallocated the cell, it is available for setting one again. Shared cells are most often used for background, border, and cursor colors.

Alternately, some clients have to be able to change the color of graphics they have already drawn. This requires another kind of cell, called private, which can't be shared. A typical use of a private cell would be for the pallete of a color mixing application. Such a program might have three bars of each primary color, and a box which shows the mixed color. The primary bars would use shared cells, while the mixed color box would use a private cell.

In summary, some programs define colorcells to be read-only and shareable, while others define the colorcells to be read/write and private.

To top it off, there are even clients that may temporarily swap in a whole private colormap of their own. Because of the way color is implemented, if this happens, all other applications will be displayed in unexpected, or "false" colors.

In order to minimize such conflicts, you should request precise colors only when necessary. By preference, use color names or hexadecimal specifications that you specified for other applications.

Font Specification

Many clients allow you to specify the font to be used when displaying text in the window. The option varies from client to client. For *xterm*, the option is −fn. For example, the command line:

```
% xterm -fn fg-16 &
```

creates an *xterm* window in which text will be displayed with the font named *fg-16*.

Table 6-2. Fonts in the Standard Distribution

Fixed-width Fonts			Variable-width Fonts			
6x10	fgb1-25	oldera	apl-s25	hbr-s40	vg-25	vr-30
6x12	fgb1-30	rot-s16	arrow3	krivo	vg-31	vr-31
6x13	fgi-20	sans12	chp-s25	met25	vg-40	vr-40
8x13	fgi1-25	sansb12	chs-s50	mit	vgb-25	vrb-25
8x13bold	fgs-22	sansi12	cursor	plunk	vgb-31	vrb-30
9x15	fixed	serif10	cyr-s25	runlen	vgbc-25	vrb-31
crturz	fqxb-25	serif12	cyr-s30	stan	vgh-25	vrb-35
dancer	fr-25	serifb10	cyr-s38	sub	vgi-20	vrb-37
fg-13	fr-33	serifb12	ent	subsub	vgi-25	vri-25
fg-16	fr1-25	serifi10	fcor-20	sup	vgi-31	vri-30
fg-18	fr2-25	serifi12	fgb-13	supsup	vgl-40	vri-31
fg-20	fr3-25	stempl	fgb-25	sym-s25	vgvb-31	vri-40
fg-22	frb-32	swd-s30	fri-33	sym-s53	vmic-25	vsg-114
fg-25	ipa-s25	vtbold	fri1-25	variable	vply-36	vsgn-57
fg-30	lat-s30	vtsingle	ger-s35	vbee-36	vr-20	vshd-40
fg-40	micro	xif-s25	grk-s25	vctl-25	vr-25	vxms-37
fg1-25			grk-s30	vg-13	vr-27	vxms-43
			hbr-s25	vg-20		

There are quite a few fonts. Pictures of the characters in each font are provided in Appendix C, or they can be displayed on the screen with *xfd* as described in Chapter 5. The font names are listed above. They are divided into fixed-width fonts (typewriter style) and variable-width fonts (proportional). Use only fixed-width fonts for text in an *xterm* window. (Variable-width fonts would be treated as constant width, and would be spaced unevenly.)

Use variable-width fonts only with programs designed to use them, such as a PostScript pre-viewer or *wysiwyg* editor.

Fonts are located in */usr/lib/X11/fonts*. When a font is referenced by an X client, the font is taken from this directory unless an explicit path name to another font directory is provided, using the fp option to *xset* described in Chapter 9.

Reverse Video

There are three options to control whether or not the application will display in reverse video—that is, with the foreground and background colors reversed. -rv or -reverse are used to request reverse video.

+rv is used to override any reverse video request that might be specified in a resource file (see Chapter 7). This is important, because not all clients handle reverse video correctly, and even those that do usually do so only on black and white displays.

7

Setting Application Defaults

This chapter describes how to set default values for application features (or "resources") such as color, geometry, fonts, and so on. It describes the syntax of resource definition files such as .Xdefaults, as well as the operation of xrdb, a client that can be used to dynamically change resource definitions, as well as to make them available to clients running on other machines.

In This Chapter:

7
Setting Application Defaults

Virtually all X clients are customizable. You can specify how the client looks on the screen—its size and placement, its border and background color or pattern, whether or not the window has title and scroll bars, and so on. These features are generically referred to as "user preferences."

Traditional UNIX applications rely on command-line options to allow users to customize the way they work. As we've already discussed in Chapter 6, X applications support command line options too, but often not for all their features. There can be so many customizable features in a application that a command line to set them all would be completely impractical. (Imagine the aggravation of misspelling an option in a command that was three lines long.)

X solves this problem by providing several different files in which you can place specifications. These files are more than just command-line options placed in a file. They are read in and processed in a certain order within an application by a set of routines called the resource manager. The resource manager applies certain rules when processing these files, so you can set an option for many applications with a single line. You can also set an option that controls only one window within one instance of a single application. These rules give you maximum flexibility in setting options, but with the minimum amount of text. It is also important to note that command line options normally take precedence over any option settings found in these files, so you can set the files to control the way you *normally* want your application to work, and then use command line options to specify changes you need for only one or two instances of the application.

The options that a given application allows depends on its features and on how it was programmed. There is a certain set of standard options, like geometry, foreground and background color, and font, but there is no guarantee that all programmers will implement these options in exactly the same way. However, all applications programmed using the same toolkit will have a common set of options, and this fact is noted on the reference page for each of these applications. The option handling of the applications described in this book are quite standard.

Prior to Release 2 of X11, there was only one user preference file called *.Xdefaults*, placed in the user's home directory. Starting with Release 2, the *.Xdefaults* file will be read if present, but more commonly, default values for user preferences can be stored in any file you like, and are "loaded" into the X server with a program called *xrdb* (X resource database manager), which is normally run from your *.login* file.

Remember that X allows clients to run on different machines across a network, not just on the machine that supports the X server. The problem with the older *Xdefaults* mechanism was that users who were running clients on multiple machines had to maintain multiple *Xdefaults* files, one on each machine. By contrast, *xrdb* stores the user preferences directly in the server, thus making them available to all clients, regardless of the machine the clients are running on. *xrdb* also allows applications to dynamically change the preferences without editing files.

For Release 2, many of the common clients were rewritten to use the X Toolkit. As described in Chapter 5, Toolkits are a mechanism for simplifying the design and coding of applications, and making them operate in a consistent way. Toolkits provides a standard set of objects, or "widgets," such as menus, command buttons, dialog boxes, scrollbars, and so on. The naming syntax for user preferences was extended in Release 2 to match the class and object hierarchy that is built into toolkit programs.

In this chapter, we'll first look at the syntax of entries in a user preference file, and then describe how to use *xrdb*.

In discussing the naming syntax, we'll explain both the basic mechanism, which will work with either Release 1 or Release 2 clients, and the more complex naming syntax for applications written with the X Toolkit.

All users should read the section entitled *Resource Naming Syntax*. If you are running clients on multiple machines, or want to change preferences dynamically, read the section *Using xrdb*.

Resource Naming Syntax

The syntax of *Xdefaults* or any other resource definition file is quite simple. Each client defines various variables that can be used to specify user preferences. The variables for each client are documented on its reference page in Part Three of this manual. Clients that use a toolkit will have a common set of variables that may not be shown on each reference page.

Each line in a resource definition file consists of the name of a client, followed by a period or an asterisk and the name of a variable. A colon and whitespace separate the client and variable names from the actual value. For example:

```
xterm*scrollbar:    on
```

If the name of the client is omitted, the variable applies to all clients. If the same variable is specified as a global variable and a client-specific variable, the client-specific variable takes precedence for that client. Note, however, that if the name of the client is omitted, the line must begin with an asterisk, not a period.

Be sure that you don't inadvertently omit the colon at the end of a resource specification. This is an easy mistake to make and there are normally no error messages. The value you set will simply not take effect.

If you do want error messages to be printed, specify the value "on" for the resource `StringConversionWarnings`. If you want such warnings for all applications, put the line:

```
*StringConversionWarnings:   on
```

in your resource file. To specify that warnings be provided for a particular application, put the
name of the application at the start of the line. For example, for *xterm*, you would specify the
resource:

```
xterm*StringConversionWarnings:   on
```

Comment lines are introduced with an exclamation point (!). Release 1 used a sharp sign (#),
but this was found to conflict with options using hexadecimal color specifications.

If the last character on a line is a backslash (\), the resource definition on that line is assumed
to continue on the next line.

Tight Bindings and Loose Bindings

In Release 1, most applications had only a single level of preference specification. That is, a
resource definition had the form:

client.option: *value*

In Release 2, however, the resource manager was rewritten to work more naturally with toolkits. As mentioned above, Toolkit applications are made up of predefined components called
widgets. There can be widgets within widgets (e.g. a command button within a dialog box).
The syntax of preference specifications was expanded to provide control over each level of the
widget hierarchy. Accordingly, you should think of a preference specification as having the
following format:

object.subobject[.*subobject*...].*attribute*: *value*

The final term might be an object (such as a label), but is frequently an attribute of an object
(such as its background color.)

The value of the final term should usually be self-evident from the type of resource or from
the description on the reference page. Most of these values are similar to those used with the
command-line options described in Chapter 6. For example, various resources, such as `bor-
derColor` or `background`, take color specifications; `geometry` takes a geometry string;
`font` takes a font name, and so on. The cases that can be somewhat confusing are logical
values, such as `scrollBar`. In some cases, logical values are specified as `on` or `off`; in
others, `True` or `False` are used instead. Check the reference page for each client, and if it is
ambiguous, try both forms.

The rewrite of an application such as *xterm* to use the Toolkit resource-handling mechanism is
something of a retrofit. The "widget" hierarchy is quite simple: the VT102 window is considered one widget, the Tektronix window another, and the menu a third.

This means that to request that *xterm* windows be created with a scrollbar, you should theoretically specify:

```
xterm.vt100.scrollbar:  on
```

instead of the Release 1 specification:

```
xterm.scrollbar:   on
```

Unfortunately, in practice *xterm* doesn't match its documentation. In fact, there seems to be another undocumented widget before *vt100* in the hierarchy. And this is where the * separator comes in. An asterisk is a kind of wildcard, referred to as a "loose binding." When you use the asterisk as a separator, you say: "I don't care how many levels in the widget hierarchy occur between these two points." So you can say:

```
xterm*scrollbar:   on
```

without having to know what widgets have been introduced.*

A period, by contrast, is considered a "tight binding" between two levels in the hierarchy. It specifies an exact relationship.

In an application that supports multiple levels of widgets, you can mix asterisks and periods. In general, though, the developers of X recommend always using * rather than . as the separator even with simple applications, since this gives application developers the freedom to insert new levels in the hierarchy as they produce new releases of an application.

The reference page for each client should always tell you what widget the variable belongs to, so you can specify the hierarchy correctly. If you are in doubt, use the * separator.

Instances and Classes

Each component of a resource specification has an associated *class*. Several different widgets, or widget attributes, may have the same class. For example, in the case of *xterm*, the foreground color for drawing, the pointer color, and the text cursor color are all defined as *instances* of the class Foreground. This makes it possible to set the value of all three with a single preference specification. That is, if you wanted to make the text, the pointer and the cursor dark blue, you could specify either:

```
xterm*foreground:    darkblue
xterm*cursorColor:   darkblue
xterm*pointerColor:  darkblue
```

or:

```
xterm*Foreground:    darkblue
```

Capitalization is used to distinguish class names from instance names. Class names always begin with a capital letter, while instance names always begin with a lowercase letter. Note however that if an instance name is a compound word (such as cursorColor), the second word is capitalized. It is only the case of the initial character that is significant.

_____

*You can tell this without looking at the code, simply by testing different resource specifications.

```
xterm.vt100.scrollbar:     on      doesn't work
xterm*vt100.scrollbar:     on      works
xterm*vt100.scrollbar:     on      works
xterm*scrollbar:           on      works
```

One shouldn't judge *xterm* too harshly for this. In the words of its authors', it is a "historical relic." It has been ported from X10 and added to so many times by so many people that the authors believe it badly needs a rewrite.

The real power of class and instance naming is not apparent in applications with a simple window hierarchy like *xterm*. In complex applications written with the X Toolkit, it allows you to do things such as to say that you want all buttons in dialog boxes to be blue, but one particular button to be red. For example, in a hypothetical application, you might have a resource file that reads:

```
xmail*buttonbox*Buttons:     blue
xmail*buttonbox*delete:      red
```

This type of thing works because an instance name always overrides the corresponding class name. Class names thus allow default values to be specified for all instances of a given type of object. Instance names can be used to specify exceptions to the rules outlined by the class names.

Note that class names can also be used with the rules for interpretation of tight and loose bindings to generalize a preference file. For example, the following specification would say that the foreground colors for all clients should be blue:

```
*Foreground:  blue
```

The reference page for a given program should always give you both instance and class names for every resource variable you can set. You'll notice that in many cases, the class name is identical to the instance name, with the exception of the initial capital. Often (but not always) this means that there is only one instance of that class. In other cases, the instance with the same name is simply the primary or most obvious instance.

Precedence Rules for Resource Specification

As described later in the section on *xrdb*, there are several possible sources of resource specifications, which must be evaluated and merged by a client. In the event of conflicting specifications, there are a number of rules that are followed by clients in deciding which resource specification should take effect.

We've already seen two of these rules, which can be used (even in a single source of resource definitions, such as an *.Xdefaults* file) to specify general rules and exceptions to those rules:

- Instance names take precedence over class names.

- Tight bindings take precedence over loose bindings.

From just these two rules, you can deduce the general principle that the more specific a resource definition is, the more likely it is to be honored in the case of a conflict. However, for cases in which you want to set things up very carefully, you should know a bit about how programs interpret resource specifications.

For each resource it manages, the program has a complete, fully-specified, tightly-bound instance name and class name. In evaluating ambiguous user specifications, the program compares the specification against both the full instance name and the full class name. If a component in the user specification matches either name, it is accepted. If it matches more than one element in either name, it is evaluated according to the following precedence rules, in order of preference:

1. The levels in the hierarchy specified by the user must match the program's expectations, or the entry will be ignored. For example, if the program expects:

   ```
   xmail.scrollbar.background          name
   Xmail.Scrollbar.Background          class
   ```

   the following preference specification won't work:

   ```
   xmail.scrollbar:   on
   ```

2. Tight bindings take precedence over loose bindings. That is, entries with instance or class prefixed by a dot (".") are more specific than those prefixed by an asterisk ("*"). For example, the entry `xterm.geometry` will take precedence over the entry `xterm*geometry`.

3. Instances take precedence over specific classes. For example, the entry `*scrollbar.background` will take precedence over `*Scrollbar.Background`.

4. An instance or class name that is explicitly stated takes precedence over one that is omitted. For example, the entry `Scrollbar*Background` is more specific than the entry `*Background`.

5. Left components carry more weight than right components. For example, the entry `xterm*background` will take precedence over `scrollbar*background`.

As an example of these rules, assume the following user preference specifications for a hypothetical Toolkit application called *xmail*:

```
xmail*background:          red
*command.font:    8x13
*command.background:      blue
*Command.Foreground:      green
xmail.toc*Command.activeForeground:      black
xmail.toc.border:        3
```

A query by the program for the name

```
xmail.toc.messageFunctions.include.activeForeground
```

and class

```
Xmail.Box.SubBox.Command.Foreground
```

would match `xmail.toc*Command.activeForeground` and return "black." However, it also matches `*Command.Foreground` but with lower preference, so it would not return "green." The foreground color of the include button in its active state would be set to "black."

Some Common Resources

Most applications written using the Toolkit have a set of class and instance names in common. Those that you might be able to set include:

Table 7-1. Core Toolkit Resources

Instance Name	Default	Description
background	white	background color
backgroundPixmap	none	background pattern
borderColor	black	border color
borderPixmap	none	border pattern
borderWidth	1	border width in pixels
foreground	black	foreground color

Note that in a complex Toolkit application, these values can occur at every level in a widget hierarchy. For example, our hypothetical *xmail* application might support the following complete instance names:

```
xmail.background
xmail.buttonBox.background
xmail.buttonBox.commandButton.background
xmail.buttonBox.commandButton.quit.background
```

Of course, the specification:

```
xmail*background
```

would match any and all of them.

A Sample .Xdefaults File

Example 7-1 shows a sample *Xdefaults* file. This file sets the border width for all clients to a default value of 3 pixels, and sets other specific variables for *xclock* and *xterm*. The meaning of each variable is fairly obvious from its name (for example, xterm*scrollbar: on means that *xterm* windows should be created with a scrollbar. For a detailed description of each possible variable, see Part Three of this manual.

Example 7-1. A Sample .Xdefaults File

```
!
! global preferences
!
*StringConversionWarnings:  on
!
! clock preferences
```

Example 7-1. A Sample .Xdefaults File (continued)

```
!
xclock*analog          1
xclock*BorderWidth:    5
xclock*Geometry:       64x64
!
! xterm preferences
!
xterm*curses:          on
xterm*cursor:          skyblue
xterm*iconBitmap:      /usr/lib/X11/bitmaps/shell
xterm*jumpScroll:      off
xterm*saveLines:       300
xterm*scrollBar:       on
xterm*scrollKey:       on
xterm*visualBell:      off
xterm*background:      black
xterm*border:          blue
xterm*borderWidth:     3
xterm*foreground:      white
xterm*font:            8x13
xterm*mouse:           white
```

Two Useful Options

Two command-line options that are supported by all clients written with the Xt Toolkit can be useful in conjunction with preference specifications.

The -xrm Option

The -xrm option allows you to specify on the command line any line that you would other-wise put into a preference-setting file. For example:

```
% xterm -xrm "xterm*Foreground: blue"
```

Note that this is most useful for setting classes, since there are usually individual named options that correspond to the variables for each instance name. (For example, -fg would set the foreground attribute of a window, whereas -xrm must be used to set Foreground.)

The -name Option

If a program has been designed to support the -name option, you can list instance resources under an arbitrary program alias name that you specify with the -name option to a program. For example, you could put the following entries into a preference file such as *Xdefaults*.

```
XTerm*Font: 6x10
smallxterm*Font:      3x5
smallxterm*Geometry: 80x10
bigxterm*Font:   9x15
bigxterm*Geometry: 80x55
```

You could then use the following commands to create *xterm*s of different sizes:

```
% xterm &
```

would create a normal *xterm*.

```
% xterm -name smallxterm &
```

would create a small *xterm*.

```
% xterm -name bigxterm &
```

would create a big *xterm*.

Note that the class name of *xterm* is *XTerm*, not *Xterm* as you might expect. This is a bug, and should be fixed in Release 5.

Using xrdb

The *xrdb* program saves you from the difficulty of maintaining multiple *.Xdefaults* files if you run clients on multiple machines. It stores user preferences in the X server, where they are accessible to all clients using that server. (Technically speaking, the values of variables are stored in a data structure referred to as the RESOURCE_MANAGER property of the root window of screen 0 for that server. From time to time, we may refer to this property colloquially simply as the Resource Database.)

xrdb is normally invoked at login, or from some other startup file, although it can also be invoked interactively. It has the following syntax:

xrdb [*options*] [*filename*]

There are a number of options; all of them are documented on the *xrdb* reference page. Several of the most useful are discussed below. (Those that are not discussed here have to do with *xrdb*'s ability to interpret C preprocessor-style defined symbols; this is an advanced topic. For more information, see the reference page in Part Three, and the *cpp*(1) manual page in your *UNIX Reference Manual*.)

The optional *filename* argument specifies the name of a file from which the values of client variables (resources) will be read. If no filename is specified, *xrdb* will expect to read its data from standard input. That is, the program will appear to hang, until you type some data, followed by an end-of-file (CTRL-D). Note that whatever you type will override the previous contents of the RESOURCE_MANAGER property, so if you inadvertently type *xrdb* without a filename argument, and then quit with CTRL-D, you will delete any previous values.

You can also load resource values with the -load option. Explicit use of this option is encouraged, but not necessary. For example, to load the contents of your *.Xdefaults* file into the RESOURCE_MANAGER, you would type:

```
% xrdb -load .Xdefaults
```

Other Sources of Resource Definition

If *xrdb* has not been run, the RESOURCE_MANAGER property will not be set. Instead, clients will look for the *Xdefaults* file in your home directory.

Whether or not *xrdb* has been run, the following sources of resource definition will also be consulted:

- Any values stored in a file with the same name as the application, in the directory */usr/lib/X11/app-defaults* will be loaded into the resource manager.

- Next, the contents of any file specified by the shell environment variable XENVIRONMENT will be loaded. If this variable is not defined in the environment, programs looks for a file named *Xdefaults-hostname* in your home directory, where **hostname** is the name of the host where the client is executing.

- Finally, any values specified on the command line with the −xrm option will be loaded.

All of these various sources of defaults will be loaded and merged, according to the precedence rules described above in the section *Precedence Rules for Resource Specification*.

The client will then merge these various defaults specified by the user with its own internal defaults, if any.

If the user has specified any options on the command line (other than with the −xrm option), these values will override those specified by resource defaults, regardless of their source.

Querying the Resource Database

You can find out what options are currently set by using the −query option. For example:

```
% xrdb -query
Xterm*ScrollBar:    true
Xterm.statusLine:   on
bigxterm*font:      9x15
bigxterm*Geometry: 80x55
smallxterm*Font:        3x5
smallxterm*Geometry:    80x10
xterm*borderWidth: 3
```

If *xrdb* has not been run, this command will produce no output.

Loading New Values into the Resource Database

By default, *xrdb* reads its input (either a file or standard input) and stores the results into the Resource Database. If instead, you want to merge new values (say by specifying a single value from standard input), you can use the −merge option instead. Only the new values will be changed; variables that were already set will be preserved rather than overwritten with empty values.

For example, let's say you wanted to add new preferences listed in the file *new.values.* You could say:

```
% xrdb -merge new.values
```

As another example, if you wanted to dynamically add scrollbars to all *xterm* windows, you could use standard input, and say:

```
% xrdb -merge
xterm*ScrollBar: on
```

and then press Control-D to end the standard input. Note that because of precedence rules for resource naming, you may not automatically get what you want. For example, if you specify:

```
xterm*scrollBar:   on
```

and the more specific value:

```
xterm*vt100.scrollBar: off
```

has already been set, your new, less-specific setting will be ignored. You didn't use the −merge option incorrectly—you got caught by the rules of precedence.

If your specifications don't seem to work, use the −query option to list the values in the RESOURCE_MANAGER property, and look for conflicting specifications. Note also that when you add new specifications, they won't affect any programs already running, but only programs started after the new resource specifications are in effect.

Saving the Resource Definitions in a File

Assume that you've loaded the RESOURCE_MANAGER property from an *.Xdefaults* or other file. However, you've dynamically loaded a different value using the −merge option, and you'd like to make the new value your default.

You don't need to edit the file manually (although you certainly could.) The −edit option allows you to write out the current value of the RESOURCE_MANAGER property into a file. If the file already exists, it is overwritten with the new values. However, *xrdb* is smart enough to preserve any comments and preprocessor declarations in the file, replacing only the resource definitions.

For example:

```
% xrdb -edit ~/.Xdefaults
```

will save the current contents of the RESOURCE_MANAGER property in the file *.Xdefaults* in your home directory.

If you want to save a backup copy of an existing file, use the −backup option as follows:

```
% xrdb -edit .mydefaults -backup old
```

The string following the −backup option is used as an extension to be appended to the old filename. In the above example, the previous copy of *.mydefaults* would be saved as *.mydefaults.old*

Removing Resource Definitions

You can delete the definition of the RESOURCE_MANAGER property from the server by calling *xrdb* with the −remove option.

There is no way to delete a single resource definition, other than to read the current *xrdb* values to a file. For example:

```
% xrdb -query > filename
```

Use an editor to edit and save the file, deleting the resource definitions you no longer want:

```
% vi filename
```

And read the edited values back into the RESOURCE_MANAGER with *xrdb*:

```
% xrdb filename
```

8
Customizing the Window Manager

This chapter describes the syntax of the .uwmrc startup file that can be used to customize the operation of the uwm *window manager. It describes how to bind functions to keys, and how to define your own* uwm *menus. An alternate .uwmrc file is presented in full.*

In This Chapter:

8
Customizing the Window Manager

Hard as it may be to believe, every function of the window manager described in Chapters 2 and 3 of this manual can be modified by the user. The function itself will remain the same (for example, you will still move a window by holding down a key and mouse button simultaneously and dragging the mouse), but the keys and/or menu items used to invoke the function may be completely different.

The operation of the window manager, as distributed, is controlled by a text file called */usr/lib/X11/uwm/default.uwmrc.* This file has three parts:

- A variables section, which contains various settings, such as the font with which menus should be displayed, the volume of the keyboard bell, and so on.

- A key bindings section, which defines the keys, mouse buttons, and key/mouse-button combinations that will be used to invoke each window manager function (including the display of menus).

- A menus section, which defines the contents of the menus.

As users gain experience with the window manager, each can create a file called *.uwmrc* in his or her home directory. This file can simply extend *default.uwmrc*, resetting a variable or two, perhaps changing a key binding or adding a menu item—or it can replace it completely, changing every aspect of the way the window manager operates. As one of its creators remarked, this flexibility makes *uwm* "the bane of trade show demonstrators and the joy of experienced users."[*]

Rather than abstractly explaining the syntax of these various sections in a *.uwmrc* file, let's plunge right in, by looking at the *default.uwmrc* file from the MIT X11 distribution. (Note that if you are using a commercial version of X, this file may be significantly different. However, in that case, you most likely have a user's guide specific to your system—perhaps even a customized version of this one!)

---

[*]Joel Gancarz, "UWM: A User Interface for X Windows," in *USENIX Conference Proceedings*, Summer 1986, p. 431.

Example 8-1. The default.uwmrc file from the MIT distribution

```
# Copyright (c) 1987 by the Massachusetts Institute of Technology.
#
# This is a startup file for uwm that produces an xwm lookalike,
# but adds two useful menus.  It is patterned on the public
# distribution ../lib/X/uwm/jg.uwmrc file by Jim Gettys.
#
resetbindings
resetvariables
resetmenus
noautoselect
delta=5
freeze
grid
zap
pushabsolute
push=1
hiconpad=5
viconpad=5
hmenupad=3
vmenupad=0
iconfont=fixed
menufont=fixed
resizefont=fixed
volume=0

# FUNCTION        KEYS  CONTEXT          MOUSE BUTTON       ACTIONS
f.newiconify=  meta  :window|icon:  delta left
f.raise=       meta  :window|icon:  delta left
f.lower=       meta  :window|icon:  left up
f.raise=       meta  :window:       middle down
f.resize=      meta  :window:       delta middle
f.iconify=     meta  :icon:         middle up
f.raise=       meta  :window|icon:  right down
f.move=        meta  :window|icon:  delta right
f.circledown=  meta  :root:         left down
f.circleup=    meta  :root:         right down
f.circledown=  m|s   ::             left down
f.menu=              :root:         middle down     : "WindowOps"
f.menu=        m|s   ::             middle down     : "WindowOps"
f.menu=        m|s   ::             middle down     : "Preferences"
f.circleup=    m|s   ::             right down
f.iconify=     m|c   :window|icon:  left down
f.newiconify=  m|l   :window|icon:  left down
f.raise=       m|l   :window|icon:  left up
f.pushright=   m|l   :window|icon:  right down
f.pushleft=    m|c   :window|icon:  right down
f.pushup=      m|l   :window|icon:  middle down
f.pushdown=    m|c   :window|icon:  middle down

menu = "WindowOps" {
New Window:     !"xterm&"
RefreshScreen: f.refresh
Redraw:            f.redraw
Move:              f.move
Resize:            f.resize
```

```
Lower:          f.lower
Raise:          f.raise
CircUp:         f.circleup
CircDown:       f.circledown
AutoIconify:    f.iconify
LowerIconify:   f.newiconify
NewIconify:     f.newiconify
Focus:          f.focus
Freeze:         f.pause
UnFreeze:       f.continue
Restart:        f.restart
}
menu = "Preferences" {
Bell Loud:      !"xset b 7&"
Bell Normal:    !"xset b 3&"
Bell Off:       !"xset b off&"
Click Loud:     !"xset c 8&"
Click Soft:     !"xset c on&"
Click Off:      !"xset c off&"
Lock On:        !"xset led on&"
Lock Off:       !"xset led off&"
Mouse Fast:     !"xset m 4 2&"
Mouse Normal:   !"xset m 2 5&"
Mouse Slow:     !"xset m 1 1&"
}
```

If you wish to change the operation of the window manager, you shouldn't change the *default.uwmrc* file. Instead, copy it to your home directory, under the name *.uwmrc*, and make changes to that copy. Or else, if you are planning only small changes, you can create a *.uwmrc* file from scratch. Settings in *default.uwmrc* and your own local *.uwmrc* file are cumulative (unless you explicitly override *default.uwmrc* as explained in the next section), so all you need to enter in your *.uwmrc* are values you wish to change.

Setting .uwmrc Variables

The first section of the file sets global variables. Some variables are Boolean—that is, their presence or absence "toggles" some attribute of the window manager—while others have the form:

```
variable=value
```

where *value* is either a number or a text string.

An example of a Boolean variable is `autoselect`, which, if present, causes the pointer to automatically appear in the first menu item whenever a menu is invoked. Note however that there are inconsistencies in the way *uwm* specifies Boolean variables. Some, like `reset-variables`, take effect if present; they must be deleted from the file or commented out by placing a sharp sign (#) at the start of the line if you don't want them to take effect. Others, such as `normali` (which makes sure that icons aren't placed partially offscreen when created), have an opposite toggle (`nonormali`, which must be used if you want the opposite effect. If two corresponding on/off toggles are both mistakenly placed in a file, whichever is specified later in the file takes effect.

An example of a text string variable is:

```
menufont=fixed
```

which names the font that should be used in all menus. (See Appendix C for a list and illustration of all fonts in the standard X11 distribution.)

An example of a numeric variable is:

```
volume=4
```

which sets the volume of the keyboard bell on a scale ranging from 0 to 7.

The available variables are described in detail on the *uwm* reference page in Part Three of this manual, so we won't go into detail on each of them here. Three variables that are worthy of note, though, are `resetvariables`, `resetbindings`, and `resetmenus`. You may recall that settings in your local *.uwmrc* file are cumulative with those in the *default.uwmrc* file. That is, you need define only changed or added variable values, function bindings or menus if you are happy with the basic operations set forth in *default.uwmrc*. If, however, you want to start with a clean slate, you should use one or more of the three *reset* variables which reset, respectively, the three sections of the *.uwmrc* file. By convention, if specified, these variables should always head the list of variables.

One additional note of syntax that is not obvious from the *default.uwmrc* example shown above: variable definitions need not be written on separate lines; instead, they can be separated by a semicolon and space. For example:

```
resetvariables; resetbindings; resetmenus
```

Button-Key Bindings

The second section of the *.uwmrc* file specifies which combination of keys and buttons (and in which context) will be used to invoke each predefined *uwm* function. Let's see how this works, by looking at the first two lines of the function binding section of *default.uwmrc*.

```
# FUNCTION      KEYS CONTEXT       MOUSE BUTTON    ACTIONS
f.newiconify=  meta :window|icon:  delta left
```

The first line we've shown is just a comment line, which labels each of the fields in the line below. The first field is separated from the others by an equals sign; subsequent fields are separated by colons. In *default.uwmrc*, fields are separated by tabs for clarity, making the colons (falsely) appear to be delimiters only for the context field; they could instead follow each other without intervening whitespace.

Let's talk about each of the fields in turn.

Function Names

The first field in a key binding contains the name of a function, followed by an equals sign.

uwm has a number of predefined functions. Each of these functions has a name beginning with "f.". The meaning of most of these functions should be fairly obvious to you from the name, if not from your experience using the window manager. For example, f.resize is used to resize a window, f.move to move a window, or f.iconify to change a window to an icon.

Others are less obvious. The function shown in the example, f.newiconify, is used to turn a window into an icon, or an icon into a window, and then to move it to a new location.

Each of the functions is described in detail on the reference page for *uwm* in Part Three of this manual.

Keys

The second field lists keys, if any, which must be held down while invoking the specified function. *uwm* recognizes a small number of keys (discussed more fully in Chapter 9), the most common of which are shift, control, lock and meta. These names must be entered in the *.uwmrc* file in lower case, and can be abbreviated s, c, l, and m.

If two keys must be held down at once, the names should be separated by a vertical bar (|). For example, c|s would mean that the control and shift keys should be pressed simultaneously. It is not permissible to bind a function to three keys at once. If the field is left blank, no key needs to be pressed while invoking the function.

Control, Shift and Lock should be familiar to most users. But what is a "Meta" key? There isn't a key by that name on many keyboards—instead, Meta is a user-definable control key that can be mapped to an actual key on the physical keyboard using the *xmodmap* client as described in Chapter 9. Most implementations of X will include a mapped Meta key. Type *xmodmap* without any arguments to display the map. The *default.uwmrc* specifies the Meta key in many keyboard bindings. On workstations without a special key corresponding to Meta, you will have to use *xmodmap* to find out or change the definition of Meta to something reasonable.

Meta could be (and often is) mapped to Control, although this could potentially lead to conflicts with applications that want to use the Control key. In particular, certain functions of *xedit* will operate strangely or not at all if Meta is mapped to Control.

If you want to map the Meta key, it is best to choose a keyboard key that's within easy reach and is not used frequently for other applications (perhaps an "Alt" or "Funct" key). Left- or right-handedness could also be a factor in choosing a Meta key.

The developers of *uwm* warn against binding functions to the shift key alone, since they say certain applications use it as a control key. If you use it in *uwm*, it will perform both functions simultaneously, which is likely to be confusing. For the same reason, you should not bind functions to buttons without modifier keys, except in the context of the root window.

Context

The third field defines the context—the location the pointer must be in before the function can be invoked. This field may be blank, or may contain one or more of: window, icon, or root. Multiple context specifications should be separated by vertical bars.

If the context is blank, it means that the pointer can be anywhere. If root is specified, it means that the pointer must be in the root (background) window, and not in any other window or icon. If the context is window or icon, the pointer must be in a window or icon for the function to be invoked.

The context field makes perfect sense if you consider our sample function binding:

```
f.newiconify= meta :window|icon: delta left
```

`f.newiconify` turns a window into an icon, or an icon into a window. Obviously, the pointer must be in a window or an icon for the function to be used.

Mouse Buttons

The fourth field defines the state of the mouse buttons used to invoke the function.

uwm is designed to be used with a three button mouse, and keeps separate track of when the button is pressed and when it is released. It can also tell when the mouse is moved.

Accordingly, a button specification has two parts:

- The name of a button: left, middle or right. These must be in lower case, and can be abbreviated l, m and r.

- The state of the button: down, up (just released), or delta (held down while the mouse is moving). The distance in pixels the mouse must be moved in order to trigger the delta state is set by the `delta` variable, and is set to 5 in *default.uwmrc.* The actual translation of pixels to distance will vary from system to system, and you will probably want to experiment to find a value that you are comfortable with. The context for the delta state is the context at the point the button was first pressed, not its position at the time it has moved a *delta* number of pixels.

The button name and state can be specified in either order.

Going back to our sample function binding:

```
f.newiconify= meta :window|icon: delta left
```

you can now understand that the `f.newiconify` function is invoked by moving the pointer to either a window or an icon, pressing the meta key and the left mouse button, and dragging the mouse in any direction.

All of the other function definitions should be equally readable to you. Go back for a moment and review the bindings shown in the *default.uwmrc* file in Example 8-1.

You'll notice that it is possible to bind the same function to more than one set of keys, buttons and/or contexts. For example, the WindowOps menu can be invoked anywhere by pressing the meta and shift keys together with the middle button on the mouse. But when the pointer is in the root window, the WindowOps menu can be invoked by pressing only the middle button on the mouse. The reason for this become obvious if you realize that when the pointer is on a window or an icon, the middle mouse button alone might have some other meaning to the application running in that window. In order to avoid conflict with other applications, *uwm* uses the more complex key/button combination. But when the pointer is in the root window, there is no possibility of conflict, and it can take a more forgiving approach.

Action

The fifth field, labeled "Action," is typically used only for the f.menu function, which allows you to invoke menus. The fifth field specifies the name of a menu, whose contents are defined in the third section of the *.uwmrc* file. If the menu name contains quotes, special characters, parentheses, tabs or blanks, it must be enclosed in double quotes. For consistency, you may want to always quote menu names. For example:

```
f.menu=                   :root:      middle down: "WindowOps"
f.menu=       m|s         ::          middle down: "WindowOps"
f.menu=       m|s         ::          middle down: "Preferences"
```

Defining Menus

The third section of a *.uwmrc* file contains menu definitions. These definitions have the format:

menu = *menu_name* {
item_name : *action*

.
.
.

}

The menu name must exactly match a name specified with the f.menu function.

Each item on the menu is given a label, which will be printed on the menu. This is followed by a colon and the action to be performed. The action may be one of *uwm*'s functions, or if prefixed by a ! character, it can be a system commands to be executed, as if in an *xterm* window. As shown in example 8-2, the WindowOps menu defined in *default.uwmrc* shows both types of action.

Example 8-2. The WindowOps Menu

```
menu = "WindowOps" {
New Window:       !"xterm&"
```

Example 8-2. The WindowOps Menu (continued)

```
RefreshScreen:   f.refresh
Redraw:          f.redraw
Move:            f.move
Resize:          f.resize
Lower:           f.lower
Raise:           f.raise
CircUp:          f.circleup
CircDown:        f.circledown
AutoIconify:     f.iconify
LowerIconify:    f.newiconify
NewIconify:      f.newiconify
Focus:           f.focus
Freeze:          f.pause
UnFreeze:        f.continue
Restart:         f.restart
}
```

New Window is accomplished by running another instance of *xterm*. The other functions are accomplished simply by invoking one of *uwm*'s predefined functions.

The Preferences menu shown in Example 8-3 simply invokes *xset* with a number of different options:

Example 8-3. The Preferences Menu

```
menu = "Preferences" {
Bell Loud:     !"xset b 7&"
Bell Normal:   !"xset b 3&"
Bell Off:      !"xset b off&"
Click Loud:    !"xset c 8&"
Click Soft:    !"xset c on&"
Click Off:     !"xset c off&"
Lock On:       !"xset led on&"
Lock Off:      !"xset led off&"
Mouse Fast:    !"xset m 4 2&"
Mouse Normal:  !"xset m 2 5&"
Mouse Slow:    !"xset m 1 1&"
}
```

Neither of these menus demonstrates a couple of other useful techniques you can put to use.

Submenus

Frankly, we consider the menus defined by the *default.uwmrc* file to be rather awkward and far from complete. Among other things, the WindowOps menu has too many infrequently-used functions mixed right in with those you need all the time.

For the moment, let's assume that we want to leave the variable definitions and function key bindings alone, but want to redefine the menus. We might create a local *.uwmrc* file that contained a menu definition like the one shown in Example 8-4.

Example 8-4. Window operations divided into two menus

```
resetmenus
menu = "WindowOps" {
Move:          f.move
Resize:        f.resize
Raise:         f.raise
Lower:         f.lower
(De)Iconify:   f.iconify
New window:    !"xterm -sb&"
Refresh screen:  f.refresh
Restart window manager:    f.restart
More Window Operations:    f.menu:"More Window Operations"
}

menu = "More Window Operations" {
(De)Iconify and move:      f.newiconify
Circulate windows up:      f.circleup
Circulate windows down:    f.circledown
Focus keyboard on window:  f.focus
Freeze server:             f.pause
Unfreeze server:           f.continue
}
```

To get from one menu to another, we simply define f.menu as the action for one item on the menu. No key, button or context is defined, so we go right to the next menu when selecting that item.

Slip off menus

In Example 8-4, there was no keyboard binding for the menu More Window Operations. That menu could only be invoked by selecting it from the WindowOps menu. Another way to divide the window into two would be to give both the same key/button/context binding, as shown in Example 8-5.

Example 8-5. Window Operations as two slip-off menus

```
resetbindings
# Note that if you resetbindings, you must recreate all desired
# operations.  If you are doing this kind of thing, you'd best copy
# the entire default.uwmrc to your home .uwmrc and edit it

f.menu=          :root:   middle down  : "WindowOps"
f.menu=          :root:   middle down  : "More Window Operations"
f.menu=   m|s    ::       middle down  : "WindowOps"
f.menu=   m|s    ::       middle down  : "More Window Operations"
```

If two menus have the same context and buttons, you can cause the second (or third, if more than two are defined) to appear simply by selecting nothing from the first, and, while continuing to hold down the specified mouse button (you can let go of the key), sliding the pointer off the menu to the right or left. The first menu will be replaced by the second.

If the labels of menu items are short, the menu can be too narrow, and hence difficult to use: you spend much more time sliding off menus unintentionally than you do selecting items. You can either train yourself to make pointer movements exactly perpendicular, or you can add horizontal menu padding as suggested in the revamp of *uwm* at the end of this chapter.

Executing System Commands from a Menu

We mentioned above that it is possible to specify a system command as a menu action simply by placing an exclamation point in front of the string to be executed. As we saw, the menus defined in *default.uwmrc* use this mechanism to create a new *xterm* window.

It is quite easy to cook up a menu that contains a miscellany of useful commands, as shown in Example 8-6.

Example 8-6. A Useful Commands Menu

```
f.menu=            :root:    middle down          : "Useful Commands"
                .
                .
                .
menu = "Useful Commands" {
Analog clock:      !"xclock -g =125x125-10+10&"
Digital clock:     !"xclock -digital -g =125x125-10+10&"
Edit File:         !"xterm -e vi"
Calculator:        !"xcalc -g =126x230-200+10&"
Mailbox:           !"xbiff -g =65x65-340+10&"
Display keyboard mappings: !"xmodmap&"
}
```

As you can quickly see, you can run any window-based programs directly, but you need to run other programs using *xterm*'s **-e** option. You are limited only by your imagination in what commands you might want to put on a menu. Each command runs in its own window, but that isn't necessarily the case, as we'll see in a moment.

Cut Buffer Strings

Another useful feature of *uwm*'s menus is that you can define the action for a menu item to be the insertion of a string into the server's "cut buffer." As discussed in Chapter 4, you can use this cut buffer from within *xterm* to cut and paste text between windows. Well, you can also use it from within *uwm* to define strings that will be placed in the cut buffer, ready for pasting into your window.

This feature is particularly useful for specifying command strings that you want to have executed in an existing *xterm* window.

A string prefixed with a vertical bar will be loaded into the cut buffer with no trailing newline. This means that you can paste the string into a window and keep typing to add to the command line. A string prefixed with a caret will be terminated with a newline, which means that if it is a command, and you paste it at the shell prompt in an *xterm* window, it will be executed immediately.

For example, we could add the following lines to our "Useful Commands" menu:

Example 8-7. Useful commands using cut buffer strings

```
menu = "Useful Commands" {
     .
     .
     .
Check disk space:  ^"df"
Remote login:      |"rlogin"
}
```

The last item on the menu uses I instead of ^, so that when the string is pasted into an *xterm* window, you can type in the name of the system to connect to. (If you tended to connect to a number of different systems on a regular basis, you could also just create a submenu with the names of various systems as menu items, and execute the correct command to login to each system from there.)

Of course, cut buffer strings are not just useful for pasting in commands at the shell prompt! You could also associate editing macros or frequently-used text with menu items for use with a text editor.

Color Menus

So far, we've assumed that all menus are black and white. But you can also create color menus. You can even assign different colors to the menu title, the highlighting bar (the horizontal band that follows the pointer within the menu and shows which item is selected) and the individual selections on the menu.

Colors are added to menus using the following syntax:

```
menu = "menu name" (title_fg:title_bg:highlight_fg: highlight_bg) {
"item name": (item_fg:item_bg):  "action"
     .
     .
     .

}
```

Up to four different colors can be defined for the overall menu:

title_fg	The foreground color of the menu title (i.e. the color of the lettering).
title_bg	The background color of the menu title.
highlight_fg	The foreground color of the highlighting bar (i.e. the color of the lettering within the bar).
highlight_bg	The background color of the highlighting bar.

Two colors can be defined for each menu item:

item_fg   The foreground color of the item (i.e. the color of the letter-
                                    ing).

item_bg   The background color of the item.

Colors can be specified either with color names or hex strings, as described in Chapter 6.

Here's a color menu that works well on a Sun-3 workstation. Keep in mind that the colors in
the color database may look different on different servers.

```
menu = "WindowOps" (darkslategrey:plum:darkslategrey:plum) {
   Move:                     (slateblue:lightblue):f.move
   Resize:                   (slateblue:lightblue):f.resize
   Raise:                    (slateblue:lightblue):f.raise
   Lower:                    (slateblue:lightblue):f.lower
   Iconify/DeIconify:        (slateblue:lightblue):f.iconify
   New window:               (slateblue:lightblue):!"xterm&"
   Refresh screen:           (slateblue:lightblue):f.refresh
   Restart window manager:   (slateblue:lightblue):f.restart
}
```

The total number of colors that can be allocated by the window manager for its own use is
specified by the `maxcolors` variable. If you try to use more than `maxcolors` colors, the
additional colors will default to the colors of the root window. This can also happen if the
server runs out of free colormap entries.

Some releases of *uwm* seem to include a color menu bug. If all menu items in the file are
specified in color, all menus default to black and white. One quick fix is to leave the final
item on the final menu in the file in black and white. More recent versions of X have
corrected the problem.

A Complete Revamp of Uwm

This section puts together the various techniques described in this chapter, and shows how to
develop a completely new user interface for *uwm*— one that we think works better than the
one defined in *default.uwmrc.*

```
# use this sample file as a starting point for your own customization

resetbindings; resetvariables; resetmenus
noautoselect
delta=5
freeze
grid
zap
pushabsolute
push=1
hiconpad=16
viconpad=16
hmenupad=22
```

```
vmenupad=1
iconfont=fg-16
menufont=fixed
resizefont=fixed
volume=0

# FUNCTION       KEYS CONTEXT        MOUSE BUTTON      ACTIONS
f.newiconify=    meta :window|icon:  delta left
f.raise=         meta :window|icon:  delta left
f.lower=         meta :window|icon:  left up
f.raise=         meta :window:       middle down
f.resize=        meta :window:       delta middle
f.iconify=       meta :icon:         middle up
f.raise=         meta :window|icon:  right down
f.move=          meta :window|icon:  delta right
f.circledown=    m|s  ::             left down
f.circledown=    meta :root:         left down
f.circleup=      meta :root:         right down
f.menu=               :root:         middle down       : "WindowOps"
f.menu=               :root:         middle down       : "More Window Operations"
f.menu=               :root:         middle down       : "Useful Commands"
f.menu=               :root:         middle down       : "Preferences"
f.menu=          m|s  ::             middle down       : "WindowOps"
f.menu=          m|s  ::             middle down       : "More Window Operations"
f.menu=          m|s  ::             middle down       : "Useful Commands"
f.menu=          m|s  ::             middle down       : "Preferences"
f.circleup=      m|s  ::             right down
f.iconify=       m|c  :window|icon:  left down
f.newiconify=    m|l  :window|icon:  left down
f.raise=         m|l  :window|icon:  left up
f.pushright=     m|l  :window|icon:  right down
f.pushleft=      m|c  :window|icon:  right down
f.pushup=        m|l  :window|icon:  middle down
f.pushdown=      m|c  :window|icon:  middle down

menu = "WindowOps" {
  Move:                 f.move
  Resize:               f.resize
  Raise:                f.raise
  Lower:                f.lower
  Iconify/DeIconify:    f.iconify
  New window:           !"xterm -sb &"
  Refresh screen:       f.refresh
  Restart window manager:      f.restart
}

menu = "More Window Operations" {
  Iconify and move:          f.newiconify
  Circulate windows up:      f.circleup
  Circulate windows down:    f.circledown
  Focus keyboard on window:  f.focus
  Freeze server:             f.pause
  Unfreeze server:           f.continue
  Create color window:       !"xterm -d unix:0.1 -fg darkslategrey
                             -bg lightblue -bd plum -bw 5&"
}
```

```
menu = "Useful Commands" {
    Analog clock:       !"xclock -hd darkslategrey -hl darkslategrey
                        -fg mediumorchid -bg lightblue -bd plum -bw 5
                        -g =162x162-10+10&"
    Digital clock:      !"xclock -digital -fg darkslategrey  -bg lightblue
                        -bd plum -bw 5 -g =162x37-10+174&"
    Calculator:         !"xcalc -g =126x230-200+10&"
    Mailbox:            !"xbiff -bg lightblue -fg lightslategrey -bd plum
                        -bw 3 -g =65x65-340+10&"
    Display keyboard mappings:      !"xmodmap&"
    Check disk space: ^"df"
    Remote login:       |"rlogin"
}

menu = "Preferences" {
    Bell Loud:      !"xset b 7&"
    Bell Normal:    !"xset b 3&"
    Bell Off:       !"xset b off&"
    Click Loud:     !"xset c 9&"
    Click Soft:     !"xset c 2&"
    Click Off:      !"xset c off&"
    Lock On:        !"xset led 1&"
    Lock Off:       !"xset -led 1&"
    Mouse Fast:     !"xset m 4 5&"
    Mouse Normal:   !"xset m 2 5&"
    Mouse Slow:     !"xset m 1 1&"
}
```

9
Setup Clients

This chapter describes three useful setup clients that can be used to customize the appearance of your display, and the operation of your keyboard and pointer. It also discusses how to run X clients from a single startup shell script.

In This Chapter:

Setup Clients

This chapter describes how to use the *xset* and *xsetroot* clients to control various aspects of server operation and how to use the *xmodmap* client to customize your keyboard. It also describes how to use a shell script run from your *.login* file as a way of automatically running these clients and opening a few standard windows to boot.

xmodmap: Modifier Key Customization Client

As described in Chapter Two, keys such as Shift, Control, Caps Lock, etc. are called "modifier" keys because they modify the action of other keys. The names and numbers of modifier keys differ from workstation to workstation. Every keyboard is likely to have a Shift, Caps Lock, and Control key, but after that, the babel begins. One workstation might have an "Alt" key, another might have a "Funct" key, and yet another a "Gold" key. On the Sun-3 keyboard, there are no less than three additional modifier keys, labeled Alternate, Right, and Left.

Because of the differences between keyboards, X programs are designed to work with "logical" modifier keynames that can be mapped by the user to any physical key on the keyboard with the *xmodmap* client.

The logical keynames that X recognizes are:

- shift
- lock
- ctrl
- mod1 (also 1 or meta in *uwm*)
- mod2 (also 2 in *uwm*)
- mod3 (also 3 in *uwm*)
- mod4 (also 4 in *uwm*)
- mod5 (also 5 in *uwm*)

These keynames are case insensitive.

Of these keys, only Shift, Caps Lock, Control, and Meta are in common use. Additional keys may be used by future applications—or you can decide to define them yourself. Note that *uwm* also recognizes the mod keys simply by number alone (1-5) and recognizes mod1 as meta (i.e., mod1, 1 and meta are equivalent).

Hypothetically, any key on the keyboard can function as a Shift, Control or Meta key, etc. For example, you could choose to map the Shift function to a single key called "Shift", to two "Shift" keys (one on either side of the keypad), to an "Alt" key, or to any other convenient key or keys on the physical keyboard. A left-handed person might choose to map modifier keys on the right side of the keyboard that more often are found on the left side, such as Control.

In practical terms, each server will have a default keyboard configuration. Shift, Caps Lock and Control will be mapped to obvious keys.

xmodmap can be used to print out the current keyboard assignments, or to change them.

Displaying the Current Map

With no arguments, *xmodmap* displays the current map of keynames to actual keys. Type *xmodmap* and you get a display similar to this:

```
xmodmap: up to 2 keys per modifier, (keycodes in parentheses):

shift       Shift_L (0x6a), Shift_R (0x75)
lock        Caps_Lock (0x7e)
control     Control_L (0x53)
mod2
mod3
mod4
mod5
```

Unfortunately, as you can see, the *xmodmap* output doesn't really tell you which key is which. As it turns out, what *xmodmap* prints out are two codes which are quite meaningless to the uninitiated.

For each logical keyname, *xmodmap* lists one or more *keysyms*, each followed in parentheses by an actual hardware *keycode*. A keysym is a symbol that theoretically represents the label on a key. A keycode is the actual value (represented in hex) that the key generates.

Every key on the keyboard has an associated keysym. Unfortunately, the keysym doesn't always correspond to the key label. For example, the keysym for the key labeled "H" is *h*, and the keysym for the key labeled "Return" is *Return*—but on the Sun-3 workstation, the keysym for the key labeled "Alternate" is *Break*, and the keysym for the key labeled "Right" is *Meta_R*.

As you can understand, this can make it difficult to figure out from the *xmodmap* display just which key is currently being used as meta.

For this reason, we've included a small program in Appendix F that you can type in and compile. This program, called *xshowkey*, prints out the keysym for each key you press.

If the keysyms that *xmodmap* prints out aren't meaningful to you, type in the program and compile it according to the instructions in Appendix F. Then type:

```
% xshowkey
```

Place the window anywhere on the screen, and leave the pointer in the window. As you press each key, the keysym corresponding to that key will be printed to standard output in the window from which you originally invoked the *xshowkey* program.* The message looks something like this:

```
The key you just pressed is keysym Meta_R, keycode 129 (0x81)
```

Press a few likely keys until you find the one you're looking for. Type CTRL-C in the window from which you invoked *xshowkey* to terminate the program.

Changing the Map with xmodmap

xmodmap executes an expression or list of expressions that are interpreted as instructions to modify the map.

An expression can be executed from the command line using the `-e expression` option (see *Options* and *Expression Grammar* following); or an expression or list of expressions can be entered in a file and the file used as an argument to *xmodmap*.

Options

xmodmap has the syntax

xmodmap [*options*] [*filename*]

and accepts the following options:

`-help`	Lists the valid command line arguments. This is also done whenever an invalid argument is specified for *xmodmap*.
`-grammar`	Returns a help message describing the expression grammar used in files and with `-e expressions`.
`-verbose`	Indicates that *xmodmap* should print logging information as it parses its input.
`-quiet`	Turns off the verbose logging. This is the default.
`-n`	Indicates that *xmodmap* should not change the mappings as specified in the `filename`, but should display what it would do. A handy test.

`-e expression`

Specifies an expression to be executed (as an instruction to modify the map). Any number of expressions may be specified from the command line. `expression` should be enclosed in quotes.

`-p`	Prints the current modifier map on the standard output.
`-`	A lone dash means that the standard input should be used as the input file.

---

*We're aware that this is a terribly inelegant implementation. However, we thought it better to keep the program as short as possible so that it would be easy to type in.

filename specifies a file containing *xmodmap* expressions to be executed (as instructions to modify the map). This file is usually kept in the user's home directory with a name like *.keymap*.

Expression Grammar

The following is a list of allowable expressions. Those expressions that include an equal sign require a space before and after the sign.

`keycode` *NUMBER* = *KEYSYMNAME*

> Assigns the keysym to the indicated keycode (which may be specified in decimal, hex or octal). Usually only one keysym is assigned to a given code. See */usr/include/X11/keysymdef.h* for a list of keysyms and keycodes.

`keysym` *KEYSYMNAME* = *KEYSYMNAME*

> Assigns the keysym on the right to the keycode of the keysym on the left. Note that if you have the same keysym bound to multiple keys, this might not work.

`clear` *MODIFIERNAME*

> Removes all entries in the modifier map for the given modifier, where valid name are: shift, lock, control, mod1, mod2, mod3, mod4 and mod5 (case does not matter in modifier names, although it does matter for all other names). For example, the expression `clear Lock` will remove all keys that were bound to the Shift Lock modifier.

`add` *MODIFIERNAME* = *KEYSYMNAME*

> Adds the given keysym to the indicated modifier map. The keysym name is evaluated after all input expressions are read to make it easy to write expressions to swap keys.

`remove` *MODIFIERNAME* = *KEYSYMNAME*

> Removes the given keysym from the indicated modifier map (unmaps it). Unlike with the `add` expression, the keysym names are evaluated as the line is read in. This allows you to remove keys from a modifier without having to worry about whether or not they have been reassigned.

Expressions can be used on the *xmodmap* command line or entered in a file that is then used as an argument to *xmodmap*. Note that if you want to change the mapping of a modifier key, you must first remove it from the current modifier map.

For example, to swap the left Control and CapsLock keys, you would first need to unmap both physical keys (Caps_Lock, Control_L) from the modifier keynames (lock, control):

```
remove lock = Caps_Lock
remove control = Control_L
```

And then reverse the mappings:

```
add lock = Caps_Lock
add control = Control_L
```

If you then type *xmodmap* without options, you see the new map.

```
xmodmap: up to 2 keys per modifier, (keycodes in parentheses):

shift        Shift_L (0x6a), Shift_R (0x75)
lock         Control_L (0x53)
control      Caps_Lock (0x7e)
mod1         Meta_L (0x7f), Meta_R (0x81)
mod2
mod3
mod4
mod5
```

The key marked Control_L functions as a lock key and the key marked Caps_Lock functions as a control key.

Perhaps somewhat more useful, you might make the backspace key function as a delete key, using the following:

```
% xmodmap -e "keysym BackSpace = Delete"
```

xset: User Setup Client

The *xset* client allows you to set an assortment of user preference options for the display and keyboard. Some of these are followed by *on* or *off* to set or unset the option. Note that *xset* is inconsistent in its use of – as an option flag. Some options use a preceding "–" to indicate that some feature be disabled; this can be confusing at first to users accustomed to seeing "–" as an introductory symbol on all options.

Although *xset* can be run any time, it is suggested that you run it at startup. These settings reset to the default values when you log out. Not all X implementations are guaranteed to honor all of these options.

Keyboard Bell

The b option controls bell volume (as a percentage of its maximum), pitch (in hertz), and duration (in milliseconds). It accepts up to three numerical parameters:

```
b volume pitch duration
```

If no parameters are given, the system defaults are used. If only one parameter is given, the bell volume is set to that value. If two values are listed, the second parameter specifies the bell pitch. If three values are listed, the third one specifies the duration.

For example, the command

```
% xset b 70 1000 100
```

sets the volume of the keyboard bell to 70 percent of the maximum, the pitch to 1000 hertz, and the duration to 100 milliseconds.

Note that bell characteristics vary with different hardware. The X server sets the characteristics of the bell as closely as it can to the user's specifications.

The b option also accepts the parameters on or off. If you specify xset b on, system defaults for volume, pitch and duration are used.

The bell can also be turned off with the option -b, or by setting the volume parameter to 0 (xset b 0).

Keyclick Volume

The c option sets the volume of the keyboard's keyclick and takes the form:

c volume

volume can be a value from 0 to 100, indicating a percentage of the maximum volume. For example,

% xset c 75

sets a moderately loud keyclick. The X server sets the volume to the nearest value that the hardware can support.

The c option also accepts the parameters on or off. If you specify xset c on, the system default for volume is used.

The keyclick can also be turned off with the option -c, or by setting the volume paramter to 0 (xset c 0).

On some hardware, a volume of 0 to 50 turns the keyclick off, and a volume of 51 to 100 turns the keyclick on.

Enabling or Disabling Auto-repeat

The r option controls the keyboard's auto-repeat feature. (Auto-repeat causes a keystroke to be repeated over and over when the key is held down.)

Use xset r or xset r on to enable key repeat. Use xset -r or xset r off to disable key repeat. On some keyboards (notably Apollo), only some keys repeat, regardless of the state of this option.

Search Other Font Directories

As mentioned earlier, programs that take font specification options look by default in the directory */usr/lib/X11/fonts*. The `fp` (font path) option directs X to search other directories for fonts called by a client. The option is followed by a comma-separated list of directories, e.g.,

```
% xset fp /work/adrian/fonts,/usr/lib/X11/newfonts
```

To restore the default font path, type:

```
% xset fp default
```

Keyboard LEDs

The `led` option controls the turning on or off of one or all of the keyboard's LEDs. It accepts the parameters `on` or `off` to turn all of the LEDs on or off. A preceding dash also turns all of the LEDs off (`-led`).

You can also turn individual LEDs on or off by supplying a numerical parameter (a value between 1 and 32) that corresponds to a particular LED. The `led` option followed by a numerical argument turns that LED on. The `led` option preceded by a dash and followed by a numerical argument turns that LED off. For example,

```
% xset led 3
```

would turn LED #3 on, while

```
% xset -led 3
```

would turn LED #3 off.

Note that the particular LED values may refer to different LEDs on different hardware.

Pointer Acceleration

The `m` (mouse) option controls the rate at which the mouse or pointer moves across the screen. This option takes two parameters: `acceleration` and `threshold`. They must be positive integers. (The acceleration can also be written as a numerator/denominator combination separated by a '/', for example, 5/4.)

The mouse or pointer moves `acceleration` times as fast when it travels more than the `threshold` number of pixels in a short time. This way, the mouse can be used for precise alignment when it is moved slowly, yet it can be set to travel across the screen in a flick of the wrist when desired. If only one parameter is given, it is interpreted as the acceleration.

For example, the command

```
% xset m 5 10
```

sets the mouse movement so that if you move the mouse more than ten pixels, the mouse cursor moves five times as many pixels on the screen as you moved the mouse on the pad.

If no parameter or the value `default` is used, the system defaults will be set.

If you want to change the threshold and leave the acceleration unchanged, enter the value `default` for acceleration.

Screen Saver

X supports a screen saver to blank or randomly change the screen when the system is left unattended for an extended period. This avoids the ''burn in'' that can occur when the same image is displayed on the screen for a long time. The s (screen saver) option to *xset* determines how long the server must be inactive before the screen saver is started.

The s option takes two arguments: *time* and `cycle`. The screen goes blank if the server has not received any input for the time interval specified by the *time* parameter. The contents of the screen reappear upon receipt of any input. If the display is not capable of blanking the screen, then the screen is shifted a pixel in a random direction at time intervals set by the `cycle` parameter. The parameters are specified in seconds.

For example, the command

`% xset s 600`

sets the length of time before the screen saver is invoked to 600 seconds (ten minutes).

For a display not capable of blanking the screen, the command

`% xset s 600 10`

sets the length of time before the screen saver is invoked to ten minutes and shifts the screen every ten seconds.

The s option also takes the parameters:

default	Reset the screen save option to the default.
blank	Turn on blanking and override any previous settings and override previous settings.
noblank	Display a background pattern rather than blanking the screen; override any previous settings.
off	Turn off the screen saver option and override any previous settings.
expose	Allow window exposures (the server can discard window contents).
noexpose	Disable screen saver unless the server can regenerate the screens without causing exposure events (i.e. without forcing the applications to regenerate their own windows.)

Color Definition

On color displays, every time a client requests a private read/write colorcell, a new color definition is entered in the display's color map. The p option sets one of these color map entries even though they are supposed to be private. The parameters are a positive integer identifying a cell in the colormap to be changed, and a color name:

p *entry_number color_name*

The root window colors can be changed on some servers. An error results if the map entry is a read-only color.

For example, the command

% **xset p 3 blue**

sets the third cell in the colormap to the color blue, but only if some client has allocated this cell read/write.

The client that allocated the cell is likely to change it again sometime after you try to set it, since this is the usual person for allocating a read/write cell.

Help with xset Options

The following options can be useful when you want to know the current value of *xset* preferences:

q   List the values of the current settings.

xsetroot: Root Window Setup Client

You can use the *xsetroot* client to tailor the appearance of the background (root) window on a display running X. If no options are specified, *xsetroot* resets the root window to its default state.

Although *xsetroot* can be run any time, it is suggested that you run it at startup either from your *.login* file or as a shell script, as described at the end of this chapter.

The settings reset to the default values when you log out. Not all X implementations are guaranteed to honor all of these options. Some of them may not work on all hardware devices.

The *xsetroot* client understands the following command line options. The solid, gray, grey, bitmap and mod options are mutually exclusive.

-help   lists all the options to *xsetroot*.

-def   resets unspecified attributes to the default values. Restores the background to the familiar grey and the pointer to the X shape. -def can be specified along with other options and only the non-specified characteristics are reset to the default state.

Setup
Clients

`-bitmap` *filename*

specifies a bitmap file to be the window pattern. The entire background will be made up of repeated "tiles" of the bitmap. You can use any of the bitmaps that are in the directory */usr/include/X11/bitmaps* or make your own bitmap files using the *bitmap* client (see Chapter 5). The default is grey.

`-cursor` *cursor_file mask_file*

changes the shape of the pointer when it is in the root window. *cursor_file* and *mask_file* are bitmaps that are in the directory */usr/include/X11/bitmaps* or you can make your own with the *bitmap* client (see Chapter 5).

For example, the command

```
% xsetroot -bitmap /usr/my_dir/bitmaps/my_face
                    -fg red -bg blue
```

fills the root window with a tiling of the bitmap */usr/my_dir/bitmaps/my_face* using the colors red and blue.

You should make the mask file all black until you get used to the way masks work.

`-fg` *color*

sets the foreground color of the root window when using the mod or bitmap options. Default is black.

`-bg` *color*

sets the background color of the root window when using the mod or bitmap options. Default is white.

`-gray` or `grey`

makes the root window gray by tiling a pattern rather than using a solid color.

`-mod` *x y*

makes a plaid-like grid pattern on your screen. The parameters x and y are integers ranging from 1 to 16. Zero and negative numbers are taken as 1. Try different combinations to see the results.

`-name` *string*

sets the name of the root window to *string*. There is no default value. This option is used so that a client can refer to the root window by name.

`-rv`

reverses the foreground and background colors when used with another option such as `-mod` *x y*. Normally the foreground color is black and the background color is white.

`-solid` *color*

sets the color of the root window to a solid color. See Chapter 6 for information on how to specify colors.

For example, the command

```
% xsetroot -solid lightblue
```

sets the color of the root window to lightblue.

When you set a color with the -solid option to *xsetroot*, the client allocates a color cell, sets the color, and deallocates the color cell. The root window changes to that color. If another client is started that sets a new color, it allocates the next available color cell—which may be the one *xsetroot* deallocated. This results in that color changing to the new color. The root window also change to the new color. If this happens, you can run *xsetroot* again and if there are other color cells available, the root window changes to the new color. If all color cells are allocated, any call to change a color cell results in an error message.

A Startup Shell Script

It's a basic principle of UNIX to "let the computer do the work." Accordingly, you'd no doubt like to run various X clients automatically whenever you log in.

There are two ways to do this:

- Start the X server from the */etc/ttys* file as described in Appendix A. This will bring up an *xterm* window with a login prompt. Other clients can be run simply by adding the commands to start them a script that is run from your *.login* file.

- Create a script containing the commands to start the various clients you want to run, and use it as an argument to *xinit*. *xinit* normally runs a single *xterm* as a client, but if you give it an argument beginning with a period or a slash, it interprets the argument as a command to be executed instead of *xterm*.

Even in the first case, it is desirable to segregate X clients into a separate script rather than invoking them directly from your *.login* file. The reason is that running *xterm* from inside a shell script only works if the script executes quickly—or doesn't terminate at all.

The problem involves the way that *xterm* sets up its controlling terminal (*/dev/tty*). If the *xterm*'s parent process has died by the time the *xterm* gets around to doing this, then */dev/tty* is redefined properly. If the parent has not died, however, *xterm* uses the parent's controlling terminal as its own. If the parent dies at any time after that, */dev/tty* will become undefined for that *xterm* (and all processes spawned by it).

A C shell script that starts up a few *xterm*s and then exits will probably work because the *xterm*'s parent process (the script) has exited by the time the *xterm*s start defining their */dev/tty*. If, however, there is a sleep or another command that takes a long time in the script after the line invoking the *xterm*, the parent may still be around when the *xterm* defines */dev/tty*. Then, when the script finally exits, */dev/tty* becomes undefined for those *xterm*s.

The problem is avoided by making the script an executable Bourne shell script, and making the last command in the script be one that opens a window, and by running that command in the foreground. In this case, the script will not terminate until that final foreground command terminates—that is, when you kill the window. In this case, all the *xterm*s will have the script's controlling tty, but since the script is guaranteed to hang around, this causes no problem.

Setup
Clients

You should also be sure to set the DISPLAY variable inside the script, or else call each of the clients with a -display option, since otherwise the clients won't know which display to connect to. (Normally, *xterm* sets the DISPLAY variable. Since you are invoking the other clients not from a shell in an *xterm* window, but from a standard shell, it will not automatically be set.)

We use a script called *.xinit.* On systems where the X server is started from */etc/ttys,* and we actually login to an *xterm* window, we include the following line at the end of our *.login* file:

```
.xinit
```

On systems where we must start the server from the *.login* file, we instead use the command:

```
xinit ~/.xinit &
```

Example 9-1 shows the actual *.xinit* script.

Example 9-1. A script to start up X clients

```
#!/bin/sh

# Set DISPLAY variable; change this to whatever is
# reasonable at your site.

DISPLAY=unix:0; export DISPLAY

# Be informed if mail arrives

xbiff =+1040+350 &

# Display both analog and digital clocks

xclock =100x100+1050+200  &
xclock -d =120x25+1040+300 &

# Start some xterm windows in convenient positions

xterm -j -sb =80x32+520+0 &
xterm -j -sb =80x40+0+350 &
xterm -j -sb =100x34+520+430  &

# Read resource definitions from .Xdefaults

xrdb -load .Xdefaults

# Set keyclick off and invoke the screen saver
# after ten minutes of screen idleness

xset c off s 600

# Start the window manager

uwm &

# Start a console xterm window.  This is the only xterm that should be
# run in the foreground, since it replaces the normal xterm login window.
# Typing exit in this window will bring down the whole shooting match,
```

Example 9-1. A script to start up X clients (continued)

```
# just like the login window normally started by xinit

xterm -j -sb -geometry +1+1 -C
```

Note that all programs that create windows (and hence don't run quickly and then go away) are run in the background, with the exception of the final *xterm* window, which is placed in the standard position given to the login window. This will cause the script to simulate the behavior of the *xterm* normally started by *xinit*.

Setup
Clients

Part Three:

Client Reference Manual

This part of the book provides UNIX-style "man-pages" for each of the X programs. These pages are arranged alphabetically for ease of reference, and contain detailed information (such as all options to a program) that is not covered in the earlier parts of the book.

Intro

Name

Intro — overview of man page format.

Syntax

This section describes the command line syntax for invoking the client.

Description

This section explains the operation of the client.

Options

This section lists available command line options. In some cases, reference is made to "all of the standard X Toolkit command-line options." These toolkit options are listed in Chapter 6 of this manual.

Defaults

This section lists the resource variable names that can be specified in an *.XDefaults* file or other file used by xrdb. In some cases, reference is made to "all the core resource names and classes." For full information, see the MIT X Toolkit documentation. A list of core names and classes of most interest to the average user is given in Chapter 7.

Environment

If present, this section lists shell environment variables used by the client. This section does not list the DISPLAY and XENVIRONMENT variables, which are used by all clients. They are used as follows:

DISPLAY   to get the default host and display number.

XENVIRONMENT

to get the name of a resource file that overrides the global resources stored in the RESOURCE_MANAGER property.

See Also

This section lists other pages in this section that may also be of interest. Note that versions of these pages may have been installed in the usual on-line manual hierarchy, and may be available via *man (1)* command. References such as *stat (2)*, are to the standard UNIX documentation. References such as *XGetDefault (3x)* should be interpreted as references to pages in Volume 2, *Xlib Reference Manual*.

Bugs

If present, this section lists areas in which the author of the program thinks it could be improved. In a few cases, we've added additional bugs we've noted.

Author

The authors of the program, and (almost always) the man page as well. Note that the pages in this section are all subject to the copyright provisions in the Copyright section of the X man page.

Where appropriate, additional copyrights are noted on individual pages.

Note, however, that those portions of this document that are based on the original X11 documentation and other source material have been significantly revised, and that all such revisions are copyright © 1987, 1988 O'Reilly & Associates, Inc. Inasmuch as the proprietary revisions can't be separated from the freely copyable MIT source material, the net result is that copying of this document is not allowed. Sorry for the doublespeak!

Name

X - a portable, network transparent window system.

Synopsis

X is a network transparent window system developed at MIT which runs under a wide variety of operating systems. The standard distribution from MIT works on Ultrix-32 Version 1.2 (and higher), 4.3BSD Unix, SunOS 3.2 (and higher), HP-UX 6.01, and DOMAIN/IX 9.7. In addition, many vendors support the X Window System under other operating systems.

The Official Names

The official names of the software are:

X

X Window System

X Version 11

X Window System, Version 11

X11

Note that the phrases X.11, X-11, X Windows or any permutation thereof, are explicitly excluded from this list and should not be used to describe the X Window System (window system should be thought of as one word).

X Window System is a trademark of the Massachusetts Institute of Technology.

Description

X window system servers run on computers with bitmap displays. The server distributes user input to, and accepts output requests from various client programs through a variety of different interprocess communication channels. Although the most common case is for the client programs to be running on the same machine as the server, clients can be run transparently from other machines (including machines with different architectures and operating systems) as well.

X supports overlapping hierarchical subwindows and text and graphics operations, on both monochrome and color displays.

When you first log in on a display running X, you are usually using the *xterm* terminal emulator program. You need not learn anything extra to use a display running X as a terminal beyond moving the mouse cursor into the login window to log in normally.

The core *X* protocol provides mechanism, not policy. Windows are manipulated (including moving, resizing and iconifying) not by the server itself, but by a separate program called a "window manager" of your choosing. This program is simply another client and requires no special privileges. If you don't like the ones that are supplied (see *uwm* and *wm*), you can write your own.

The number of programs that use *X* is growing rapidly. Of particular interest are: a terminal emulator (*xterm*), window managers (*wm* and *uwm*), a mailer reader (*xmh*), a bitmap editor (*bitmap*), an access control program (*xhost*), user preference setting programs (*xset, xsetroot,* and *xmodmap*), a load monitor (*xload*), clock (*xclock*), a font displayer (*xfd*), a protocol translator for running X10 programs (*x10tox11*), and various demos (*ico, muncher, puzzle*, etc.).

Display Specification

When you first log in, the environment variable DISPLAY will be set to a string specifying the name of the machine on which the server is running, a number indicating which of possibly several servers to use, and possibly a number indicating the default screen of the server (usually this is omitted and defaults to 0). By convention, servers on a particular machine are numbered starting with zero. The format of the DISPLAY string depends on the type of communications channel used to contact the server. The following connection protocols are supported:

TCP/IP

DISPLAY should be set to "*host:dpy.screen*" where *host* is the symbolic name of the machine (e.g. expo), *dpy* is the number of the display (usually 0), and *screen* is the number of the screen. The *screen* and preceding period are optional, with the default value being zero (0). Full Internet domain names (e.g. expo.lcs.mit.edu) are allowed for the host name.

Unix domain

DISPLAY should be set to "unix:*dpy.screen*", where *dpy* is the display number and *screen* is the screen number; *screen* and the preceding period are optional, with the default value being zero (0).

DECnet

DISPLAY should be set to "*nodename::dpy.screen*" where *nodename* is the symbolic name of the machine, *dpy* is the display number, and *screen* is the screen number; *screen* and the preceding period are optional, with the default value being zero (0).

Most programs accept a command line argument of the form "-display *display*" that can be used to override the DISPLAY environment variable.

Geometry Specification

One of the advantages of using window systems over hardwired terminals is that applications don't have to be restricted to a particular size or location on the screen. Although the layout of windows on a display is controlled by the window manager that the user is running, most applications accept a command line argument that is treated as the preferred size and location for this particular application's window.

This argument, usually specified as "-geometry WxH+X+Y", indicates that the window should have a width of W and height of H (usually measured in pixels or characters, depending on the application), and the upper left corner X pixels to the right and Y pixels below the upper left corner of the screen (origin (0,0)). "WxH" can be omitted to obtain the default application size, or "+X+Y" can be omitted to obtain the default application position (which is usually then left up to the window manager or user to choose). The X and Y values may be negative to position the window off the screen. In addition, if minus signs are used instead of plus signs (e.g. WxH-X-Y), then (X,Y) represents the location of the lower right hand corner of the window relative to the lower right hand corner of the screen.

By combining plus and minus signs, the window may be place relative to any of the four corners of the screen. For example:

555x333+11+22

> requests a window 555 pixels wide and 333 pixels tall, with the upper left corner located at (11,22).

300x200-0+0

> requests a window measuring 300 by 200 pixels in the upper right hand corner of the screen.

48x48—5—10

> requests a window measuring 48 by 48 pixels whose lower right hand corner is 5 pixel off the right edge and the screen and 10 pixels off the bottom edge.

Command Line Arguments

Most X programs attempt to use a common set of names for their command line arguments. The X Toolkit automatically handles the following arguments:

-bg *color*, -background *color*
> Either option specifies the color to use for the window background.

-bd *color*, -bordercolor *color*
> Either option specifies the color to use for the window border.

-bw *number*, -borderwidth *number*
> Either option specifies the width in pixels of the window border.

-display *display*
> This option specifies the name of the X server to use.

-fg *color*, -foreground *color*
> Either option specifies the color to use for text or graphics.

-fn *font*, -font *font*
> Either option specifies the font to use for displaying text.

-geometry *geometry*
> This option specifies the initial size and location of the window.

-iconic
> This option indicates that application should start out in an iconic state. Note that how this state is represented is controlled by the window manager that the user is running.

-name   This option specifies the name under which resources for the application should be found. This option is useful in shell aliases to distinguish between invocations of an application, without resorting to creating links to alter the executable file name.

-rv, -reverse
> Either option indicates that the program should simulate reverse video if possible, often by swapping the foreground and background colors. Not all programs honor this or implement it correctly. It is usually only used on monochrome displays.

`+rv`   This option indicates that the program should not simulate reverse video. This is used to override any defaults since reverse video doesn't always work properly.

`-synchronous`

This option indicates that requests to the X server should be sent synchronously, instead of asynchronously. Since *Xlib* normally buffers requests to the server, errors do not necessarily get reported immediately after they occur. This option turns off the buffering so that the application can be debugged. It should never be used with a working program.

`-title` *string*

This option specifies the title to be used for this window. This information is sometimes used by a window manager to provide some sort of header identifying the window.

`-xrm` *resourcestring*

This option specifies a resource name and value to override any defaults. It is also very useful for setting resources that don't have explicitly command line arguments.

Resources

To make the tailoring of applications to personal preferences easier, X supports several mechanisms for storing default values for program resources (e.g. background color, window title, etc.) Resources are specified as strings of the form *"name*subname*subsubname . . . : value"* (see Chapter 11 in *Volume 1, Xlib Programming Manual* for more details) that are loaded into a client when it starts up. The *Xlib* routine *XGetDefault* and the resource utilities within the X Toolkit obtain resources from the following sources:

RESOURCE_MANAGER root window property

Any global resources that should be available to clients on all machines should be stored in the RESOURCE_MANAGER property on the root window using the *xrdb* program.

application-specific directory

Any application- or machine-specific resources can be stored in the class resource files located in the XAPPLOADDIR directory (this is a configuration parameter that is */usr/lib/X11/app-defaults* in the standard distribution).

XENVIRONMENT

Any user- and machine-specific resources may be specified by setting the XENVIRONMENT environment variable to the name of a resource file to be loaded by all applications. If this variable is not defined, the X Toolkit looks for a file named .Xdefaults-*hostname*, where *hostname* is the name of the host where the application is executing.

`-xrm` *resourcestring*

Applications that use the X Toolkit can have resources specified from the command line. The *resourcestring* is a single resource name and value as shown above. Note that if the string contains characters interpreted by the shell (e.g., asterisk), they must be quoted. Any number of `-xrm` arguments may be given on the command line.

Program resources are organized into groups called "classes," so that collections of individual "instance" resources can be set all at once. By convention, the instance name of a resource begins with a lowercase letter and class name with an upper case letter. Multiple word resources are concatentated with the first letter of the succeeding words capitalized. Applications written with the X Toolkit will have at least the following resources:

`background` (class `Background`)
> This resource specifies the color to use for the window background.

`borderWidth` (class `BorderWidth`)
> This resource specifies the width in pixels of the window border.

`borderColor` (class `BorderColor`)
> This resource specifies the color to use for the window border.

Most X Toolkit applications also have the resource `foreground` (class `Foreground`), specifying the color to use for text and graphics within the window.

By combining class and instance specifications, application preferences can be set quickly and easily. Users of color displays will frequently want to set Background and Foreground classes to particular defaults. Specific color instances such as text cursors can then be overridden without having to define all of the related resources.

When a named resource is unavailable (for example, a color named chartreuse or a font named teeneyweeney), normally no error message will be printed; whether or not useful results ensue is dependent on the particular application. If you wish to see error messages (for example, if an application is failing for an unknown reason), you may specify the value "on" for the resource named "StringConversionWarnings." If you want such warnings for all applications, specify "*StringConversionWarnings:on" to the resource manager. If you want warnings only for a single application named "zowie", specify "zowie*StringConversionWarnings:on" to the resource manager.

Diagnostics
The default error handler uses the Resource Manager to build diagnostic messages when error conditions arise. The default error database is stored in the file *XErrorDB* in the directory specified by the LIBDIR configuration parameter (*/usr/lib/X11* in the standard distribution). If this file is not installed, error messages will tend to be somewhat cryptic.

See Also
xterm, bitmap, ico, muncher, plaid, puzzle, resize, uwm, wm, x10tox11, xbiff, xcalc, xclock, xedit, xfd, xhost, xinit, xload, xlogo, xlsfonts, xmh, xmodmap, xpr, xprkbd, xprop, xrdb, xrefresh, xset, xsetroot, xwd, xwininfo, xwud, Xserver, Xapollo, Xqdss, Xqvss, Xsun, kbd_mode, todm, tox, biff, init(8), ttys(5), *Volume 1, Xlib Programming Manual* .

Copyright
The following copyright and permission notice outlines the rights and restrictions covering most parts of the standard distribution of the X Window System from MIT. Other parts have additional or different copyrights and permissions; see the individual source files.

Authors

It is no longer feasible to list all people who have contributed something to X, but see doc/contributors in the standard sources.

Name
X - X Window System server

Syntax
X displaynumber [-option ...] ttyname

Description
X is the window system server. On operating systems derived from 4.3bsd, it is run automatically by *init(8)*, otherwise it is started from the *xinit* program. The *displaynumber* argument is used by clients in their DISPLAY environment variables to indicate which server to contact (large machines may have several displays attached). This number is usually in the range of 0-6 and is also used in determining the names of various startup files. The *ttyname* argument is passed in by *init* and isn't used. The executable that is invoked when *X* is run is actually one of a collection of programs that depend on the hardware that is installed on the machine. Any additional features are described in the documentation for that server.

The individual server (e.g. Xsun) should be renamed or linked to X, so that *init* will run properly.

The sample server has support for the following protocols:

TCP/IP
> The server listens on port htons(6000+N), where N is the display number.

Unix Domain
> The file name for the socket is X_UNIX_PATH* where X_UNIX_PATH is a configuration parameter (*/tmp/.X11-unix/X* in the standard release) and ``*'' is the display number.

DECnet
> The server responds to connections to object ``X*'', where ``*'' is the display number. When the sample server starts up, it takes over the display. If you are running on a workstation whose console is the display, you cannot log into the console while the server is running.

Options
The following options can be given on the command line to any X server, usually when it is started by *init* using information stored in the file */etc/ttys*. (see *ttys(5)* for details):

-a *number*
> sets pointer acceleration (i.e. the ratio of how much is reported to how much the user actually moved the pointer).

-c
> turns off key-click.

ac *volume*
> sets key-click *volume* (allowable range: 0-8).

-f *volume*
> sets beep (bell) *volume* (allowable range: 0-7).

-logo turns on the X Window System logo display in the screen-saver. There is currently no way to change this from a client.

nologo turns off the X Window System logo display in the screen-saver. There is currently no way to change this from a client.

-p *minutes*
> sets screen-saver pattern cycle time in minutes.

-r turns off auto-repeat.

ar turns on auto-repeat.

-s *minutes*
> sets screen-saver timeout time in minutes.

-t *numbers*
> sets pointer acceleration threshold in pixels (i.e. after how many pixels pointer acceleration should take effect).

-to *seconds*
> sets default screensaver timeout in seconds.

av sets video-on screen-saver preference.

-v sets video-off screen-saver preference

-co *filename*
> sets name of RGB color database

-help prints a usage message

-fp *fontPath*
> sets the search path for fonts

-fc *cursorFont*
> sets default cursor font

-fn *font*
> sets the default font Specific implementations may have other command line options.

Running From *init*

On operating systems such as 4.3bsd and Ultrix, the server and your login window are normally started automatically by *init(8)*.

By convention, the pseudoterminal with the highest minor device number (e.g. */dev/ttyqf* and */dev/ptyqf*) is renamed for the lowest display number (e.g. */dev/ttyv0* and */dev/ptyv0*). Machines that have more than one display can repeat this process using *ttyqe* for *ttyv1*, and so on. With this done, you can set up */etc/ttys* to run *X* and *xterm* by adding the following entry:

> ttyv0 ''/etc/xterm -L -geometry -1+1 -display :0'' xterm on secure window="/etc/X :0 -c -1''

on the client machine.

Important note: some versions of *init* have relatively small program name buffer sizes, so you may find that you can't list many *xterm* options. In addition, some *init*'s will treat the sharp signs that are used in specifying colors (such as for window backgrounds) as comments for the whole line. If you run into problems such as this you may want to write a small program that just exec's *xterm* with the proper arguments and have *init* run that instead.

If all else fails, set the display up to be a dumb terminal and use the *xinit* program after logging in.

Security

X uses an access control list for deciding whether or not to accept a connection from a given cleint. This list initially consists of the machine on which the server is running, and any hosts listed in the file */etc/X*.hosts* (where * is the display number). This file should contain one line per host name, with no white space. If a name ends in "::", it is assumed to be a DECnet host, otherwise it is interpreted as an Internet host.

The user can manipulate a dynamic form of this list in the server using the *xhost* program from the same machine as the server.

Unlike some window systems, *X* does not have any notion of window operation permissions or place any restrictions on what a client can do; if a program can connect to a display, it has full run of the screen. There is support for using authentication services on connection startup beyond the simple host name check, but it is not used in the standard distribution.

Signals

X will catch the SIGHUP signal sent by *init(8)* after the initial process (usually the login *xterm*) started on the display terminates. This signal causes all connections to be closed (thereby "disowning" the terminal), all resources to be freed, and all defaults restored.

Diagnostics

Too numerous to list them all. If run from *init(8)*, errors are logged in the file */usr/adm/X*msgs,*

Files

/etc/X*.hosts	Initial access control list
/usr/lib/X11/fonts	Font directory
/usr/lib/X11/rgb.txt	Color database
/tmp/.X11-unix/X*	Unix domain socket
/usr/adm/X*msgs	
	Error log file

See Also

X, xinit, xterm, uwm, xhost, xset, xsetroot, ttys(5), init(8), *X Window System Protocol, Definition of the Porting Layer for the X v11 Sample Server, Strategies for Porting the X v11 Sample Server, Godzilla's Guide to Porting the X V11 Sample Server*

Bugs

The option syntax is inconsistent with itself and *xset*.

The acceleration option should take a numerator and a denominator like the protocol.

If *X* dies before its clients, new clients won't be able to connect until all existing connections have their TCP TIME_WAIT timers expire.

The color database is missing a large number of colors. However, there doesn't seem to be a better one available that can generate RGB values.

Copyright

Copyright 1988, Massachusetts Institute of Technology.
See *X* for a full statement of rights and permissions.

Authors

The sample server was originally written by Susan Angebranndt, Raymond Drewry, Philip Karlton, and Todd Newman, with support from a cast of thousands. See also the *doc/contributors* file.

Name

bitmap — system bitmap editor.

Syntax

bitmap *filename* [*options*] [*WIDTH***x***HEIGHT*]

Description

bitmap allows you to create and edit small bitmaps which you can use to create backgrounds, icons, and pointers. A bitmap is a grid of pixels, or picture elements, each of which is white, black, or, in the case of color displays, a color.

The window that *bitmap* creates has three sections (see Figure 5-6 in this guide). The largest section is the checkerboard grid, which is a magnified version of the bitmap you are editing. On the right-hand side of the window is a list of commands in command boxes that you can invoke with any mouse button. Beneath the commands is an actual size picture of the bitmap you are editing; and below this is an inverted version of the same bitmap. Each time the grid changes, the same change occurs in the actual-size bitmap and its inverse.

Menu Commands

Clear All

Turns all the grid squares white and sets all bitmap bits to 0. This is irreversible, so invoke it with care.

Set All

Turns all the grid squares black and sets all bitmap bits to 1. This is also irreversible, so invoke it with care.

Invert All

Inverts all the grid squares and bitmap bits, as if you had pressed the middle mouse button over each square. This can be reversed by selecting it again.

Clear Area

Clears a rectangular area of the grid, turning it white and setting the corresponding bitmap bits to 0. After you click over this command, the cursor turns into a corner cursor representing the upper-left corner of the area you want to clear. Press and hold down any mouse button while moving the mouse to the lower-right corner of the area you want to clear, then let the button up.

While you are holding down the button, the selected area is covered with X's, and the cursor changes to a lower-right corner cursor. If you now wish to abort the command without clearing an area, either press another mouse button, move the cursor outside the grid, or move the cursor to the left of or above the upper-left corner.

Set Area

Turns a rectangular area of the grid black and sets the corresponding bitmap bits to 1. It works the same way as the *Clear Area* command.

Invert Area

Inverts a rectangular area of the grid. It works the same way as the *Clear Area* command.

Copy Area

Copies a rectangular area from one part of the grid to another. First, you select the rectangle to be copied, in the manner described under *Clear Area* above. Then, the cursor changes to an "upper-left corner" cursor. When you press a mouse button, a destination rectangle overlays the grid; moving the mouse while holding down the button moves this destination rectangle. The copy occurs when you let up the button. To cancel the copy, move the mouse outside the grid and then let up the button.

Move Area

Works identically to *Copy Area, except* it clears the source rectangle after copying to the destination.

Line

Draws a line between two points. The cursor changes to a dot shape. First, position the cursor over the first point of the line you want and click any mouse button. Then position the cursor over the end point of the line and click any mouse button. A black line is drawn between the two points.

Circle

Draws a circle. The cursor changes to a dot shape. First, position the cursor over the point you want to specify the center and click any mouse button. Then position the cursor over the point you want to specify the radius and click any mouse button. A black circle is drawn.

Filled Circle

Draws a filled circle given the center and radius of the circle as with *Circle*.

Set HotSpot

Designates a point on the bitmap as the "hot spot." If a program is using your bitmap as a cursor, the hot spot indicates which point on the bitmap is the "actual" location of the cursor. For instance, if your cursor is an arrow, the hot spot could be the tip of the arrow; if your cursor is a cross, the hot spot should be where the perpendicular lines intersect.

Clear HotSpot

Removes any hot spot that was defined for this bitmap.

Write Output

Writes the current bitmap value to the file specified in the command line. If the file already exists, the original file is first renamed to **filename~** (in the manner of *emacs(1)* and other text editors).

If either the renaming or the writing cause an error (for example 'Permission denied'), a dialog window appears, asking if you want to write the file */tmp/filename* instead. If you say yes, all future "Write Output" commands are written to */tmp/filename* as well. See below for the format of the output file.

Quit

Exits the *bitmap* program. If you have edited the bitmap and have not invoked *Write Output,* or you have edited it since the last time you invoked *Write Output,* a dialog window appears, asking if you want to save changes before quitting. "Yes" does a "Write Output" before exiting. "No" just exits, losing the edits. "Cancel" means you decided not to quit after all and you can continue with your editing.

File Format

bitmap reads and writes files in the following format, which is suitable for including (*#include*) in a C program:

```
#define name_width9
#define name_height13
#define name_x_hot 4
#define name_y_hot 6
static char name_bits[] = {
    0x10, 0x00, 0x38, 0x00, 0x7c, 0x00, 0x10, 0x00, 0x10, 0x00, 0x10, 0x00,
    0xff, 0x01, 0x10, 0x00, 0x10, 0x00, 0x10, 0x00, 0x7c, 0x00, 0x38, 0x00,
    0x10, 0x00};
```

The variables ending with *_x_hot* and *_y_hot* are optional; they must be present only if a hotspot has been defined for this bitmap. The other variables must be present.

In place of name, the five variables are prefixed with a string derived from the name of the file that you specified on the original command line by deleting the directory path (all characters up to and including the last "/", if one is present), or, deleting the extension (the first ".", if one is present, and all characters beyond it).

For example, invoking *bitmap* with filename */usr/include/bitmaps/cross.bitmap* produces a file with variable names `cross_width`, `cross_height`, and `cross_bits` (and `cross_x_hot` and `cross_y_hot` if a hotspot is defined).

To define a bitmap or pointer in an X program include (*#include*) a bitmap file and refer to its variables. For instance, to use a pointer defined in the files *this.cursor* and *this_mask.cursor*, write:

```
#include "this.cursor"
#include "this_mask.cursor"
Pixmap source = XCreateBitmapFromData (display, drawable, this_bits,
   this_width, this_height);
Pixmap mask = XCreateBitmapFromData (display, drawable, this_mask_bits,
   this_mask_width, this_mask_height);
Cursor cursor = XCreatePixmapCursor (display, source, mask, foreground,
   background, this_x_hot, this_y_hot);
```

where `foreground` and `background` are `XColor` values.

An X program can also read a *bitmap* file at runtime by using the function `XReadBitmapFile`.

The bits are in `XYBitmap` format, with `bitmap_unit`=`bitmap_pad`=8, and `byte_order`=`bitmap_bit_order`=`LSBFirst` (least significant bit and byte are leftmost).

Options

-help	Prints a brief description of the allowable options.
-bw *number*	Specifies the border width in pixels of the *bitmap* window. Default is 3 pixels.
-fn *font*	Specifies the font to be used in the command boxes (refer to the Bitmap Command Boxes discussion below). Default is *fixed*, a 6x13 pixel, mono-spaced font.
-fg *color*	Specifies the color to be used for the foreground. Default is black.
-bg *color*	Specifies the color to be used for the background. Default is white.
-hl *color*	Specifies the color to be used for highlighting.
-bd *color*	Specifies the color to be used for the window border.
-ms *color*	Specifies the color to be used for the pointer (mouse). Default is black.
-nodashed	Specifies that the grid lines in the bitmap window are drawn as solid lines not as dashed lines. Default is dashed lines.

WIDTHxHEIGHT

Two numbers separated by the letter "x" which specify the size of the checkerboard grid within the *bitmap* window (e.g., 9x13). The first number is the grid's width; the second number is its height. Default is 16x16.

-geometry =*geometry*

The bitmap is created with the specified size and location determined by the supplied geometry specification. The -geometry option can be (and often is) abbreviated to -g, unless there is a conflicting option that begins with "g." The argument to the geometry option (*geometry*) has the form *widthxheight±xoff±yoff*.

-display [*host*]:*server*[.*screen*]

Allows you to specify the host, server and screen on which to create the *bitmap* window. *host* specifies which machine to create the *bitmap* window on, *server* specifies the server number, and *screen* specifies the screen number. For example,

bitmap -display *your_node*:**0.1**

creates a *bitmap* window on screen 1 of server 0 on the machine *your_node*. If the host is omitted, the local machine is assumed. If the screen is omitted, screen 0 is assumed; the colon (:) is necessary in either case.

Defaults

The following resources can be specified in your *Xdefaults* file. The foreground, background, and highlight colors are ignored unless you specify new values for all three options.

Background   determines the window's background color. Bits which are 0 in the bitmap are displayed in this color. Default is white.

BodyFont   determines the text font. Default: *fixed*, a 6x13 pixel mono-spaced font.

BorderColor   determines the color of the border. Default is black.

BorderWidth   determines the border width. Default is 3 pixels.

Foreground   determines the foreground color. Bits which are 1 in the bitmap are displayed in this color. Default is black.

Highlight   determines the highlight color. *bitmap* uses this color to show the hotspot and to indicate rectangular areas that are affected by the Move Area, Copy Area, Set Area, Clear Area, and Invert Area commands. If a highlight color is not given, then *bitmap* highlights by inverting. For example, if you have a black rectangular area selected for a move, white X's appear in the rectangle.

Mouse   determines the pointer's color. Default is black.

Geometry   determines the size and location of the *bitmap* window.

WIDTHxHEIGHT

        determines the WIDTHxHEIGHT of the checkerboard grid within the *bitmap* window. Default is 16x16.

Files

Many standard bitmaps can be found in the directory /usr/include/X11/bitmaps.

Author

Ron Newman, MIT Project Athena.

Additional Information

For additional information on *bitmap*, refer to Chapter 5 of this guide, or to Volume 1, *Xlib Programmer's Guide*.

Name

uwm — a window manager for X.

Syntax

uwm [*options*]

Description

The *uwm* program is a window manager client application of the window server.

When *uwm* is invoked, it searches a predefined search path to locate any *uwm* startup files. If no startup files exist, *uwm* initializes its built-in defaults.

If startup files exist in any of the following locations, it adds the variables to the default variables. In the case of contention, the variables in the last file found override previous specifications. Files in the *uwm* search path are:

> */usr/lib/X11/uwm/system.uwmrc*
> *$HOME/.uwmrc*

To use only the settings defined in a single startup file, include the variables, `resetbindings`, `resetmenus`, `resetvariables` at the top of that specific startup file.

Options

`-f` *filename*   Names an alternate file as a *uwm* startup file.

`-display` [*host*]:*server*[*.screen*]

> Allows you to specify the host, server and screen on which to run the window manager. For example,

> **uwm -display** *your_node*:**0.1**

> specifies screen 1 on server 0 on the machine *your_node*. If the host is omitted, the local machine is assumed. If the screen is omitted, the screen 0 is assumed; the colon (:) is necessary in either case.

Startup File Variables

Variables are typically entered first, at the top of the startup file. By convention, `reset-bindings`, `resetmenus`, and `resetvariables` head the list.

`autoselect/noautoselect`

> places menu cursor in first menu item. If unspecified, menu cursor is placed in the menu header when the menu is displayed.

`delta=pixels`

> indicates the number of pixels the cursor is moved before the action is interpreted by the window manager as a command. (Also refer to the `delta` mouse action.)

`freeze/nofreeze`

> locks all other client applications out of the server during certain window manager tasks, such as move and resize.

grid/nogrid displays a finely-ruled grid to help you position an icon or window during resize or move operations.

hiconpad=*n* indicates the number of pixels to pad an icon horizontally. The default is five pixels.

hmenupad=*n* indicates the amount of space in pixels, that each menu item is padded above and below the text.

iconfont=*fontname*
  names the font that is displayed within icons. Font names for a given server can be obtained using *xlsfonts*.

maxcolors=*n* limits the number of colors the window manager can use in a given invocation. If set to zero, or not specified, *uwm* assumes no limit to the number of colors it can take from the color map. maxcolors counts colors as they are included in the file.

normali/nonormali
  places icons created with f.newiconify within the root window, even if it is placed partially off the screen. With nonormali the icon is placed exactly where the cursor leaves it.

normalw/nonormalw
  places window created with f.newiconify within the root window, even if it is placed partially off the screen. With nonormalw the window is placed exactly where the cursor leaves it.

push=n moves a window *n* number of pixels or a relative amount of space, depending on whether pushabsolute or pushrelative is specified. Use this variable in conjunction with f.pushup, f.pushdown, f.pushright, or f.pushleft.

pushabsolute/pushrelative
  pushabsolute indicates that the number entered with push is equivalent to pixels. When an f.push (left, right, up, or down) function is called, the window is moved exactly that number of pixels.

  pushrelative indicates that the number entered with the push variable represents a relative number. When an f.push function is called, the window is invisibly divided into the number of parts you entered with the push variable, and the window is moved one part.

resetbindings, resetmenus, resetvariables
  resets all previous function bindings, menus, and variables entries, specified in any startup file in the *uwm* search path, including those in the default environment. By convention, these variables are entered first in the startup file.

resizefont=*fontname*
  identifies the font of the indicator that displays in the corner of the window as you resize windows.

reverse/noreverse
  defines the display as black characters on a white background for the window manager windows and icons.

viconpad=*n* indicates the number of pixels to pad an icon vertically. Default is five pixels.

vmenupad=*n* indicates the amount of space in pixels that the menu is padded on the right and left of the text.

volume=*n* increases or decreases the base level volume set by the *xset*(1) command. Enter an integer from 0 to 7, 7 being the loudest.

zap/nozap causes ghost lines to follow the window or icon from its previous default location to its new location during a move or resize operation.

Binding Syntax

function=[*control key(s)*]:[*context*]:*mouse events*: "*menu name*"

Function and mouse events are required input. Menu name is required with the *f.menu* function definition only.

Function

f.beep emits a beep from the keyboard. Loudness is determined by the volume variable.

f.circledown
  causes the top window that is obscuring another window to drop to the bottom of the stack of windows.

f.circleup exposes the lowest window that is obscured by other windows.

f.continue releases the window server display action after you stop action with the f.pause function.

f.focus directs all keyboard input to the selected window. To reset the focus to all windows, invoke f.focus from the root window.

f.iconify when implemented from a window, this function converts the window to its respective icon. When implemented from an icon, f.iconify converts the icon to its respective window.

f.lower lowers a window that is obstructing a window below it.

f.menu invokes a menu. Enclose 'menu name' in quotes if it contains blank characters or parentheses.

f.move   moves a window or icon to a new location, which becomes the default location.

f.moveopaque
                  moves a window or icon to a new screen location. When using this function, the entire window or icon is moved to the new screen location. The grid effect is not used with this function.

f.newiconify
                  allows you to create a window or icon and then position the window or icon in a new default location on the screen.

f.pause   temporarily stops all display action. To release the screen and immediately update all windows, use the f.continue function.

f.pushdown   moves a window down. The distance of the push is determined by the push variables.

f.pushleft   moves a window to the left. The distance of the push is determined by the push variables.

f.pushright   moves a window to the right. The distance of the push is determined by the push variables.

f.pushup   moves a window up. The distance of the push is determined by the push variables.

f.raise   raises a window that is being obstructed by a window above it.

f.refresh   results in exposure events being sent to the window server clients for all unobscured or partially obscured windows. The windows will not refresh correctly if the exposure events are not handled properly.

f.resize   resizes an existing window. Note that some clients, notably editors, react unpredictably if you resize the window while the client is running.

f.restart   causes the window manager application to restart, retracing the *uwm* search path and initializing the variables it finds.

Control Keys

By default, the window manager uses meta as its control key. It can also use ctrl, shift, lock, or null (no control key). Control keys must be entered in lowercase, and can be abbreviated as: c, l, m, s for ctrl, lock, meta, and shift, respectively.

You can bind one, two, or no control keys to a function. Use the bar (|) character to combine control keys.

Note that client applications other than the window manager use the shift as a control key. If you bind the shift key to a window manager function, you can not use other client applications that require this key.

Context

The context refers to the screen location of the pointer when a command is initiated. When you include a context entry in a binding, the pointer must be in that context or the function will not be activated. The window manager recognizes the following four contexts: icon, window, root, (null).

The root context refers to the root, or background window, A (null) context is indicated when the context field is left blank, and allows a function to be invoked from any screen location. Combine contexts using the bar (|) character.

Mouse Buttons

Any of the following mouse buttons are accepted in lowercase and can be abbreviated as l, m, or r, respectively: left, middle, right.

With the specific button, you must identify the action of that button. Mouse actions can be:

down   function occurs when the specified button is pressed down.

up   function occurs when the specified button is released.

delta   indicates that the mouse must be moved the number of pixels specified with the delta variable before the specified function is invoked. The mouse can be moved in any direction to satisfy the delta requirement.

Menu Definition

After binding a set of function keys and a menu name to f.menu, you must define the menu to be invoked, using the following syntax:

```
menu = "menu name" {
"item name" : "action"
    .
    .
    .
}
```

Enter the menu name exactly the way it is entered with the f.menu function or the window manager will not recognize the link. If the menu name contains blank strings, tabs or parentheses, it must be quoted here and in the f.menu function entry. You can enter as many menu items as your screen is long. You cannot scroll within menus.

Any menu entry that contains quotes, special characters, parentheses, tabs, or strings of blanks must be enclosed in double quotes. Follow the item name by a colon (:).

Menu Action

Window manager functions
                Any function previously described (e.g., f.move or f.iconify).

Shell commands Begin with an exclamation point (!) and set to run in background. You cannot include a new line character within a shell command.

Text strings   Text strings are placed in the window server's cut buffer.

Strings starting with an up arrow (^) will have a new line character appended to the string after the up arrow (^) has been stripped from it.

Strings starting with a bar character (|) will be copied as is after the bar character (|) has been stripped.

Color Menus

Use the following syntax to add color to menus:

```
menu = "menu name" (color1:color2:color3:color4) {
"item name" :(color5 :color6)   : " action "

    .

    .

    .

}
```

where:

color1   Foreground color of the header.

color2   Background color of the header.

color3   Foreground color of the highlighter, the horizontal band of color that moves with the cursor within the menu.

color4   Background color of the highlighter.

color5   Foreground color for the individual menu item.

color6   Background color for the individual menu item.

Color Defaults

Colors default to the colors of the root window under any of the following conditions: If you run out of color map entries, either before or during an invocation of *uwm*. If you specify a foreground or background color that does not exist in the RGB color database of the server (see */usr/lib/X11/rgb.txt* for a sample). If you omit a foreground or background color. If the total number of colors specified in the startup file exceeds the number specified in the *maxcolors* variable. If you specify no colors in the startup file.

Examples

The following sample startup file shows the use of window manager options:

```
# Global variables
#
resetbindings;resetvariables;resetmenus
autoselect
delta=25
freeze
grid
```

```
hiconpad=5
hmenupad=6
iconfont=oldeng
menufont=timrom12b
resizefont=9x15
viconpad=5
vmenupad=3
volume=7
#
# Mouse button/key maps
#
# FUNCTION       KEYS   CONTEXT   BUTTON      MENU(if any)
# ========       ====   =======   ======      =============
f.menu =         meta   :         :left down   :"WINDOW OPS"
f.menu =         meta   :         :middle down :"EXTENDED WINDOW OPS"
f.move =         meta   :w|i      :right down
f.circleup =     meta   :root     :right down
#
# Menu specifications
#
menu = "WINDOW OPS" {
"(De)Iconify":f.iconify
Move:f.move
Resize:f.resize
Lower:f.lower
Raise:f.raise
}

menu = "EXTENDED WINDOW OPS" {
Create Window:!"xterm &"
Iconify at New Position:f.lowericonify
Focus Keyboard on Window:f.focus
Freeze All Windows:f.pause
Unfreeze All Windows:f.continue
Circulate Windows Up:f.circleup
Circulate Windows Down:f.circledown
}
```

Restrictions

The color specifications have no effect on a monochrome system.

Files

/usr/lib/X11/uwm/system.uwmrc
$HOME/.uwmrc

See Also
X, Xserver, xset, xlsfonts

Author
M. Gancarz, DEC Ultrix Engineering Group, Merrimack, New Hampshire, using some algorithms originally by Bob Scheifler, MIT Laboratory for Computer Science. Copyright 1985, 1986, 1987, 1988 Digital Equipment Corporation, Maynard, MA.

xbiff

Name

xbiff — mailbox flag for X.

Syntax

xbiff [`options`]

Description

The *xbiff* program displays a little image of a mailbox. When there is no mail, the flag on the mailbox is down. When mail arrives, the flag goes up and the mailbox beeps.

Options

xbiff accepts all of the standard X Toolkit command line options along with the additional options listed below:

`-help`
This option indicates that a brief summary of the allowed options should be printed on the standard error.

`-update` *seconds*
This option specifies the frequency in seconds at which *xbiff* should update its display. If the mailbox is obscured and then exposed, it will be updated immediately.

`-file` *filename*
This option specifies the name of the file which should be monitored. By default, it watches /usr/spool/mail/*username*, where *username* is your login name.

`-bg` *color*
This option specifies the color to use for the background of the window. The default is "white."

`-bd` *color*
This option specifies the color to use for the border of the window. The default is "black."

`-bw` *number*
This option specifies the width in pixels of the border surrounding the window.

`-fg` *color*
This option specifies the color to use for the foreground of the window. The default is "black."

`-rv`
This option indicates that reverse video should be simulated by swapping the foreground and background colors.

`-geometry` =*geometry*
Specifies the size and location of the mailbox window. The `-geometry` option can be (and often is) abbreviated to `-g`, unless there is a conflicting option that begins with "g." The argument to the geometry option (*geometry*) is referred to as a "standard geometry string," and has the form *width*x*height*±*xoff*±*yoff*.

-display [*host*]:*server*[.*screen*]

>Allows you to specify the host, server and screen on which to create the mailbox window. *host* specifies which machine to create the mailbox window on, *server* specifies the server number, and *screen* specifies the screen number. For example,

>>**xbiff -display** *your_node***:0.1**

>creates a mailbox on screen 1 of server 0 on the machine *your_node*. If the host is omitted, the local machine is assumed. If the screen is omitted, screen 0 is assumed; the colon (:) is necessary in either case.

-xrm *resourcestring*

>Specifies a resource string to be used. This is especially useful for setting resources that do not have separate command line options.

Defaults

This program uses the *Mailbox* widget in the X Toolkit. It understands all of the core resource names and classes as well as:

file (class File)

>Specifies the name of the file to monitor. The default is to watch */usr/spool/mail/username*, where *username* is your login name.

width (class Width)

>Specifies the width of the mailbox.

height (class Height)

>Specifies the height of the mailbox.

update (class Interval)

>Specifies the frequency in seconds at which the mail should be checked.

foreground (class Foreground)

>Specifies the color for the foreground. The default is ''black'' since the core default for background is ''white.''

reverseVideo (class ReverseVideo)

>Specifies that the foreground and background should be reversed.

See Also

X, stat(2), xrdb

Author

Jim Fulton, MIT X Consortium.

xcalc

Name

xcalc — scientific calculator for X.

Syntax

xcalc [*options*]

Description

xcalc is a scientific calculator desktop accessory that can emulate a TI-30, an HP-10C, and a slide rule.

Options

−bw *pixels*   This option specifies the border width in pixels.

−stip   This option indicates that the background of the calculator should be drawn using a stipple of the foreground and background colors. On monochrome displays this makes for a nicer display.

−rv   This option indicates that reverse video should be used.

−rpn   This option indicates that Reverse Polish Notation should be used. In this mode the calculator will look and behave like an HP-10C. Without this flag, it will emulate a TI-30.

−analog   This option indicates that a slide rule should be used.

−geometry =*geometry*
The *xcalc* display is created with the specified size and location determined by the supplied geometry specification. The −geometry option can be (and often is) abbreviated to −g, unless there is a conflicting option that begins with "g." The argument to the geometry option (*geometry*) is referred to as a "standard geometry string," and has the form *widthxheight±xoff±yoff*.

−display [*host*]:*server*[.*screen*]
Allows you to specify the server to contact. For example,

      xcalc −display *your_node*:**0.1**

specifies screen 1 on server 0 on the machine *your_node*. If the host is omitted, the local machine is assumed. If the screen is omitted, the screen 0 is assumed; the colon (:) is necessary in either case.

Calculator Operations

Pointer Operation: The left button is the only one (really) used to operate the calculator. Pressing the AC key with the right button terminates the calculator.

Key Usage (Normal Mode): The number keys, the +/- key, and the +, -, *, /, and = keys all do exactly what you would expect them to. It should be noted that the operators obey the standard rules of precedence. Thus, entering 3+4*5= results in 23, not 35. Parentheses can be used to override this. For example, (1+2+3) * (4+5+6) = results in "6*15" which equals 90. The non-obvious keys are detailed below.

1/x replaces the number in the display with its reciprocal.

x^2 squares the number in the display.

SQRT takes the square root of the number in the display.

CE/C when pressed once, clears the number in the display without clearing the state of the machine. Allows you to re-enter a number if you screw it up. Pressing it twice clears the state, also.

AC clears everything, the display, the state, the memory, everything. Pressing it with the right button 'turns off' the calculator, in that it exits the program.

INV inverts the meaning of the function keys. See the individual function keys for details.

sin computes the sine of the number in the display, as interpreted by the current DRG mode (see DRG, below). If inverted, it computes the arcsine.

cos computes the cosine, or arccosine when inverted.

tan computes the tangent, or arctangent when inverted.

DRG changes the DRG mode, as indicated by 'DEG', 'RAD', or 'GRAD' at the bottom of the display. When in 'DEG' mode, numbers in the display are taken as being degrees. In 'RAD' mode, numbers are in radians, and in 'GRAD' mode, numbers are in gradians. When inverted, the DRG key has the nifty feature of converting degrees to radians to gradians and vice-versa. Example: put the calculator into 'DEG' mode, and type 45 INV DRG. The display should now show something along the lines of .785398, which is 45 degrees converted to radians.

e is the constant 'e'. (2.7182818 . . .)

EE is used for entering exponential numbers. For example, to enter "-2.3E-4" you'd type 2 . 3 +/- EE 4 +/-.

log calculates the log (base 10) of the number in the display. When inverted, it raises 10.0 to the number in the display. For example, typing 3 INV log should result in 1000.

ln calcuates the log (base e) of the number in the display. When inverted, it raises "e" to the number in the display. For example, typing e ln should result in 1.

y^x raises the number on the left to the power of the number on the right. For example 2 y^x 3 = results in 8, which is 2^3. For a further example, (1+2+3) y^x (1+2) = equals "6 y^x 3" which results in 216.

PI the constant 'pi'. (3.1415927 . . . .)

x! computes the factorial of the number in the display. The number in the display must be an integer in the range 0-500, though, depending on your math library, it might overflow long before that.

STO copies the number in the display to the memory location.

RCL copies the number from the memory location to the display.

SUM adds the number in the display to the number in the memory location.

EXC swaps the number in the display with the number in the memory location.

Key Usage (RPN mode): The number keys, CHS (change sign), +, -, *, /, and ENTR keys all do exactly what you would expect them to. Many of the remaining keys are the same as in normal mode. The differences are detailed below.

<- is a backspace key that can be used while typing a number. It will erase digits from the display.

ON clears everything, the display, the state, the memory, everything. Pressing it with the right button 'turns off' the calculator, in that it exits the program.

INV inverts the meaning of the function keys. This would be the "f" key on an HP calcula-tor, but xcalc does not have the resolution to display multiple legends on each key. See the individual function keys for details.

10^x raises 10.0 to the number in the top of the stack. When inverted, it calculates the log (base 10) of the number in the display.

e^x raises "e" to the number in the top of the stack. When inverted, it calcuates the log (base e) of the number in the display.

STO copies the number in the top of the stack to a memory location. There are 10 memory locations. The desired memory is specified by following this key with pressing a digit key.

RCL pushes the number from the specified memory location onto the stack.

SUM adds the number on top of the stack to the number in the specified memory location.

x:y exchanges the numbers in the top two stack positions.

R v rolls the stack downward. When inverted, it rolls the stack upward.

blank these keys were used for programming functions on the HP11-C. Their functionality has not been duplicated here.

Keyboard Equivalents

If you have the pointer in the *xcalc* window, you can use the keyboard to speed entry, as almost all of the calculator keys have keyboard equivalents. The number keys, the operator keys, and the parentheses all have the obvious equivalent. The less-obvious equivalents are as follows:

```
n:  +/-              !:  x!
p:  PI               e:  EE
l:  ln               ^:  y^x
i:  INV              s:  sin
c:  cos              t:  tan
d:  DRG              BS, DEL:  CE/C ("<-" in RPN mode)
CR: ENTR             q:  quit
```

Color Usage

xcalc uses a lot of colors, given the opportunity. In the default case, it will just use two colors (Foreground and Background) for everything. This works out nicely. However, if you're a color fanatic you can specify the colors used for the number keys, the operator (+, -, *, /, =) keys, the function keys, the display, and the icon.

Defaults

The program uses the Xlib routine XGetDefault(3X) to read defaults, so its resource names are all capitalized.

BorderWidth Specifies the width of the border. The default is 2.

ReverseVideo

Indicates that reverse video should be used.

Stipple   Indicates that the background should be stippled. The default is on for monochrome displays, and off for color displays.

Mode   Specifies the default mode. Allowable values are are "rpn", "analog".

Foreground   Specifies the default color used for borders and text.

Background   Specifies the default color used for the background.

NKeyFore, NKeyBack

Specifies the colors used for the number keys.

OKeyFore, OKeyBack

Specifies the colors used for the operator keys.

FKeyFore, FKeyBack

Specifies the colors used for the function keys.

DispFore, DispBack

Specifies the colors used for the display.

IconFore, IconBack

Specifies the colors used for the icon.

Examples

If you're running on a monochrome display, you shouldn't need any *Xdefaults* entries for *xcalc*. On a color display, you might want to try the following in normal mode:

```
xcalc*Foreground:          black
xcalc*Background:          lightsteelblue
xcalc*NKeyFore:            black
xcalc*NKeyBack:            white
xcalc*OKeyFore:            aquamarine
xcalc*OKeyBack:            darkslategray
xcalc*FKeyFore:            white
xcalc*FKeyBack:            #900
xcalc*DispFore:            yellow
```

```
xcalc*DispBack:          #777
xcalc*IconFore:          red
xcalc*IconBack:          white
```

See Also
X, xrdb

Bugs
The calculator doesn't resize.

The slide rule may or may not work correctly.

This application should really be implemented with the X Toolkit. It would make a very good example of a compound widget.

Base conversions are not easily done.

Authors
John Bradley, University of Pennsylvania;
Mark Rosenstein, MIT Project Athena.

Name

xclock — continuously display the time in either analog or digital form.

Syntax

xclock [*options*]

Description

xclock continuously displays the time of day, either in digital or analog form. In digital form, *xclock* displays the time using a 24-hour clock. It also displays the day, month, and year. In analog form, *xclock* displays a standard 12-hour clock face. You can set up more than one clock simultaneously.

The default clock is an analog clock with a black foreground on a white background. It is positioned in the upper-left corner of your background window. If you want to change the clock's appearance, type in the appropriate options. For example,

xclock −analog −bd slateblue −fg navyblue −hl darkslategrey &

sets up a conventional 12-hour clock with a slate blue window border, navy blue tick marks, and dark slate grey hands.

Options

xclock accepts all of the standard X Toolkit command line options along with the additional options listed below:

−analog Draws a conventional 12-hour clock face with ticks for each minute and stroke marks for each hour. This is the default.

−digital Uses digital mode. Displays the date and time in digital format.

−d Uses digital mode. Displays the date and time in digital format. Note: −display must be used to specify a display.

−bg *color* Determines the background color. The default is white.

−bd *color* Determines the border color. The default is black.

−bw *pixels* Specifies the width in pixels of the border around the *xclock* window. The default is 2 pixels.

−chime Indicates that the clock should chime once on the half hour and twice on the hour.

−fg *color* Determines the color of the text in digital mode, and the color of the tick and stroke marks in analog mode. The default is black.

−fn *font* Specifies the font to be used in digital mode. Any fixed width font may be used. The default is 6x10.

−help Displays a brief summary of *xclock*'s calling syntax and options.

−hd *color* Specifies the color of the hands on an analog clock. The default is black.

-hl *color*   Specifies the color of the edges of the hands on an analog clock. Only useful on color displays. The default is black.

-padding *pixels*

Specifies the width in pixels of the space between the window border and any portion of the *xclock* display. The default is 10 pixels in digital mode and 8 pixels in analog mode.

-rv   Produces all output in white-on-black instead of black-on-white.

-update *seconds*

Specifies the frequency in seconds with which *xclock* updates its display. If, however, the *xclock* window is obscured and then exposed, *xclock* overrides this setting and redisplays immediately. A value of less than 30 seconds will enable a second hand on an analog clock. The default is 60 seconds.

-geometry =*geometry*

Sets *xclock* window size and location according to the geometry specification. The -geometry option can be (and often is) abbreviated to -g, unless there is a conflicting option that begins with "g." The argument to the geometry option (*geometry*) is referred to as a "standard geometry string," and has the form *widthxheight±xoff±yoff*.

In digital mode, height and width are determined by the font in use, unless otherwise specified. In analog mode, width and height default is 164, unless otherwise specified. The default value for any unspecified offset is -0. All values are in pixels.

-display [*host*]:*server*[.*screen*]

Allows you to specify the host, server and screen on which to create the *xclock* window. *host* specifies which machine to create the *xclock* window on, *server* specifies the server number and *screen* specifies the screen number. For example,

        xclock –display *your_node*:**0.1**

creates an *xclock* display on screen 1 on server 0 on the machine *your_node*. If the host is omitted, the local machine is assumed. If the screen is omitted, the screen 0 is assumed; the colon (:) is necessary in either case. Note that for *xclock* the -display option can't be shortened to -d.

xrm *resourcestring*

Specifies a resource string to be used. This is especially useful for setting resources that do not have separate command line options.

Resources

xclock uses the *Clock* widget in the X Toolkit. It understands all of the core resource names and classes as well as:

width (class Width)
> Specifies the width of the clock.

height (class Height)
> Specifies the height of the clock.

update (class Interval)
> Specifies the frequency in seconds at which the time should be redisplayed.

foreground (class Foreground)
> Specifies the color for the tic marks. Using the class specifies the color for all things that normally would appear in the foreground color. The default is "black" since the core default for background is "white."

hand (class Foreground)
> Specifies the color of the insides of the clock's hands.

high (class Foreground)
> Specifies the color used to highlight the clock's hands.

analog (class Boolean)
> Specifies whether or not an analog clock should be used instead of a digital one. The default is True.

chime (class Boolean)
> Specifies whether or not a bell should be rung on the hour and half hour.

padding (class Margin)
> Specifies the amount of internal padding in pixels to be used. The default is 8.

font (class Font)
> Specifies the font to be used for the digital clock. Note that variable width fonts currently will not always display correctly.

reverseVideo (class ReverseVideo)
> Specifies that the foreground and background colors should be reversed.

See Also

X, xrdb, time(3C), Athena Clock widget

Bugs

xclock believes the system clock.

When in digital mode, the string should be centered automatically.

When specifying an offset, the grammar requires an hours field but if only minutes are given they will be quietly ignored. A negative offset of less than 1 hour is treated as a positive offset.

Digital clock windows default to the analog clock size.

Border color has to be explicitly specified when reverse video is used.

When the update is an even divisor of 60 seconds, the second hand should always be on a multiple of the update time.

There is no way to exit the program. Should be able to select the text in digital mode.

Authors

Tony Della Fera (MIT-Athena, DEC);
Dave Mankins (MIT-Athena, BBN);
Ed Moy (UC Berkeley).

xdpr

Name

xdpr — dump an X window directly to the printer.

Syntax

xdpr [*options*]

Description

xdpr runs the commands *xwd*, *xpr*, and *lpr* to dump an X window, process it for a laser printer, and print it out. This is the easiest way to get a printout of a window. *xdpr* by default will print the largest possible representation of the window on the output page.

Options

-P*printer*   This option specifies the name of the printer to be used.

-display [*host*]:*server*[.*screen*]

Allows you to specify the server to connect to. *host* specifies the machine, *server* specifies the server number, and *screen* specifies the screen number. For example,

% **xdpr –display** *your_node*:**0.1**

prints a dump of an X window on screen 1 of server 0 on the machine *your_node*. If the host is omitted, the local machine is assumed. If the screen is omitted, screen 0 is assumed; the colon (:) is necessary in either case.

Any other arguments will be passed as arguments to the *xpr* command.

See Also

X(1), xwd, xpr, xwud

Authors

Michael R. Gretzinger, MIT Project Athena;
Jim Gettys, MIT Project Athena.

xedit

Name
xedit — simple text editor for X.

Syntax
xedit [*options*] [*filename*]

Description
xedit provides a window consisting of the following three areas:

Commands Menu

        Lists editing commands (for example, Undo or Search).

Message Window

        Displays *xedit* messages. In addition, this window can be used as a scratch pad.

Edit Window   Displays the text of the file that you are editing or creating.

Options
xedit accepts all of the standard X Toolkit command line options, plus:

filename   Specifies the file that is to be loaded during start-up. If a file is not specified, *xedit* lets you load a file or create a new file after it has started up.

Commands
Quit   Quits the current editing session. If any changes have not been saved, *xedit* displays a warning message and allows you to save the file.

Save   Stores a copy of the original, unedited file in *file*.BAK. Then, overwrites the original file with the edited contents.

Edit   Allows the text displayed in the Edit window to be edited.

Load   Loads the specified file and displays it in the Edit window.

Undo   Undoes the last edit only.

More   Undoes each edit previous to the last edit, which must first be undone with the Undo command.

Jump   Advances the cursor from the beginning of the file to the text line that corresponds to the selected line number.

<<   Searches from the cursor back to the beginning of the file for the string entered in the Search input box. If you do not enter a string in the Search input box, *xedit* automatically copies the last string that you selected from any X application into the Search input box and searches for that string.

Search >>   Searches from the cursor forward to the end of the file for the string entered in the search input box. If you do not enter a string in the Search input box, *xedit* automatically copies the last string that you selected from any X application into the Search input box and searches for that string.

Replace   Replaces the last searched-for string with the string specified in the Replace input box. If no string has been previously searched for, searches from the insert cursor to the end of the file for the next occurrence of the search string and highlights it.

All   Repositions the cursor at the beginning of the file and replaces all occurrences of the search string with the string specified in the Replace input box.

Resources

xedit is written using the X toolkit, and therefore it supports all the core resources of the toolkit as well as the resource for each of its widgets. The application contains four types of widgets and the following are the valid class identifiers.

```
ButtonBox       (the two boxes containing command buttons)
Command         (all command buttons)
Scrollbar       (the two scroll bars)
Text            (the two text areas)
```

The name identifiers for the various buttons are the same as the string on each button. The resources for individual buttons can be set using these names. All of the buttons can be affected by using the Command class.

```
All
Edit
Jump
Load
More
Quit
Replace
Save
Undo
```

The resources for the two text windows can be modified using the names EditWindow and MessageWindow.

Beyond the standard resources, xedit's resources are:

EnableBackups
              Specifies that, when edits made to an existing file are saved, *xedit* is to copy the original version of that file to *file*.BAK before it saves the changes. If the value of this option is specified as off, a backup file is not created.

background   Specifies the background color to be displayed in command buttons. The default is white.

border   Specifies the border color of the *xedit* window.

borderWidth   Specifies the border width, in pixels, of the *xedit* window.

`font`   Specifies the font displayed in the *xedit* window.

`foreground`   Specifies the foreground color of the *xedit* window. The default is black.

`geometry`   Specifies the geometry (window size and screen location) to be used as the default for the *xedit* window.

`internalHeight`
Specifies the internal horizontal padding (spacing between text and button border) for command buttons.

`internalWidth`
Specifies the internal vertical padding (spacing between text and button border) for command buttons.

Key Bindings

Each specification included in the *.XtActions* file modifies a key setting for the editor that *xedit* uses. When defining key specifications, you must use the following resource specification:

`text.EventBindings:`   `.XtActions`

Each key specification assigns an editor command to a named key and/or mouse combination and has the format:

`key:function`

`key`   Specifies the key or mouse button that is used to invoke the named function.

`function`   Specifies the function to be invoked when the named key is pressed.

For more information about specifications in the *.XtActions* file, see *X(1)*.

Files

~/.XtActions
/usr/lib/X11/.XtActions

See Also

X, xrdb

Restrictions

Large numbers of certain edit functions (for example, Undo or More) tend to degrade performance over time. If there is a noticeable decrease in response time, save and reload the file.

Author

Copyright © 1988, Digital Equipment Corporation.

Reference
Pages

Name

xfd — X window font displayer.

Syntax

xfd [*options*] [*fontname*]

Description

xfd creates a window in which the characters in the named font are displayed. The characters are shown in increasing order from left to right, top to bottom. The first character displayed at the top left will be character number 0 unless the −start option has been supplied in which case the character with the number given in the −start option will be used.

The characters are displayed in a grid of boxes, each large enough to hold any character of the font. If the −gray option has been supplied, the characters will be displayed using the Xlib routine XDrawImageString using the foreground and background colors on a gray background. This permits determining exactly how XDrawImageString will draw any given character. If −gray has not been supplied, the characters will simply be drawn using the foreground color on the background color.

All the characters in the font may not fit in the window at once. To see additional characters, click the right mouse button on the window. This will cause the next window full of characters to be displayed. Clicking the left mouse button on the window will cause the previous window full of characters to be displayed. *xfd* will beep if an attempt is made to go back past the 0th character.

Note that if the font is a 8 bit font, the characters 256-511 (0x100-0x1ff), 512-767 (0x200-0x2ff), etc. will display exactly the same as the characters 0-255 (0x00-0xff). *xfd* by default creates a window of size sufficient to display the first 256 characters using a 16 by 16 grid. In this case, there is no need to scroll forward or backward window fulls in order to see the entire contents of a 8 bit font. Of course, this window may very well not fit on the screen.

Clicking the middle button on a character will cause that character's number to be displayed in both decimal and hexidecimal at the bottom of the window. If verbose mode is selected, additional information about that particular character will be displayed as well. The displayed information includes the width of the character, its left bearing, right bearing, ascent, and its descent. If verbose mode is selected, typing '<' or '>' into the window will display the minimum or maximum values respectively taken on by each of these fields over the entire font.

The fontname is interpreted by the X server. To obtain a list of all the fonts available, use *xlsfonts*.

If no fontname is given on the command line, *xfd* displays the font "fixed".

The window stays around until the xfd process is killed or one of 'q', 'Q', ' ', or Control-C is typed into the *xfd* window.

Options

-bw *number*   Allows you to specify the width of the window border in pixels.

-rv   The foreground and background colors will be switched. The default colors are black on white.

-fw   Overrides a previous choice of reverse video. The foreground and background colors will not be switched.

-fg *color*   On color displays, determines the foreground color (the color of the text).

-bg *color*   On color displays, determines the background color.

-bd *color*   On color displays, determines the color of the border.

-bf *fontname*   Specifies the font to be used for the messages at the bottom of the window.

-tl *title*   Specifies that the title of the displayed window should be *title*.

-in *iconname*   Specifies that the name of the icon should be *iconname*.

-icon *filename*

Specifies that the bitmap in file *filename* should be used for the icon.

-verbose   Specifies that verbose mode should be used.

-gray   Specifies that a gray background should be used.

-start *charnum*

Specifies that character number *charnum* should be the first character displayed.

-geometry *=geometry*

Specifes the size and location of the *xfd* window. The **-geometry** option can be (and often is) abbreviated to **-g**, unless there is a conflicting option that begins with "g." The argument to the geometry option (*geometry*) is referred to as a "standard geometry string," and has the form *widthxheight±xoff±yoff*.

-display *[host]:server[.screen]*

Allows you to specify the host, server and screen on which to create the *xfd* window. For example,

xfd -display *your_node:0.1*

creates a window on screen 1 of server 0 on the machine *your_node*. If the host is omitted, the local machine is assumed. If the screen is omitted, the screen 0 is assumed; the colon (:) is necessary in either case.

Defaults

The *xfd* program uses the routine *XGetDefault(3X)* to read defaults, so its resource names are all capitalized.

BorderWidth Set the border width of the window in pixels.

BorderColor Set the border color of the window.

ReverseVideo
       If "on", reverse the definition of foreground and background color.

Foreground Set the foreground color.

Background Set the background color.

BodyFont Set the font to be used in the body of the window (i.e., for messages). This is not the font that *xfd* displays; it is the font used to display information about the font being displayed.

IconName Set the name of the icon.

IconBitmap Set the file we should look in to get the bitmap for the icon.

Title Set the title to be used.

See Also
Xlsfonts

Bugs
It should display the name of the font somewhere.

It should be rewritten to use the X toolkit.

It should skip over pages full of non-existent characters.

Author
Mark Lillibridge, MIT Project Athena.

xhost

Name

xhost — server access control program for X.

Syntax

xhost [*options*]

Description

The *xhost* program is used to add and delete hosts to the list of machines that are allowed to make connections to the X server. This provides a rudimentary form of privacy control and security. It is only sufficient for a workstation (single user) environment, although it does limit the worst abuses. Environments which require more sophisticated measures should use the hooks in the protocol for passing authentication data to the server.

The server initially allows network connections only from programs running on the same machine or from machines listed in the file */etc/X*.hosts* (where * is the display number of the server). The *xhost* program is usually run either from a startup file or interactively to give access to other users.

Hostnames that are followed by two colons (::) are used in checking DECnet connections; all other hostnames are used for TCP/IP connections.

If no command line arguments are given, the list of hosts that are allowed to connect is printed on the standard output along with a message indicating whether or not access control is currently enabled. This is the only option that may be used from machines other than the one on which the server is running.

Options

xhost accepts the command line options described below. For security, the options that affect access control may only be run from the same machine as the server.

[+]*hostname*   The given *hostname* (the plus sign is optional) is added to the list of machines that are allowed to connect to the X server.

−*hostname*   The given *hostname* is removed from the list of machines that are allowed to connect to the server. Existing connections are not broken, but new connection attempts will be denied. Note that the current machine is allowed to be removed; however, further connections (including attempts to add it back) will not be permitted. Resetting the server (thereby breaking all connections) is the only way to allow local connections again.

+   Access is granted to everyone, even if they aren't on the list of allowed hosts (i.e. access control is turned off).

−   Access is restricted to only those machines on the list of allowed hosts (i.e. access control is turned on).

Files

/etc/X*.hosts

See Also

X, Xserver

Bugs

You can't specify a display on the command line because −display indicates that you want to remove the machine named *display* from the access list.

Authors

Bob Scheifler, MIT Laboratory for Computer Science;
Jim Gettys, MIT Project Athena (DEC).

xinit

Window System Initializer—

Name

xinit — X Window System initializer.

Syntax

xinit [[*client*] *options*] [-- [*server_program*]
    [-display [*host*]:*server* [.*screen*]] *options*]

Options

client   Specifies the client to be started with the server.

server_program

         Specifies the server program to be used.

-display [*host*]:*server*[.*screen*]

         Specifies the host, server and screen on which you are initializing the X Window System. For example,

           xinit -display *your_node***:0.1**

         specifies screen 1 on server 0 on the machine *your_node*. If the host is omitted, the local machine is assumed. If the screen is omitted, the screen 0 is assumed; the colon (:) is necessary in either case.

Description

The *xinit* program is used to start the X Window System server program and a first client program (usually a terminal emulator) on systems that cannot start X directly from */etc/init* or in environments that use multiple window systems. When this first client exits, *xinit* will kill the X server program and then terminate.

Unless otherwise specified on the command line, *xinit* assumes that there are programs called "X" and "xterm" in the current search path. It starts the server program on screen 1 of server 0 on the machine *your_node* and then runs an *xterm* using the following command line:

    xterm –geometry +1+1 -n login –display *your_node***:0.1**

(Systems that don't support UNIX domain sockets will be started with host:0 instead).

Additional arguments can be added to the *xinit* command line, and they will simply be appended to the *xterm* command shown above. This makes it possible to add arguments (for example, foreground and background colors) without having to retype the whole command line.

An alternate client and/or server program may be specified on the command line.

To specify a particular server program command line, append a double dash (--) to the *xinit* command line (after any client and arguments) followed by the desired server comand. For example:

    % **xinit -- Xsun**

If you want to specify a different client than the *xterm* command shown above, the desired client and its arguments should be given as the first command line arguments to *xinit*. The

192   *X Window System User's Guide*

client program name must begin with a slash (/) or a period (.). Otherwise, it is treated as an argument to be appended to the existing startup command. This makes it possible to construct a script to invoke a series of X clients, and to start it from the command line. For example:

```
% xinit /usr/tim/startx
```

You can also put a line like this into your *.login* file if the X server is not started automatically from */etc/ttys*. See Chapter 9 for additional details.

If an explicit server program name is not given and the first argument following the double dash (−−) is a digit, *xinit* will use that number as the server number instead of zero. All remaining arguments are appended to the server program command line.

Examples

The following examples show various permutations of *xinit* options. The first simply appends arguments to the normal *xterm* invocation. The second adds an argument and also runs a server other than the default X. The third example runs a CPU-intensive client on a remote system with the horsepower to handle it.

```
xinit −geometry =80x65+10+10 −fn 8x13 −j −fg white −bg navy

xinit −e widgets −− Xsun −l −c

xinit rsh fasthost cpupig −display workstation:1 −− 1 −a 2 −t 5
```

See Also

X, Xserver, xterm

Author

Bob Scheifler, MIT Laboratory for Computer Science.

xload

Name
xload — load average display for X.

Syntax
xload [*–toolkitoptions*] [*options*]

Description
The *xload* program displays a periodically updating histogram of the system load average.

Options
xload accepts all of the standard X Toolkit command line options along with the additional options listed below:

-scale *integer*

This option specifies the minimum number of tick marks in the histogram, where one division represents one load average point. If the load goes above this number, *xload* will create more divisions, but it will never use fewer than this number. The default is 1.

-update *seconds*

This option specifies the frequency in seconds at which *xload* updates its display. Expose events will cause automatic updating. The minimum as well as default time is 5 seconds.

The following standard X Toolkit arguments are commonly used with *xload*.

-bd *color*   This option specifies the border color. The default color is "black".

-bg *color*   This option specifies the background color. The default color is "white".

-bw *pixels*   This option specifies the width in pixels of the border around the window. The default value is 2.

-fg *color*   This option specifies the graph color. The default color is "black".

-fn *fontname* This option specifies the font to be used in displaying the name of the host whose load is being monitored. The default is "6x10."

-rv   This option indicates that reverse video should be simulated by swapping the foreground and background colors.

-geometry *=geometry*

Specifies the size and location of the window. The **-geometry** option can be (and often is) abbreviated to **-g**, unless there is a conflicting option that begins with "g." The argument to the geometry option (*geometry*) is referred to as a "standard geometry string," and has the form *widthxheight±xoff±yoff*.

-display [*host*]:*server*[.*screen*]

Allows you to specify the host, server and screen on which to create the *xload* window. *host* specifies which machine to create the *xload* window on, `server` specifies the server number, and `screen` specifies the screen number. For example,

xload -display *your_node*:0.1

creates an *xload* window on screen 1 of server 0 on the machine *your_node*. If the host is omitted, the local machine is assumed. If the screen is omitted, screen 0 is assumed; the colon (:) is necessary in either case.

-xrm *resourcestring*

This option specifies a resource string to be used. This is especially useful for setting resources that do not have separate command line options.

Defaults

This program uses the *Load* widget in the X Toolkit. It understands all of the core resource names and classes as well as:

width (class Width)

Specifies the width of the load average graph.

height (class Height)

Specifies the height of the load average graph.

update (class Interval)

Specifies the frequency in seconds at which the load should be redisplayed.

scale(class Scale)

Specifies the initial number of ticks on the graph. The default is 1.

minScale (class Scale)

Specifies the minimum number of ticks that will be displayed. The default is 1.

foreground (class Foreground)

Specifies the color for the graph. Using the class specifies the color for all things that normally would appear in the foreground color. The default is "black" since the core default for background is "white."

label (class Label)

Specifies the label to use on the graph. The default is the hostname.

font (class Font)

Specifies the font to be used for the label. The default is "fixed."

reverseVideo (class ReverseVideo)

Specifies that the foreground and background should be reversed.

See Also

X, xrdb, mem(4), Athena Load widget

Diagnostics

Unable to open display or create window. Unable to open */dev/kmem*. Unable to query window for dimensions. Various X errors.

Bugs

This program requires the ability to open and read */dev/kmem*. On most systems, this requires the suid bit set with root ownership or the sgid bit set and membership in the same group as */dev/kmem*.

Reading */dev/kmem* is inherently non-portable.

Border color has to be explicitly specified when reverse video is used.

Authors

K. Shane Hartman (MIT-LCS) and Stuart A. Malone (MIT-LCS);
with features added by Jim Gettys (MIT-Athena), Bob Scheifler (MIT-LCS), and Tony Della Fera (MIT-Athena).

xlogo

Name

xlogo — X Window System logo.

Synopsis

xlogo [-*options*]

Description

The *xlogo* program displays the X Window System logo. This program is nothing more than a wrapper around the Athena Logo widget.

Options

xlogo accepts all of the standard X Toolkit command line options, of which the following are commonly used:

-bg *color*   This option specifies the color to use for the background of the window. The default is "white." A correct color for the background is something like "maroon."

-bd *color*   This option specifies the color to use for the border of the window. The default is "black."

-bw *number*   This option specifies the width in pixels of the border surrounding the window.

-fg *color*   This option specifies the color to use for displaying the logo. The default is "black". A correct color for the background is something like "silver," which you can approximate with a shade of gray, like #aa9.

-rv   This option indicates that reverse video should be simulated by swapping the foreground and background colors.

-geometry =*geometry*

The *xlogo* window is created with the specified size and location determined by the supplied geometry specification. The -geometry option can be (and often is) abbreviated to -g, unless there is a conflicting option that begins with "g." The argument to the geometry option (*geometry*) is referred to as a "standard geometry string," and has the form *widthxheight±xoff±yoff*.

-display [*host*]:*server*[.*screen*]

Allows you to specify the host, server and screen on which to create the *xlogo* window. (See *X(1)*.) *host* specifies which machine to create the *xlogo* window on, *server* specifies the server number, and *screen* specifies the screen number. For example,

xlogo -display *your_node*:**0.1**

creates an *xlogo* window on screen 1 of server 0 on the machine *your_node*. If the host is omitted, the local machine is assumed. If the screen is omitted, screen 0 is assumed; the colon (:) is necessary in either case.

-xrm *resourcestring*
> This option specifies a resource string to be used. This is especially useful for setting resources that do not have separate command line options.

Defaults

This program uses the *Logo* widget in the X Toolkit. It understands all of the core resource names and classes as well as:

width (class Width)
> Specifies the width of the logo.

height (class Height)
> Specifies the height of the logo.

foreground (class Foreground)
> Specifies the color for the logo. The default is "black" since the core default for background is "white."

reverseVideo (class ReverseVideo)
> Specifies that the foreground and background should be reversed.

See Also

X, xrdb

Authors

Ollie Jones of Apollo Computer wrote the logo graphics routine, based on a graphic design by Danny Chong and Ross Chapman of Apollo Computer.

Name

xlsfonts — server font list displayer for X.

Syntax

xlsfonts [*options*] [*pattern*]

Description

xlsfonts lists the fonts that match the given *pattern*. The wildcard character "*" may be used to match any sequence of characters (including none), and "?" to match any single character. If no pattern is given, "*" is assumed.

The "*" and "?" characters must be quoted or escaped to prevent them from being expanded by the shell.

Options

-display [*host*]:*server*[.*screen*]

Allows you to specify the host, server and screen. For example,

xlsfonts –display *your_node*:**0.1**

specifies screen 1 on server 0 on the machine *your_node*. If the host is omitted, the local machine is assumed. If the screen is omitted, the screen 0 is assumed; the colon (:) is necessary in either case.

-l   This option indicates that a long listing should be generated for each font.

-m   This option indicates that long listings should also print the minimum and maximum bounds of each font.

-C   This option indicates that listings should use multiple columns.

-1   This option indicates that listings should use a single column.

See Also

X, Xserver, xset, xfd

Bugs

Doing xlsfonts -l can tie up your server for a very long time. This is really a bug with single-threaded non-preemptible servers, not with this program.

Author

Mark Lillibridge, MIT Project Athena.

xmodmap

Name

xmodmap — keyboard modifier utility.

Syntax

xmodmap [*options*] [*filename*]

Description

xmodmap is a utility for displaying and altering the X keyboard modifier map and keysym table on the specified server and host. It is intended to be run from a user's X startup script to setup the keyboard according to personal tastes.

With no arguments, *xmodmap* displays the current map.

Options

-display [*host*]:*server*[.*screen*]

Allows you to specify the host, server and screen to use. See *X(1)*. For example,

xmodmap –display *your_node*:**0.1**

specifies the screen 1 on server 0 on the machine *your_node*. If the host is omitted, the local machine is assumed. If the screen is omitted, the screen 0 is assumed; the colon (:) is necessary in either case.

-help   This option indicates that a brief description of the command line arguments should be printed on the standard error. This will be done whenever an unhandled argument is given to *xmodmap*.

-grammar   This option indicates that a help message describing the expression grammar used in files and with -e expressions should be printed on the standard error.

-verbose   This option indicates that *xmodmap* should print logging information as it parses its input.

-quiet   This option turns off the verbose logging. This is the default.

-n   This option indicates that *xmodmap* should not change the mappings, but should display what it would do, like *make*(1) does when given this option.

-e *expression*

This option specifies an expression to be executed. Any number of expressions may be specified from the command line.

-p   This option indicates that the current modifier map should be printed on the standard output.

–   A lone dash means that the standard input should be used as the input file.

The *filename* specifies a file containing *xmodmap* expressions to be executed. This file is usually kept in the user's home directory with a name like "*.keymap.km*".

For compatibility with an older version, *xmodmap* also accepts the following obsolete single letter options:

-[SLC12345]

> These options indicate that all current keys for the Shift, Lock, Control, or Mod modifier sets should be removed from the modifier map. These are equivalent to `clear` expressions.

-[slc] *keysym*

> These options specify a *keysym* to be removed from the Shift, Lock, or Control modifier sets. These are equivalent to `remove` expressions.

+[slc12345] *keysym*

> These options specify a *keysym* to be added to the Shift, Lock, or Control modifier sets. These are equivalent to `add` expressions.

Expression Grammar

The *xmodmap* program reads a list of expressions and converts them into appropriate calls to the *Xlib* routines *XChangeKeyboardMapping*, *XInsertModifiermapEntry* and *XDeleteModifiermapEntry*. Allowable expressions include:

keycode *NUMBER = KEYSYMNAME* . . .

> The list of keysyms is assigned to the indicated keycode (which may be specified in decimal, hex or octal and can be determined by running the *xev* program in the examples directory). Usually only one keysym is assigned to a given code.

keysym *KEYSYMNAME = KEYSYMNAME* . . .

> The *KEYSYMNAME* on the left hand side is looked up to find its current key-code and the line is replaced with the appropriate `keycode` expression. Note that if you have the same keysym bound to multiple keys, this might not work.

clear *MODIFIERNAME*

> This removes all entries in the modifier map for the given modifier, where valid name are: Shift, Lock, Control, Mod1, Mod2, Mod3, Mod4 and Mod5 (case does not matter in modifier names, although it does matter for all other names). For example, ''clear Lock'' will remove all any keys that were bound to the shift lock modifier.

add *MODIFIERNAME = KEYSYMNAME* . . .

> This adds the given keysyms to the indicated modifier map. The keysym names are evaluated after all input expressions are read to make it easy to write expressions to swap keys.

remove *MODIFIERNAME = KEYSYMNAME* . . .

> This removes the given keysyms from the indicated modifier map. Unlike `add`, the keysym names are evaluated as the line is read in. This allows you

to remove keys from a modifier without having to worry about whether or not they have been reassigned.

Lines that begin with an exclamation mark (!) are taken as comments.

If you want to change the binding of a modifier key, you must also remove it from the appropriate modifier map.

Examples

To make the backspace key generate a delete instead, use

```
% xmodmap -e "keysym BackSpace = Delete"
```

To swap the left control and caps lock keys you could use:

```
!
! Swap Caps_Lock and Control_L
!
remove Lock = Caps_Lock
remove Control = Control_L
keysym Control_L = Caps_Lock
keysym Caps_Lock = Control_L
add Lock = Caps_Lock
add Control = Control_L
```

As a more complicated example, the following is what the author uses:

```
!
! On the HP, the following keycodes have key caps as listed:
!
!      101   Backspace
!       55   Caps
!       14   Ctrl
!       15   Break/Reset
!       86   Stop
!       89   F5
!
! I prefer using ''keycode'' over ''keysym'' so that I can
! rerun the file to fix up my keyboard.
!
! This sets the backspace key to generate Delete, flushes
! all caps lock bindings, assigned a control key to what used
! to be the caps lock key, makes the F1 generate ESC, and makes
! the Break/Reset key be a shift lock.

keycode 101 = Delete
keycode 55 = Control_R
clear Lock
```

```
add Control = Control_R
keycode 89 = Escape
keycode 15 = Caps_Lock
add Lock = Caps_Lock
```

See Also

X

Bugs

Every time a `keycode` expression is evaluated, the server generates a `MappingNotify` event on every client. This can cause some thrashing. All of the changes should be batched together and done at once. Clients that receive keyboard input and ignore `MappingNotify` events will not notice any changes made to keyboard mappings.

xmodmap should generate ''add'' and ''remove'' expressions automatically whenever a keycode that is already bound to a modifier is changed.

There should be a way to have the `remove` expression accept keycodes as well as keysyms for those times when you really mess up your mappings.

Authors

Rewritten by Jim Fulton, MIT X Consortium, from an original by David Rosenthal of Sun Microsystems.

xpr

Name
xpr — print an X window dump.

Syntax
xpr [*options*] [*filename*]

Description
xpr takes as input a window dump file produced by *xwd* and formats it for output on the DEC LN03 or LA100 PostScript printers, or the IBM PP3812 page printer. If you do not give a filename, standard input is used. By default, *xpr* prints the largest possible representation of the window on the output page. Options allow you to add headers and trailers, specify margins, adjust the scale and orientation, and append multiple window dumps to a single output file. Output is sent to standard output unless you specify -output *filename*.

Options
-scale *scale*

Affects the size of the window on the page. The LN03 and PostScript printers are able to translate each bit in a window pixel map into a grid of a specified size. For example, each bit might translate into a 3x3 grid. This is specified by -scale 3. By default, a window is printed with the largest scale that fits onto the page for the specified orientation.

-height *inches*

Specifies the maximum height of the window on the page. Inches are expressed as real numbers.

-width *inches*

Specifies the maximum width of the window. Inches are expressed as real numbers.

-left *inches*

Specifies the left margin in inches. Inches are expressed as real numbers. By default, the window is centered on the page.

-top *inches* Specifies the top margin for the picture in inches. Inches are expressed as real numbers. By default, the window is centered on the page.

-header *header*

Specifies a header string to be printed above the window. Default is no header.

-trailer *trailer*

Specifies a trailer string to be printed below the window. Default is no trailer.

-landscape Prints the window in landscape mode. By default, a window is printed such that its longest side follows the long side of the paper.

-portrait Prints the window in portrait mode. By default, a window is printed such that its longest side follows the long side of the paper.

-rv   Reverses the foreground color and the background color.

-report   Prints out the following window statistics: window name, width, height, orientation, and scale.

-compact   Compresses white pixels on PostScript printers.

-output *filename*
                   Specifies an output filename. If this option is not specified, standard output is used.

-append *filename*
                   Specifies a filename previously produced by *xpr* to which the window contents are to be appended.

-noff   When specified in conjunction with -append, the window appears on the same page as the previous window.

-split *n*   Allows you to split a window onto several pages. This might be necessary for large windows that would otherwise cause the printer to overload and print the page in an obscure manner.

-device *device*
                   Specifies the device on which the file is to be printed. Currently only the LN03 (-device ln03), LA100 (-device la100), generic PostScript printers (-device ps), IBM PP3812 (-device pp), and Apple LaserWriter (-device lw or -device ps) are supported.

Limitations

The current version of *xpr* can generally print out on the LN03 most X windows that are not larger than two-thirds of the screen. For example, it will be able to print out a large *emacs* window, but it will usually fail when trying to print out the entire screen. The LN03 has memory limitations that can cause it to incorrectly print very large or complex windows. The two most common errors encountered are "band too complex" and "page memory exceeded." In the first case, a window may have a particular band (a row six pixels deep) that contains too many changes (from black to white to black). This will cause the printer to drop part of the line and possibly parts of the rest of the page. The printer will flash the number '1' on its front panel when this problem occurs. A possible solution to this problem is to increase the scale of the picture, or to split the picture onto two or more pages. The second problem, "page memory exceeded," will occur if the picture contains too much black, or if the picture contains complex half-tones such as the background color of a display. When this problem occurs the printer will automatically split the picture into two or more pages. It may flash the number '5' on its from panel. There is no easy solution to this problem. It will probably be necessary to either cut and paste, or rework to application to produce a less complex picture.

xpr provides some support for the LA100. However, there are several limitations on its use: The picture will always be printed in portrait mode, there is no scaling and the aspect ratio will be slightly off.

Support for PostScript output currently cannot handle the -append, -noff or -split options.

The -compact option is *only* supported for PostScript output. It compresses white space but not black space, so it is not useful for reverse-video windows.

See Also

xwd, xdpr, xwud, X

Authors

Michael R. Gretzinger, MIT Project Athena;
Jose Capo, MIT Project Athena (PP3812 support);
Marvin Solomon (University of Wisconsin).

Name

xprop — display window and font properties for X.

Syntax

xprop [*options*]

Description

The *xprop* utility is for displaying window and font properties in an X server. One window or font is selected using the command line arguments, or in the case of a window, by clicking on the desired window. A list of properties is then given, possibly with formatting information.

For each of these properties, its value on the selected window or font is printed using the supplied formatting information if any. If no formatting information is supplied, internal defaults are used. If a property is not defined on the selected window or font, "not defined" is printed as the value for that property. If no property list is given, all the properties possessed by the selected window or font are printed.

A window may be selected in one of four ways. First, if the desired window is the root window, the -root option may be used. If the desired window is not the root window, it may be selected in two ways on the command line, either by id number such as might be obtained from *xwininfo*, or by name if the window possesses a name. The -id option selects a window by id number in either decimal or hex (must start with 0x) while the -name option selects a window by name.

The last way to select a window does not involve the command line at all. If none of -font, -id, -name, and -root are specified, a crosshairs cursor is displayed and the user allowed to choose any visible window by pressing any pointer button in the desired window. If it is desired to display properties of a font as opposed to a window, the -font option may be used.

Other than the above four options and the -help option for obtaining help, and the -grammar option for listing the full grammar for the command line, all the other command line options are used in specifing both the format of the properties to be displayed and how to display them. The -len *n* option specifies that at most *n* bytes of any given property will be read and displayed. This is useful for example when displaying the cut buffer on the root window, which could run to several pages if displayed in full.

Normally each property name is displayed by printing first the property name then its type (if it has one) in parentheses followed by its value. The -notype option specifies that property types should not be displayed. The -fs option is used to specify a file containing a list of formats for properties while the -f option is used to specify the format for one property.

The formatting information for a property actually consists of two parts, a *format* and a *dformat*. The *format* specifies the actual formatting of the property (i.e., is it made up of words, bytes, or longs?, etc.) while the *dformat* specifies how the property should be displayed.

The following paragraphs describe how to construct *format*s and *dformat*s. However, for the vast majority of users and uses, this should not be necessary as the built in defaults contain the `formats` and `dformats` necessary to display all the standard properties. It should only be necessary to specify `formats` and `dformats` if a new property is being dealt with or the user dislikes the standard display format. New users especially are encouraged to skip this part.

A *format* consists of one of 0, 8, 16, or 32 followed by a sequence of one or more format characters. The 0, 8, 16, or 32 specifies how many bits per field there are in the property. Zero is a special case meaning use the field size information associated with the property itself. (this is only needed for special cases like type INTEGER which is actually three different types depending on the size of the fields of the property)

A value of 8 means that the property is a sequence of bytes while a value of 16 would mean that the property is a sequence of words. The difference between these two lies in the fact that the sequence of words will be byte swapped while the sequence of bytes will not be when read by a machine of the opposite byte order of the machine that orginally wrote the property. For more information on how properties are formatted and stored, consult Volume 1, *Xlib Programming Manual*.

Once the size of the fields has been specified, it is necessary to specify the type of each field (i.e., is it an integer, a string, an atom, or what?) This is done using one format character per field. If there are more fields in the property than format characters supplied, the last character will be repeated as many times as necessary for the extra fields. The format characters and their meaning are as follows:

a   The field holds an atom number. A field of this type should be of size 32.

b   The field is an boolean. A 0 means false while anything else means true.

c   The field is an unsigned number, a cardinal.

i   The field is a signed integer.

m   The field is a set of bit flags, 1 meaning on.

s   This field and the next ones until either a 0 or the end of the property represent a sequence of bytes. This format character is only usable with a field size of 8 and is most often used to represent a string.

x   The field is a hex number (like 'c' but displayed in hex - most useful for displaying window ids and the like)

An example *format* is 32ica which is the format for a property of three fields of 32 bits each, the first holding a signed integer, the second an unsigned integer, and the third an atom.

The format of a *dformat* (unlike that of a *format*) is not so rigid. The only limitations on a *dformat* is that it may not start with a letter or a dash. This is so that it can be distinguished from a property name or an option. A *dformat* is a text string containing special characters instructing that various fields be printed at various points in a manor similar to the formatting string used by printf. For example, the *dformat* '' is ($0, $1 \)\n'' would render the POINT 3, -4 which has a *format* of 32ii as '' is (3, -4)\n''.

Any character other than a $, ?, \, or a (in a *dformat* prints as itself. To print out one of $, ?, \, or (proceed it by a \. I.e., to print out a $, use \$. Several special backslash sequences are provided as shortcuts. \n will cause a newline to be displayed while \t will cause a tab to be displayed. \o where o is an octal number will display character number o.

A $ followed by a number n causes field number n to be displayed. The format of the displayed field depends on the formatting character used to describe it in the corrsponding *format*. I.e., if a cardinal is described by 'c' it will print in decimal while if it is described by a 'x' it is displayed in hex.

If the field is not present in the property (this is possible with some properties), <field not available> is displayed instead. $n+ will display field number n then a comma then field number n+1 then another comma then ... until the last field defined. If field n is not defined, nothing is displayed. This is useful for a property that is a list of values.

A ? is used to start a conditional expression, a kind of if-then statement. ?exp(text) will display *text* if and only if *exp* evaluates to non-zero. This is useful for two things. First, it allows fields to be displayed if and only if a flag is set. And second, it allows a value to such as a state number to be displayed as a name rather than as just a number. The syntax of *exp* is as follows:

exp   ::= *term* | *term=exp* | *!exp*

term   ::= *n* | *$n* | m*n*

The ! operator is a logical "not", changing 0 to 1 and any non-zero value to 0. = is an equality operator. Note that internally all expressions are evaluated as 32 bit numbers so -1 is not equal to 65535. = returns 1 if the two values are equal and 0 if not. n represents the constant value n while $n represents the value of field number n. mn is 1 if flag number n in the first field having format character 'm' in the corrsponding *format* is 1, 0 otherwise.

Examples: ?m3(count: $3\n) displays field 3 with a label of count if and only if flag number 3 (count starts at 0!) is on. ?$2=0(True)?!$2=0(False) displays the inverted value of field 2 as a boolean.

In order to display a property, *xprop* needs both a *format* and a *dformat*. Before *xprop* uses its default values of a *format* of 32x and a *dformat* of " = { $0+ }\n", it searches several places in an attempt to find more specific formats. First, a search is made using the name of the property. If this fails, a search is made using the type of the property. This allows type STRING to be defined with one set of formats while allowing property WM_NAME which is of type STRING to be defined with a different format. In this way, the display formats for a given type can be overridden for specific properties.

The locations searched are in order: the format if any specified with the property name (as in 8x WM_NAME), the formats defined by -f options in last to first order, the contents of the file specified by the -fs option if any, the contents of the file specified by the environmental variable XPROPFORMATS if any, and finally *xprop*'s built in file of formats.

The format of the files refered to by the −fs option and the XPROPFORMATS variable is one or more lines of the following form:

name format [*dformat*]

Where *name* is either the name of a property or the name of a type, *format* is the *format* to be used with *name* and *dformat* is the *dformat* to be used with *name*. If *dformat* is not present, " = $0+\n" is assumed.

Options

-help   Prints out a summary of command line options.

-grammar   Prints out a detailed grammar for all command line options.

-id *id*   Allows the user to select window *id* on the command line rather than using the pointer to select the target window. This is very useful in debugging X applications where the target window is not mapped to the screen or where the use of the pointer might be impossible or interfere with the application.

-name *name*   Allows the user to specify that the window named *name* is the target window on the command line rather than using the pointer to select the target window.

-font *font*   Allows the user to specify that the properties of font *font* should be displayed.

-root   Specifies that X's root window is the target window. This is useful in situations where the root window is completely obscured.

-display [*host*]:*server*[.*screen*]
               Allows you to specify the server to connect to. For example,

                       xprop -display *your_node*:**0.1**

               specifies screen 1 on server 0 on the machine *your_node*. If the host is omitted, the local machine is assumed. If the screen is omitted, the screen 0 is assumed; the colon (:) is necessary in either case.

-len *n*   Specifies that at most *n* bytes of any property should be read or displayed.

-notype   Specifies that the type of each property should not be displayed.

-fs *file*   Specifies that file *file* should be used as a source of more formats for properties.

-f *name format* [*dformat*]
               Specifies that the format for *name* should be *format* and that the dformat for *name* should be *dformat*. If *dformat* is missing, " = $0+\n" is assumed.

Examples

To display the name of the root window: xprop -root WM_NAME.

To display the window manager hints for the clock: xprop -name xclock WM_HINTS.

To display the start of the cut buffer: xprop -root -len 100 CUT_BUFFER0.

To display the point size of the fixed font: `xprop -font fixed POINT_SIZE`.

To display all the properties of window # 0x200007: `xprop -id 0x200007`.

See Also
X, xwininfo

Author
Mark Lillibridge, MIT Project Athena.

xrdb

Name

xrdb — X server resource database utility.

Syntax

xrdb [*option*] [*filename*]

Description

xrdb is used to get or set the contents of the RESOURCE_MANAGER property on the root window of screen 0. You would normally run this program from your X startup file.

The resource manager (used by the Xlib routine *XGetDefault(3X)* and the X Toolkit) uses the RESOURCE_MANAGER property to get user preferences about color, fonts, and so on for applications. Having this information in the server (where it is available to all clients) instead of on disk, solves the problem in previous versions of X that required you to maintain *defaults* files on every machine that you might use. It also allows for dynamic changing of defaults without editing files.

For compatibility, if there is no RESOURCE_MANAGER property defined (either because *xrdb* was not run or if the property was removed), clients will look for a file called *Xdefaults* in your home directory.

The `filename` (or the standard input if - or no input file is given) is optionally passed through the C preprocessor with the following symbols defined, based on the capabilities of the server being used:

`HOST=hostname`
    the hostname portion of the display to which you are connected.

`WIDTH=num`   the width of the screen in pixels.

`HEIGHT=num`   the height of the screen in pixels.

`X_RESOLUTION=num`
    the x resolution of the screen in pixels per meter.

`Y_RESOLUTION=num`
    the y resolution of the screen in pixels per meter.

`PLANES=num`   the number of bit planes for the default visual.

`CLASS=visualclass`
    one of StaticGray, GrayScale, StaticColor, PsuedoColor, TrueColor, DirectColor.

`COLOR`   only defined if the default visual's type is one of the color options.

    Lines that begin with an exclamation mark (!) are ignored and may be used as comments.

Options

xrdb accepts the following options:

-help
: This option (or any unsupported option) will cause a brief description of the allowable options and parameters to be printed.

-display [*host*]:*server*[.*screen*]
: Allows you to specify the host, server and screen to connect to. *host* specifies the machine, *server* specifies the server number, and *screen* specifies the screen number. For example:

    xrdb -display *your_node*:**0.0**

    specifies screen 0 of server 0 on the machine *your_node*. If the host is omitted, the local machine is assumed. If the screen is omitted, screen 0 is assumed; the colon (:) is necessary in either case.

-cpp *filename*
: This option specifies the pathname of the C preprocessor program to be used. Although *xrdb* was designed to use CPP, any program that acts as a filter and accepts the -D, -I, and -U options may be used.

-nocpp
: This option indicates that *xrdb* should not run the input file through a preprocessor before loading it into the RESOURCE_MANAGER property.

-symbols
: This option indicates that the symbols that are defined for the preprocessor should be printed onto the standard output. It can be used in conjunction with -query, but not with the options that change the RESOURCE_MANAGER property.

-query
: This option indicates that the current contents of the RESOURCE_MANAGER property should be printed onto the standard output. Note that since preprocessor commands in the input resource file are part of the input file, not part of the property, they won't appear in the output from this option. The -edit option can be used to merge the contents of the property back into the input resource file without damaging preprocessor commands.

-load
: This option indicates that the input should be loaded as the new value of the RESOURCE_MANAGER property, replacing whatever what there (i.e. the old contents are removed). This is the default action.

-merge
: This option indicates that the input should be merged with, instead of replacing, the current contents of the RESOURCE_MANAGER property. Since *xrdb* can read the standard input, this option can be used to the change the contents of the RESOURCE_MANAGER property directly from a terminal or from a shell script.

-remove
: This option indicates that the RESOURCE_MANAGER property should be removed from its window.

-edit *filename*
> This option indicates that the contents of the RESOURCE_MANAGER property should be edited into the given file, replacing any values already listed there. This allows you to put changes that you have made to your defaults back into your resource file, preserving any comments or preprocessor lines.

-backup *string*
> This option specifies a suffix to be appended to the filename used with -edit to generate a backup file.

-D*name*[=*value*]
> This option is passed through to the preprocessor and is used to define symbols for use with conditionals such as *#ifdef*.

-U*name*
> This option is passed through to the preprocessor and is used to remove any definitions of this symbol.

-I*directory*
> This option is passed through to the preprocessor and is used to specify a directory to search for files that are referenced with *#include*.

Files
Generalizes ~/.*Xdefaults* files.

See Also
X(1), XGetDefault(3X), Volume 1, *Xlib Programming Manual*.

Bugs
The default for no arguments should be to query, not to overwrite, so that it is consistent with other programs.

Authors
Phil Karlton, rewritten from the original by Jim Gettys. Copyright © 1988, Digital Equipment Corporation.

Name

xrefresh — refresh all or part of an X screen.

Syntax

xrefresh [*options*]

Description

xrefresh is a simple X program that causes all or part of your screen to be repainted. *xrefresh* maps a window on top of the desired area of the screen and then immediately unmaps it, causing refresh events to be sent to all applications. By default, a window with no background is used, causing all applications to repaint "smoothly." However, the various options can be used to indicate that a solid background (of any color) or the root window background should be used instead.

Options

-white   Use a white background. The screen just appears to flash quickly, and then repaint.

-black   Use a black background (in effect, turning off all of the electron guns to the tube). This can be somewhat disorienting as everything goes black for a moment.

-solid *color*
                Use a solid background of the specified color. Try green.

-root   Use the root window background.

-none   This is the default. All of the windows simply repaint.

-geometry =*geometry*
                Specifies the portion of the screen to be repainted. The -geometry option can be (and often is) abbreviated to -g, unless there is a conflicting option that begins with "g." The argument to the geometry option (*geometry*) is referred to as a "standard geometry string," and has the form *widthxheight±xoff±yoff*.

-display [*host*]:*server*[.*screen*]
                Allows you to specify the server and screen to refresh. For example, *host* specifies the machine, *server* specifies the server number, and *screen* specifies the screen number. For example,

> **xrefresh –display** *your_node*:**0.1**

specifies screen 1 of server 0 on the machine *your_node*. If the host is omitted, the local machine is assumed. If the screen is omitted, screen 0 is assumed; the colon (:) is necessary in either case.

Defaults

The *xrefresh* program uses the routine *XGetDefault(3X)* to read defaults, so its resource names are all capitalized.

`Black, White, Solid, None, Root`
          Determines what sort of window background to use.

`Geometry`   Determines the area to refresh. Not very useful.

See Also
X

Bugs
It should have just one default type for the background.

Author
Jim Gettys, Digital Equipment Corp., MIT Project Athena.

Name
xset — user preference utility for X.

Syntax
xset [*options*]

Description
xset is used to set various user preference options of the display and keyboard.

Options
Note that not all X implementations are guaranteed to honor all of these options.

-display [*host*]:*server*[.*screen*]

> Allows you to specify the host, server and screen for which to set preferences. *host* specifies the machine, *server* specifies the server number, and *screen* specifies the screen number. For example,
>
> **-display** *your_node*:**0.1** &
>
> specifies screen 1 of server 0 on the machine *your_node*. If the host is omitted, the local machine is assumed. If the screen is omitted, screen 0 is assumed; the colon (:) is necessary in either case.

b

> The b option controls bell volume, pitch and duration. This option accepts up to three numerical parameters (volume, pitch, and duration), a preceding dash (-), or an on/off flag. If no parameters are given, or the on flag is used, the system defaults will be used. If the dash or off are given, the bell will be turned off. If only one numerical parameter is given, the bell volume will be set to that value, as a percentage of its maximum. Likewise, the second numerical parameter specifies the bell pitch, in hertz, and the third numerical parameter specifies the duration in milliseconds. Note that not all hardware can vary the bell characteristics. The X server will set the characteristics of the bell as closely as it can to the user's specifications.

c

> The c option controls key click. This option can take an optional value, a preceding dash (-), or an on/off flag. If no parameter or the on flag is given, the system defaults will be used. If the dash or off flag is used, the keyclick will be disabled. If a value from 0 to 100 is given, it is used to indicate volume, as a percentage of the maximum. The X server will set the volume to the nearest value that the hardware can support.

fp

> The fp option sets the font path. It must be followed by a comma-separated list of directories or the flag default. The indicated path will be used to find fonts for clients. To restore the default font path, use fp default.

led

> The led option controls the keyboard LEDs. This controls the turning on or off of one or all of the LEDs. It accepts an optional integer, a preceding dash (-) or an on/off flag. If no parameter or the on flag is given, all LEDs are turned on. If a preceding dash or the flag off is given, all LEDs

are turned off. If a value between 1 and 32 is given, that LED will be turned on or off depending on the existence of a preceding dash. A common LED which can be controlled is the Caps Lock LED. xset led 3 would turn led #3 on. xset -led 3 would turn it off. The particular LED values may refer to different LEDs on different hardware.

m   The m option controls the mouse parameters. The parameters for the mouse are *acceleration* and *threshold*. The mouse, or whatever pointer the machine is connected to, will go *acceleration* times as fast when it travels more than *threshold* pixels in a short time. This way, the mouse can be used for precise alignment when it is moved slowly, yet it can be set to travel across the screen in a flick of the wrist when desired. One or both parameters for the m option can be omitted, but if only one is given, it will be interpreted as the acceleration. If no parameters or the flag default is used, the system defaults will be set.

p   The p option controls pixel color values. The parameters are the color map entry number in decimal, and a color specification. The root background colors may be changed on some servers by altering the entries for BlackPixel and WhitePixel. Although these are often 0 and 1, they need not be. Also, a server may choose to allocate those colors privately, in which case an error will be generated. The map entry must not be a read-only color, or an error will result.

r   The r option controls the autorepeat. If a preceding dash or the off flag is used, autorepeat will be disabled. If no parameters or the on flag is used, autorepeat will be enabled.

s   The s option lets you set the screen saver parameters. This option accepts up to two numerical parameters, a blank/noblank flag, an expose/noexpose flag, an on/off flag, or the default flag. If no parameters or the default flag is used, the system will be set to its default screen saver characteristics. The on/off flags simply turn the screen saver functions on or off. The blank flag sets the preference to blank the video (if the hardware can do so) rather than display a background pattern, while noblank sets the preference to display a pattern rather than blank the video. The expose flag sets the preference to allow window exposures (the server can freely discard window contents), while noexpose sets the preference to disable screen saver unless the server can regenerate the screens without causing exposure events. The length and period parameters for the screen saver function determines how long the server must be inactive for screen saving to activate, and the period to change the background pattern to avoid burn in. The arguments are specified in seconds. If only one numerical parameter is given, it will be used for the length.

q   The q option gives you information on the current settings.

These settings will be reset to default values when you log out.

See Also

X, Xserver, xmodmap, xrdb, xsetroot

Authors

Bob Scheifler, MIT Laboratory for Computer Science;
David Krikorian, MIT Project Athena (X11 version).

xsetroot

Name

xsetroot — parameter setting utility.

Syntax

xsetroot [*options*]

Description

xsetroot allows you to tailor the appearance of the root (background) window or pointer. You can experiment with *xsetroot* until you find a look that you like, then put the *xsetroot* command that produces it into your X startup file. If you do not specify any options or you specify -def, the window is reset to its default state.

Options

Only one of the background color/tile changing options (-solid, -gray, grey, -bitmap, or -mod) may be specified at a time.

-help   Displays a brief description of the allowable options.

-def   Resets unspecified attributes to the default values; the background to the gray mesh background and the pointer to the hollow X pointer. If you specify -def and other options, only the non-specified options are reset to their default state.

-cursor *cursorfile maskfile*
         Changes the pointer to whatever you want when the pointer is outside of any window. Pointer and mask files are bitmaps made with the *bitmap* client. Refer to the *bitmap* discussion for more information on creating bitmaps. The mask file may need to be all black until you are accustomed to the way masks work. Default is hollow X pointer.

-bitmap *filename*
         Uses the bitmap specified in the file to set the window pattern. The entire background is made up of repeated tiles of the bitmap. You can make your own bitmap files using the *bitmap* client or you can use those available with this software. Look for these available bitmaps in the following directory: */usr/include/X11/bitmaps*. Default is gray mesh.

-mod *x y*   Makes a plaid-like grid pattern on your screen. *x* and *y* are integers ranging from 1 to 16. Zero and negative numbers are taken as 1.

-gray or -grey
         Creates a grey background.

-fg *color*   Sets the foreground color of the root window when using the mod or bitmap options. Default is black.

-bg *color*   Sets the background color of the root window when using options such as -mod or -bitmap options. Default is white.

Reference
Pages

-rv   Reverses the foreground color and the background color when used with another option such as -mod. -rv without another specified option returns the root (background) window to the default state.

-solid *color*   Sets the window color to the specified color. Default is gray mesh.

-name *string*   Sets the name of the background window to string. There is no default value. Usually, a name is assigned to a window so that the window manager can use a text representation when the window is converted to an icon.

-display [*host*]:*server*[.*screen*]
                   Allows you to specify the host, server and screen of the root window. *host* specifies the machine, *server* specifies the server number, and *screen* specifies the screen number. For example,

% **xsetroot -display** *your_node*:**0.1**

specifies screen 1 of server 0 on the machine *your_node*. If the host is omitted, the local machine is assumed. If the screen is omitted, screen 0 is assumed; the colon (:) is necessary in either case.

See Also

X, xset, xrdb

Author

Mark Lillibridge, MIT Project Athena.

xterm

Name

xterm — window terminal emulator.

Syntax

xterm [*options*]

Description

The *xterm* program is a terminal emulator for the X Window System. It provides DEC VT102 and Tektronix 4014 compatible terminals for programs that can't use the window system directly. If the underlying operating system supports terminal resizing capabilities (for example, the SIGWINCH signal in systems derived from 4.3bsd), *xterm* will use the facilities to notify programs running in the window whenever it is resized.

The VT102 and Tektronix 4014 terminals each have their own window so that you can edit text in one and look at graphics in the other at the same time. To maintain the correct aspect ratio (height/width), Tektronix graphics will be restricted to the largest box with a 4014's aspect ratio that will fit in the window. This box is located in the upper left area of the window.

Although both windows may be displayed at the same time, one of them is considered the *active* window for receiving keyboard input and terminal output. This is the window that contains the text cursor and whose border highlights whenever the pointer is in either window. The active window can be choosen through escape sequences, the Modes menu in the VT102 window, and the Tektronix menu in the 4014 window.

Options

xterm understands the options described below.

-132   Causes the DECCOLM escape sequence, which switches between 80 and 132 column mode, to be recognized. Default: does not recognize the DEC-COLM escape sequence. (See Appendix D for more information on *xterm* escape sequences.)

-L   Indicates that *xterm* is being called by *init*, and presumes that its file descriptors are already open on a slave pseudo-tty, and that getty runs rather than the shell. This option is only used by *init*.

-b *border*   Sets the distance between the text and the window's border. Default is one pixel.

-bd *color*   Sets the color of the border. Default of the highlighted border is black. Default of the unhighlighted border is gray.

-bg *color*   Sets the background color of the *xterm* window. Default is white.

-bw *borderwidth*
        Specifies the width of the *xterm* window border in pixels. Default is one pixel.

-cr *color*   Sets the highlighted color of the text cursor. Default is white cursor, black border.

-cu   Enables the `curses` fix. Several programs that use the `curses` cursor motion package have some difficulties with VT102-compatible terminals. The bug occurs when you run the `more` program on a file containing a line that is exactly the width of the window and which is followed by a line beginning with a tab. The leading tabs may disappear, but this option causes the tabs to be displayed correctly.

-e *command arguments*
           Executes the specified command in the window, rather than starting a shell. The command and the arguments must appear last on the *xterm* command line, e.g., `xterm -rv -e rlogin gssb &`. This option allows you to run a single command rather than starting an entire shell.

-fb *font*   Uses the specified font instead of the default bold font (*vtbold*). This font must be the same height and width as the normal font. If only one of the normal or bold fonts is specified, it is used as the normal font and the bold font is produced by overstriking this font.

-fg *color*   Sets the color of the text (foreground). Default is black.

-fn *font*   Uses the specified font instead of the default font (*fixed*). You can use any fixed width font.

-i   Causes *xterm* to display an *xterm* icon rather than an *xterm* window when it starts up.

-j   Causes jump scrolling; when *xterm* falls behind scrolling the screen, it moves lines up several lines at a time. The VT100 escape sequences for smooth scroll can be used to enable/disable this feature from a program.

-l   Logs *xterm* input/output into a file called *xterm Log.XXXX* where *X* represents the process id number. To display your data, turn off logging using the *xterm* menu, then type *cat xtermLog.XXXX* at the *xterm* window prompt and the output file is sent to your *xterm* window. Logging allows you to keep track of the sequence of data and is particularly helpful while debugging code.

-lf *file*   Specifies the file in which the data is written to rather than the default *xterm Log.XXXX* where *XXXX* is the process identification of *xterm* (the file is created in the directory that *xterm* is started in or the home directory for a login *xterm*). If `file` begins with a "l", then the rest of the string is assumed to be a command to be executed by the shell and a pipe is opened to the process.

-ls   Makes the shell execute a login shell. If that shell is C shell, it reads and executes *.cshrc* file and then reads and executes *.login* file. If *loginshell* is not activated, the shell starts up after you log in. If that shell is C shell, it reads and executes *.cshrc* file but not the login file.

-mb   Turns on the margin bell. Default is bell off.

-ms `color`   Sets the color of the I-beam pointer. Default is white pointer, black border.

-n `windowname`

Sets the name of the *xterm* window or icon for use by a window manager. Default name is *xterm*.

-nb `number`   Sets the distance at which the margin bell rings for the right margin. Default is 10 characters.

-rv   Displays the screen with white characters on a black background, rather than the default of black on white.

-rw   Turns on the reverse-wraparound mode that allows the cursor to wraparound from the leftmost column to the rightmost column of the previous line. Allows you to backspace to the previous line and overstrike data or erase data with the spacebar.

-s   Allows *xterm* to scroll asynchronously with the display. *xterm* no longer scrolls synchronously with the display but saves data in memory which is displayed later. As a result, *xterm* does not keep the screen completely up to date while scrolling but can then run faster when network latencies are high. This is useful when using *xterm* across a large internet or many network modes.

-sb   Displays the scrollbar in the *xterm* window at startup.

-si   Disables repositioning the cursor at the bottom of the scroll region when the process sends output.

-sk   Causes the cursor to be repositioned at the bottom of the scroll region when a key is pressed.

-sl `number`   Specifies the maximum number of lines to be saved that are scrolled off the top of the window. Default is 64 lines.

-t   Causes the startup *xterm* window to be the Tektronix window rather than the VT102 window.

-vb   Causes your terminal window to flash whenever an event occurs that would ordinarily cause your terminal bell to ring.

-geometry =`geometry`

xterm takes this geometry specification for the VT102 window. The – geometry option can be (and often is) abbreviated to –g, unless there is a conflicting option that begins with ''g.'' The argument to the geometry option (`geometry`) is referred to as a ''standard geometry string,'' and has the form `widthxheight±xoff±yoff`.

%`geometry`   This geometry specification applies to the Tektronix window.

#`geometry`   This geometry specification applies to the icon position (the width and height information are optional and otherwise ignored).

```
-display [host]:server[.screen]
```
> *xterm* obtains the host and server number to use from the environment variable DISPLAY. You can, however, specify them. `host` specifies which machine to create the window on, `server` specifies the server number, and `screen` specifies the screen number. For example,
>
> **xterm -display** *your_node***:0.1**
>
> specifies screen 1 of server 0 on the machine *your_node*. If the host is omitted, the local machine is assumed. If the screen is omitted, screen 0 is assumed; the colon (:) is necessary in either case.

Defaults

The program understands all of the core X Toolkit resource names and classes as well as:

`name` (class `Name`)
> Specifies the name of this instance of the program. The default is "xterm."

`iconGeometry` (class `IconGeometry`)
> Specifies the prefered size and position of the application when iconified. It is not necessarily obeyed by all window managers.

`title` (class `Title`)
> Specifies a string that may be used by the window manager when displaying this application.

The following resources are specified as part of the "vt100" widget (class "VT100"):

`font` (class `Font`)
> Specifies the name of the normal font. The default is "vtsingle."

`boldFont` (class `Font`)
> Specifies the name of the bold font. The default is "vtbold."

`c132` (class `C132`)
> Specifies whether or not the VT102 DECCOLM escape sequence should be honored. The default is "false."

`curses` (class `Curses`)
> Specifies whether or not the last column bug in cursor should be worked around. The default is "false."

`background` (class `Background`)
> Specifies the color to use for the background of the window. The default is "white."

`foreground` (class `Foreground`)
> Specifies the color to use for displaying text in the window. Setting the class name instead of the instance name is an easy way to have everything that would normally appear in the "text" color change color. The default is "black."

cursorColor (class Foreground)
> Specifies the color to use for the text cursor. The default is "black."

geometry (class Geometry)
> Specifies the prefered size and position of the VT102 window.

tekGeometry (class Geometry)
> Specifies the prefered size and position of the Tektronix window.

internalBorder (class BorderWidth)
> Specifies the number of pixels between the characters and the window border. The default is 2.

jumpScroll (class JumpScroll)
> Specifies whether or not jump scroll should be used. The default is "false".

logFile (class Logfile)
> Specifies the name of the file to which a terminal session is logged. The default is XtermLog.*XXXXX* (where *XXXXX* is the process id of *xterm*).

logging (class Logging)
> Specifies whether or not a terminal session should be logged. The default is "false."

logInhibit (class LogInhibit)
> Specifies whether or not terminal session logging should be inhibited. The default is "false."

loginShell (class LoginShell)
> Specifies whether or not the shell to be run in the window should be started as a login shell. The default is "false."

marginBell (class MarginBell)
> Specifies whether or not the bell should be run when the user types near the right margin. The default is "false."

multiScroll (class MultiScroll)
> Specifies whether or not asynchronous scrolling is allowed. The default is "false."

nMarginBell (class Column)
> Specifies the number of characters from the right margin at which the margin bell should be run, when enabled.

pointerColor (class Foreground)
> Specifies the color of the pointer. The default is "black."

pointerShape (class Cursor)
> Specifies the name of the shape of the pointer. The default is "xterm."

reverseVideo (class ReverseVideo)
> Specifies whether or not reverse video should be simulated. The default is "false."

`reverseWrap` (class `ReverseWrap`)
> Specifies whether or not reverse-wraparound should be enabled. The default is "false."

`saveLines` (class `SaveLines`)
> Specifies the number of lines to save beyond the top of the screen when a scrollbar is turned on. The default is 64.

`scrollBar` (class `ScrollBar`)
> Specifies whether or not the scrollbar should be displayed. The default is "false."

`scrollInput` (class `ScrollCond`)
> Specifies whether or not output to the terminal should automatically cause the scrollbar to go to the bottom of the scrolling region. The default is "true."

`scrollKey` (class `ScrollCond`)
> Specifies whether or not pressing a key should automatically cause the scrollbar to go to the bottom of the scrolling region. The default is "false."

`signalInhibit` (class `SignalInhibit`)
> Specifies whether or not the entries in the xterm X11 menu for sending signals to *xterm* should be disallowed. The default is "false."

`tekInhibit` (class `TekInhibit`)
> Specifies whether or not Tektronix mode should be disallowed. The default is "false."

`tekStartup` (class `TekStartup`)
> Specifies whether or not *xterm* should start up in Tektronix mode. The default is "false."

`visualBell` (class `VisualBell`)
> Specifies whether or not a visible bell (i.e. flashing) should be used instead of an audible bell when Control-G is received. The default is "false."

The following resources are specified as part of the "tek4014" widget (class "Tek4014"):

`width` (class `Width`)
> Specifies the width of the Tektronix window in pixels.

`height` (class `Height`)
> Specifies the height of the Tektronix window in pixels.

The following resources are specified as part of the "menu" widget:

`menuBorder` (class `MenuBorder`)
> Specifies the size in pixels of the border surrounding menus. The default is 2.

`menuFont` (class `Font`)
> Specifies the name of the font to use for displaying menu items.

`menuPad` (class `MenuPad`)

> Specifies the number of pixels between menu items and the menu border. The default is 3.

Emulations

The VT102 emulation is fairly complete, but does not support the blinking character attribute nor the double-wide and double-size character sets. *termcap* entries that work with *xterm* include "xterm", "vt102", "vt100" and "ansi", and *xterm* automatically searches the termcap file in this order for these entries and then sets the TERM and the TERMCAP environment variables. Note that the *xterm termcap* entry distributed with X is not automatically installed. You can add it to */etc/termcap* yourself, if you are using the MIT distribution. However, don't bother to install it because it contains a bug that prevents `vi` from working properly. The VT100 or VT102 entries work just fine.

Many of the special *xterm* features (like logging) may be modified under program control through a set of escape sequences different from the standard VT102 escape sequences. (See Appendix D, *xterm Control Sequences*.)

The Tektronix 4014 emulation is also fairly good. Four different font sizes and five different lines types are supported. The Tektronix text and graphics commands are recorded internally by *xterm* and may be written to a file by sending the COPY escape sequence (or through the Tektronix menu; see below). The name of the file will be "`COPYyy-MM-dd.hh:mm:ss`", where `yy` , `MM`, `dd`, `hh`, `mm` and `ss` are the year, month, day, hour, minute and second when the COPY was performed (the file is created in the directory *xterm* is started in, or the home directory for a login *xterm*).

Pointer Usage

Once the VT102 window is created, *xterm* allows you to select text and copy it within the same or other windows.

The selection functions are invoked when the pointer buttons are used with no modifiers, and when they are used with the Shift key.

Pointer button one (usually left) is used to save text into the cut buffer. Move the cursor to beginning of the text, and then hold the button down while moving the cursor to the end of the region and releasing the button. The selected text is highlighted and is saved in the global cut buffer when the button is released. Double-clicking selects by words. Triple-clicking selects by lines. Quadruple-clicking goes back to characters, etc. Multiple-click is determined by the time from button up to button down, so you can change the selection unit in the middle of a selection.

Pointer button two (usually middle) 'types' (pastes) the text from the cut buffer, inserting it as keyboard input.

Pointer button three (usually right) extends the current selection. (Without loss of generality, that is you can swap "right" and "left" everywhere in the rest of this paragraph...) If pressed while closer to the right edge of the selection than the left, it extends/contracts the right edge of the selection. If you contract the selection past the left edge of the selection, *xterm* assumes you really meant the left edge, restores the original selection, then extends/contracts the left edge of the selection. Extension starts in the selection unit mode that the last selection or extension was performed in; you can multiple-click to cycle through them.

By cutting and pasting pieces of text without trailing new lines, you can take text from several places in different windows and form a command to the shell, for example, or take output from a program and insert it into your favorite editor. Since the cut buffer is globally shared among different applications, you should regard it as a 'file' whose contents you know. The terminal emulator and other text programs should be treating it as if it were a text file, i.e. the text is delimited by new lines.

The scroll region displays the position and amount of text currently showing in the window (highlighted) relative to the amount of text actually saved. As more text is saved (up to the maximum), the size of the highlighted area decreases.

Clicking button one with the pointer in the scroll region moves the adjacent line to the top of the display window.

Clicking button three moves the top line of the display window down to the pointer position.

Clicking button two moves the display to a position in the saved text that corresponds to the pointer's position in the scrollbar.

Unlike the VT102 window, the Tektronix window dows not allow the copying of text. It does allow Tektronix GIN mode, and in this mode the cursor will change from an arrow to a cross. Pressing any key will send that key and the current coordinate of the cross cursor. Pressing button one, two, or three will return the letters 'l', 'm', and 'r', respectively. If the Shift key is pressed when a pointer button is pressed, the corresponding upper case letter is sent. To distinquish a pointer button from a key, the high bit of the character is set (but this is bit is normally stripped unless the terminal mode is RAW; see *tty*(4) for details).

Menus

xterm has three different menus, named **xterm**, **Modes**, and **Tektronix**. Each menu pops up under the correct combinations of key and button presses. Most menus are divided into two section, separated by a horizontal line. The top portion contains various modes that can be altered. A check mark appears next to a mode that is currently active. Selecting one of these modes toggles its state. The bottom portion of the menu are command entries; selecting one of these performs the indicated function.

The **xterm** menu pops up when the Control key and pointer button one are pressed in a window. The modes section contains items that apply to both the VT102 and Tektronix windows. Notable entries in the command section of the menu are the **Continue, Suspend, Interrupt, Hangup, Terminate** and **Kill,** which send the SIGCONT, SIGTSTP, SIGINT, SIGHUP, SIGTERM and SIGKILL signals, respectively, to the process group of the process running under *xterm* (usually the shell). The **Continue** function is especially useful if the user has accidentally typed CTRL-Z, suspending the process.

The **Modes** menu sets various modes in the VT102 emulation, and is popped up when the Control key and pointer button two are pressed in the VT102 window. In the command section of this menu, the soft reset entry will reset scroll regions. This can be convenient when some program has left the scroll regions set incorrectly (often a problem when using VMS or

TOPS-20). The full reset entry will clear the screen, reset tabs to every eight columns, and reset the terminal modes (such as wrap and smooth scroll) to there initial states just after *xterm* has finish processing the command line options. The Tektronix menu sets various modes in the Tektronix emulation, and is popped up when the Control key and pointer button two are pressed in the Tektronix window. The current font size is checked in the modes section of the menu. The PAGE entry in the command section clears the Tektronix window.

Other Features

xterm automatically highlights the window border and text cursor when the pointer enters the window (selected) and unhighlights them when the pointer leaves the window (unselected). If the window is the focus window, then the window is highlighted no matter where the pointer is.

In VT102 mode, there are escape sequences to activate and deactivate an alternate screen buffer, which is the same size as the display area of the window. When activated, the current screen is saved and replace with the alternate screen. Saving of lines scrolled off the top of the window is disabled until the normal screen is restored. The *termcap* entry for *xterm* allows the visual editor *vi* to switch to the alternate screen for editing, and restore the screen on exit.

In either VT102 or Tektronix mode, there are escape sequences to change the name of the windows and to specify a new log file name.

Environment

xterm sets the environment variables TERM and TERMCAP properly for the size window you have created. It also uses and sets the environment variable DISPLAY to specify which bit map display terminal to use. The environment variable WINDOWID is set to the X window id number of the *xterm* window.

See Also

X, pty(4), tty(4)
Appendix D of this guide, *xterm Control Sequences*.

Bugs

xterm will hang forever if you try to paste too much text at one time. It is both producer and consumer for the pty and can deadlock.

Variable-width fonts are not handled reasonably.

This program still needs to be rewritten. It should be split into very modular sections, with the various emulators being completely separate widgets that don't know about each other. Ideally, you'd like to be able to pick and choose emulator widgets and stick them into a single control widget.

The focus is considered lost if some other client (e.g., the window manager) grabs the pointer; it is difficult to do better without an addition to the protocol.

There needs to be a dialog box to allow entry of log file name and the COPY file name.

Many of the options are not resettable after *xterm* starts.

This manual page is too long.

All programs should be written to use X directly; then we could eliminate this program.

Authors

Far too many people, including:

Loretta Guarino Reid (DEC-UEG-WSL), Joel McCormack (DEC-UEG-WSL), Terry Weissman (DEC-UEG-WSL), Edward Moy (Berkeley), Ralph R. Swick (MIT-Athena), Mark Vandevoorde (MIT-Athena), Bob McNamara (DEC-MAD), Jim Gettys (MIT-Athena), Bob Scheifler (MIT X Consortium), Doug Mink (SAO), Steve Pitschke (Stellar), Ron Newman (MIT-Athena), Jim Fulton (MIT X Consortium).

xwd

Name

xwd — place window images in a dump file.

Syntax

xwd [*options*]

Description

xwd stores window images in a specially formatted window dump file. This file can then be read by various other X utilities for redisplay, printing, editing, formatting, archiving, image processing, etc. The target window is selected by clicking the mouse in the desired window. The keyboard bell is rung once at the beginning of the dump and twice when the dump is completed.

Options

-help
: Prints out the Usage: command syntax summary.

-nobdrs
: Specifies that the window dump should not include the pixels that compose the X window border. This is useful when the window contents are included in a document as an illustration.

-out *file*
: Allows you to specify the output file on the command line. The default outputs to the standard output (*stdout*).

-xy
: This option applies to color displays only. It selects 'XY' pixmap format dumping instead of the default 'Z' pixmap format.

-display [*host*]:*server*[.*screen*]
: Allows you to specify the host, server and screen to connect to. *host* is the machine, *server* is the server number and *screen* is the screen number. For example,

  xwd -display *your_node***:0.1 &**

  specifies screen 1 on server 0 on the machine *your_node*. If the host is omitted, the local machine is assumed. If the screen is omitted, the screen 0 is assumed; the colon (:) is necessary in either case.

Files

XWDFile.h
: X Window Dump File format definition file.

See Also

xwud, xpr, xdpr, X

Author

Tony Della Fera, Digital Equipment Corp., MIT Project Athena;
William F. Wyatt, Smithsonian Astrophysical Observatory.

Name

xwininfo — window information utility for X.

Syntax

xwininfo [*options*]

Description

xwininfo is a utility for displaying information about windows. Depending on which options are choosen, various information is displayed. If no options are choosen, -stats is assumed.

The user has the option of selecting the target window with the mouse (by clicking any mouse button in the desired window) or by specifying its window id on the command line with the -id option. In addition, if it is easier, instead of specifying the window by its id number, the -name option may be used to specify which window is desired by name. There is also a special -root option to quickly obtain information on the root window.

Options

-display [*host*]:*server*[*.screen*]

> Allows you to specify the host, server and screen to connect to. *host* specifies the machine, *server* specifies the server number, and *screen* specifies the screen number. For example,

xwininfo –display *your_node*:**0.1** **&**

> specifies screen 1 of server 0 on the machine *your_node*. If the host is omitted, the local machine is assumed. If the screen is omitted, screen 0 is assumed; the colon (:) is necessary in either case.

-help   Print out the 'Usage:' command syntax summary.

-id *id*   This option allows the user to specify a target window *id* on the command line rather than using the mouse to select the target window. This is very useful in debugging X applications where the target window is not mapped to the screen or where the use of the mouse might be impossible or interfere with the application.

-name *name*   This option allows the user to specify that the window named *name* is the target window on the command line rather than using the mouse to select the target window.

-root   This option specifies that the root window is the target window. This is useful in situations where the root window is completely obscured.

-int   This option specifies that all X window ids should be displayed as integer values. The default is to display them as hexadecimal values.

-tree   This option causes the root, parent, and children windows id's and name's of the selected window to be displayed.

-stats   This option causes various attributes of the selected window having to do
                with its location and appearence to be displayed. Information displayed
                includes the location of the window, its width and height, its depth, border
                width, class, and map state.

-bits   This option causes various attributes of the selected window having to do
                with its raw bits and how it is to be stored to be displayed. Information
                displayed includes the window's window and bit gravities, the window's
                backing store hint and backing_planes value, its backing pixel, and whether
                or not the window has save-under set.

-events   This option causes the selected window's event masks to be displayed. Both
                the event mask of events wanted by some client and the event mask of
                events not to prograte are displayed.

-size   This option causes the selected window's sizing hints to be displayed. Infor-
                mation displayed includes for both the normal size hints and the zoom size
                hints the user supplied location if any, the program supplied location if any,
                the user supplied size if any, the program supplied size if any, the minimum
                size if any, the maximum size if any, the resize increments if any, and the
                minimum and maximum aspect ratios if any.

-wm   This option causes the selected window's window manager hints to be
                displayed. Information displayed may include whether or not the application
                accepts input, what the window's icon window # and name is, where the
                window's icon should go, and what the window's initial state should be.

-all   This option is a quick way to ask for all information possible.

Example

The following is a sample summary taken with no options specified:

```
xwininfo ==> Please select the window you wish
         ==> information on by clicking the
         ==> mouse in that window.

xwininfo ==> Window id: 0x8006b (fred)

         ==> Upper left X: 0
         ==> Upper left Y: 0
         ==> Width: 1024
         ==> Height: 864
         ==> Depth: 1
         ==> Border width: 0
         ==> Window class: InputOutput
         ==> Window Map State: IsUnviewable
```

See Also
X, xprop

Author
Mark Lillibridge, MIT Project Athena.

xwud

Name
xwud — X window image displayer.

Syntax
xwud [*options*]

Description
xwud is an X Window System window image undumping utility. *xwud* allows X users to display window images that were saved in a specially formatted dump file. The window image will appear at the coordinates of the original window from which the dump was taken. This is a crude version of a more advanced utility that has never been written. Monochrome dump files are displayed on a color monitor in the default foreground and background colors.

Options
-help   Print out a short description of the allowable options.

-in *file*   This option allows the user to explicitly specify the input file on the command line. The default is to take input from standard in.

-inverse   Applies to monochrome window dump files only. If selected, the window is undumped in reverse video. This is mainly needed because the display is 'write white', whereas dump files intended eventually to be written to a printer are generally 'write black'.

-display [*host*]:*server*[.*screen*]

Allows you to specify the server to connect to. For example,

        xwud -display *your_node*:0.1

specifies screen 1 on server 0 on the machine *your_node*. If the host is omitted, the local machine is assumed. If the screen is omitted, the screen 0 is assumed; the colon (:) is necessary in either case.

Files
XWDFile.h   X Window Dump File format definition file.

Bugs
Does not attempt to do color translation when the destination screen does not have a colormap exactly matching that of the original window.

See Also
xwd, xpr, xdpr, X

Author
Tony Della Fera, Digital Equipment Corp., MIT Project Athena;
William F. Wyatt, Smithsonian Astrophysical Observatory.

Part Four:

Appendices

This part of the book contains useful reference information.

System Management
Standard Cursors
Standard Fonts
xterm Control Sequences
Standard Bitmaps
The xshowkey Program
Glossary

Index

A
System Management

This appendix discusses various topics related to installing and managing the X software, mostly from the UNIX point of view.

In This Appendix:

A
System Management

X runs on so many different variations of UNIX (not to mention other operating systems) that it is difficult to be definitive about system management. Hence, we've relegated to an appendix a few hints that we hope will be useful. However, you should be sure to check your system's documentation for additional (or contrary) details.

Including X in Your Search Path

The various X clients are normally stored in the directory *lusr/bin/X11*. In order to invoke them by name like any other UNIX program, you need to make this directory part of your search path.*

This is normally done from your *.login* (C Shell) or *.profile* (Bourne shell) file, using a command similar to the following:

Bourne Shell:

```
PATH=.:/usr/ucb:/bin:/usr/bin:/usr/bin/X11:Other directories; export PATH
```

C Shell:

```
set path (. /usr/ucb /bin /usr/bin /usr/bin/X11 Other directories)
```

The exact list of directories will differ from system to system. You should be aware that directories are searched in order from left to right, so a command with the same name in an earlier directory will be found and used before one in a later directory. Many users take advantage of this fact to run customized versions of programs by putting "." (the current directory) or a local tools directory first in their search path. This works fine, but you should be aware that this provides a security loophole that can be taken advantage of by an experienced system cracker.

If you have already logged in before adding the above line to your *.profile* or *.login* file, you should logout and login again, or type in the path-setting command at your prompt, so that it takes effect for your current session.

---

*This topic isn't really part of system management, but since we assume most people know how to do it, we didn't want to clutter up Chapter Two with unnecessary discussion. On the other hand, the information is critical for those who don't already know it, so we wanted to put it somewhere!

Setting the Terminal Type

Most users set the TERM variable in their *.login* file to identify the terminal type they are using. *xterm* emulates either a vt102 or a Tektronix 4015 terminal, so you can use either of these terminal types. In addition, there is a *termcap* entry called *xterm* which comes with the standard X distribution.

Depending on which version of the shell you are using, the *termcap* entry corresponding to the terminal type you have set may be loaded into the TERMCAP environment variable. When the window is resized, *xterm* sends a SIGWINCH signal to the shell. If the shell has been designed to recognize this signal, it dynamically changes the **li** and **co** *termcap* capabilities (the number of lines and columns, respectively) to reflect the new size of the window. If not, you may have to use the *resize* client for this purpose.

Occasionally, the program running within *xterm* will not know that the window has been resized and will still keep the old size. This may happen if you resize the window in the middle of a *vi* editing session. In a case like this, you may have to quit the editor and re-enter it in order for it to re-read the changed values in the TERMCAP variable.

Starting Up X

In Chapter 2, we described how to start X manually. However, on a single-user workstation, it is likely that you might want X to come up automatically. In many commercial X ports, this may already have been done for you.

This section describes how this could be done in various different environments.

BSD 4.3: /etc/ttys

On BSD 4.3-derived systems, the preferred way to start X automatically is from the */etc/ttys* terminal initialization file.* This file normally contains a list of terminals on which a login prompt should be printed by the *getty* program. For X, this file can be used instead to start *xterm* for a pseudo-terminal. A typical line to start X from the */etc/ttys* file might have the following format:

---

*Note that the technique described here will not work on earlier BSD systems, Xenix, or other systems which use the pre-BSD 4.3 *ttys* format.

```
devname                            command                    ttytype
   |                                  |                          |
ttyv0 "/etc/xterm -L -geometry -1+1 -display :0"  xterm
              on secure window="/usr/bin/X11/X :0 -c -1"    #Start X
                   |                                            |
                 status                                      comment
```

Field   *Function in /etc/ttys*

devname   The name of the special file in the *dev* directory that corresponds to the device. For X, the pseudo-terminal with the highest minor device number (e.g. */dev/ttyqf* and */dev/ptyqf*) is normally renamed */dev/ttyv0* and */dev/ptyv0*. For systems with more than one display, the next highest pty is used for the second display, and so on.

command   The command to be run by *init*. This is normally *getty*, but can be another command, such as the command to start a window system. In this example, *xterm* is run with the -L option, which causes *getty* to be run in the *xterm* window rather than the shell. The window is placed in the top right corner of the screen. Since spaces and tabs are used to separate fields in */etc/ttys*, the entire command must be quoted.

Note that some implementations of *init* have relatively small program name buffer sizes, so you may find you can't list many *xterm* options. In addition, because the # character is used as a comment symbol in */etc/ttys*, you may have difficulty specifying colors (say for an *xterm* window background) using the hexadecimal color syntax. If you run into either of these problems, you may want to write a small program that runs *xterm* with the desired arguments, and have *init* run that instead.

ttytype   The name of the terminal attached to the line. This should be the name as defined in the */etc/termcap* terminal database. In the example above, it is specified as *xterm*.

Note that the presence of the terminal type field in the BSD 4.3 *ttys* replaces the */etc/ttytype* file that was used for this purpose in earlier BSD versions.

status   The word **on** if the *command* is to be executed, or **off** if it is not. Additional flags may be specified after **on** or **off**. The word **secure** must be present to allow root to login on a particular terminal. The flag **window="***command***"** specifies a window system command to be executed by *init* before it starts *getty*. This should be the command to start the X server, as shown in the example.

comment   Comments can appear anywhere in the file. They are introduced by #, and are terminated by a newline.

System V: /etc/rc

In the System V environment, the folks at MIT simply run *xinit* manually, as described in Chapter 2. However, at least theoretically, the job of starting up X automatically could be handled in several ways:

- Run *xinit* from the system startup file */etc/rc*, or one of its cousins. (Depending on the version of UNIX, local hacks to the startup procedure may belong in */etc/rc.local, /etc/rc2*, or some other variation. See your documentation for details.) Beware that there might be some problems with the system not being able to assign a controlling tty to the process.

- Run *xinit* from the terminal initialization file */etc/inittab*. This file is analogous to the BSD 4.3 */etc/ttys*. The */etc/inittab* file normally has an entry for each serial port on a system, plus several entries that are used during the boot process. Note that the concept of pseudo-terminals, or ptys (which X relies on) is foreign to System V. All System V servers will have had to do some system hacking to add support for ptys. How this is done will vary from system to system. As a result, we're going to beg off on describing *inittab* in detail, and refer you to your system documentation. Again, it is also possible that there will be problems with the controlling tty.

- Run *xinit* from your *.login* or *.profile* file. This third option is the only one we can recommend as a sure-fire method of starting X automatically from a System V environment. See Chapter 9 for details.

Access Control

X runs in a networked environment. Because of X's design, your workstation is no longer your private preserve, but can be accessed by any other host on the network. This is the true meaning of the server concept: your display can serve clients on any system, and clients on your system can display on any other screen.

The possibilities for abuse are limited. Nonetheless, you should know that there is a simple access control mechanism.

The */etc/X**n**.hosts* file (where **n** is the number of the server) contains a list of systems that are allowed to access the server. By default, this file contains only the name of the local host.

The client *xhost* can be used to add or delete names from this file. Specifying a host name (with an optional leading plus sign) adds the host to the list, and specifying a host name with a leading minus sign deletes a host from the list. Multiple hosts can be specified on the same line. Running *xhost* without any arguments prints the current hosts allowed to access your display.

For example, to add the hosts jupiter and saturn, and remove neptune:

```
% xhost +jupiter saturn -neptune
```

It is possible to remove the current host from the access list. Be warned that you can't undo this without logging out.

Note that when a remote system is denied access to your display, it means two things: that a person working on the remote system can't display on your screen, and that you can't use that remote system for running clients you want displayed on your screen.

Console Messages

On a single-user workstation, it is likely that the screen used for running X is also used as the system console.

If X is started manually, the console will be the first window to appear on the screen. But if X is started from your *.login* file, console messages from the kernel may sometimes appear on the screen, overlaying the X windows. They make a nasty mess of the screen, but the display can be refreshed and the console message erased by running the client *xrefresh* (described in Part Three) or by selecting the Refresh function of the window manager (*uwm*, described in Chapter 3).

Some implementations of X support a -C option to *xterm* that redirects messages sent to */dev/console* to that *xterm* window. If this option is supported, you should add the -C option to the login *xterm* started up in the */etc/ttys* file. After this window is mapped (displayed on the screen), all such messages are displayed there.

However, you should be aware that output sent to */dev/console* before the *xterm* window was started is queued and not displayed until the X server is killed. Furthermore, the processes generating the messages hang.

Log Files

The X server creates log files useful in fixing a problem that might occur. These files are located in */usr/adm* and take the form *x11log**n** where **n** is the number of the display.

You should make provisions to trim these files periodically. As with all log files, you can do this automatically with an entry in the *crontab* file.

Performance Tuning

Because the X Window System tends to have many processes running concurrently per display, it is advisable to consider increasing the values of the `files`, `procs`, `max-proc`, and `texts` lines in the system configuration files and rebuilding the kernel. See your system documentation for details on how to do this.

In addition, X needs 32 pseudo-terminals (ptys) to function effectively. Some workstations are configured with only 16 by default. To create more ptys, *cd* to the */dev* directory, and run the ./MKDEV script. See your documentation, or comments in the script, for details.

Changing the Color Name Database

The X Window System comes with a predefined set of colors, located in */usr/lib/X11/rgb*. These color names are used by clients to specify options either in command lines or in the *.Xdefaults* file. If you have the X sources, you can customize the color name database using the following procedure.

1. Edit the *rgb.txt* file to change or add colors. The format of a line in the *rgb.txt* file is

   ```
   red green blue color_name
   ```

   The red, green, and blue values are integers in the range 0 to 255, and the color name must be in lowercase characters with no spaces or special symbols. The current contents of the *rgb.txt* file on the sun sample server are:

Red	Green	Blue	English Words
112	219	147	aquamarine
50	204	153	medium aquamarine
0	0	0	black
0	0	255	blue
95	159	159	cadet blue
66	66	111	cornflower blue
107	35	142	dark slate blue
191	216	216	light blue
143	143	188	light steel blue
50	50	204	medium blue
127	0	255	medium slate blue
47	47	79	midnight blue
35	35	142	navy blue
35	35	142	navy
50	153	204	sky blue
0	127	255	slate blue
35	107	142	steel blue
255	127	0	coral
0	255	255	cyan
142	35	35	firebrick
165	42	42	brown
204	127	50	gold
219	219	112	goldenrod
234	234	173	medium goldenrod
0	255	0	green
47	79	47	dark green
79	79	47	dark olive green
35	142	35	forest green
50	204	50	lime green
107	142	35	medium forest green
66	111	66	medium sea green
127	255	0	medium spring green
143	188	143	pale green

Red	Green	Blue	English Words
35	142	107	sea green
0	255	127	spring green
153	204	50	yellow green
47	79	79	dark slate grey
47	79	79	dark slate gray
84	84	84	dim grey
84	84	84	dim gray
168	168	168	light grey
168	168	168	light gray
192	192	192	gray
192	192	192	grey
159	159	95	khaki
255	0	255	magenta
142	35	107	maroon
204	50	50	orange
219	112	219	orchid
153	50	204	dark orchid
147	112	219	medium orchid
188	143	143	pink
234	173	234	plum
255	0	0	red
79	47	47	indian red
219	112	147	medium violet red
255	0	127	orange red
204	50	153	violet red
111	66	66	salmon
142	107	35	sienna
219	147	112	tan
216	191	216	thistle
173	234	234	turquoise
112	147	219	dark turquoise
112	219	219	medium turquoise
79	47	79	violet
159	95	159	blue violet
216	216	191	wheat
252	252	252	white
255	255	0	yellow
147	219	112	green yellow

2. Run the **rgb** program using the makefile located in the *util/rgb* directory. This program converts the text file to a UNIX *dbm*(1) format file.

```
% make
```

3. Install the new *rgb* file. Type:

```
% make install
```

B
Standard Cursors

This appendix lists the standard cursor images that may be used by X programs.

B
Standard Cursors

Table B-1. *Standard Cursor Symbols*

Symbol	Value	Symbol	Value
XC_X_cursor	0	XC_iron_cross	66
XC_arrow	2	XC_left_ptr	68
XC_based_arrow_down	4	XC_left_side	70
XC_based_arrow_up	6	XC_left_tee	72
XC_boat	8	XC_leftbutton	74
XC_bogosity	10	XC_ll_angle	76
XC_bottom_left_corner	12	XC_lr_angle	78
XC_bottom_right_corner	14	XC_man	80
XC_bottom_side	16	XC_middlebutton	82
XC_bottom_tee	18	XC_mouse	84
XC_box_spiral	20	XC_pencil	86
XC_center_ptr	22	XC_pirate	88
XC_circle	24	XC_plus	90
XC_clock	26	XC_question_arrow	92
XC_coffee_mug	28	XC_right_ptr	94
XC_cross	30	XC_right_side	96
XC_cross_reverse	32	XC_right_tee	98
XC_crosshair	34	XC_rightbutton	100
XC_diamond_cross	36	XC_rtl_logo	102
XC_dot	38	XC_sailboat	104
XC_dot_box_mask	40	XC_sb_down_arrow	106
XC_double_arrow	42	XC_sb_h_double_arrow	108
XC_draft_large	44	XC_sb_left_arrow	110
XC_draft_small	46	XC_sb_right_arrow	112
XC_draped_box	48	XC_sb_up_arrow	114
XC_exchange	50	XC_sb_v_double_arrow	116
XC_fleur	52	XC_shuttle	118
XC_gobbler	54	XC_sizing	120
XC_gumby	56	XC_spider	122
XC_hand	58	XC_spraycan	124
XC_hand1_mask	60	XC_star	126
XC_heart	62	XC_target	128
XC_icon	64	XC_tcross	130

Table B-1. Standard Cursor Symbols (continued)

Symbol	Value	Symbol	Value
XC_top_left_arrow	132	XC_ul_angle	144
XC_top_left_corner	134	XC_umbrella	146
XC_top_right_corner	136	XC_ur_angle	148
XC_top_side	138	XC_watch	150
XC_top_tee	140	XC_xterm	152
XC_trek	142		

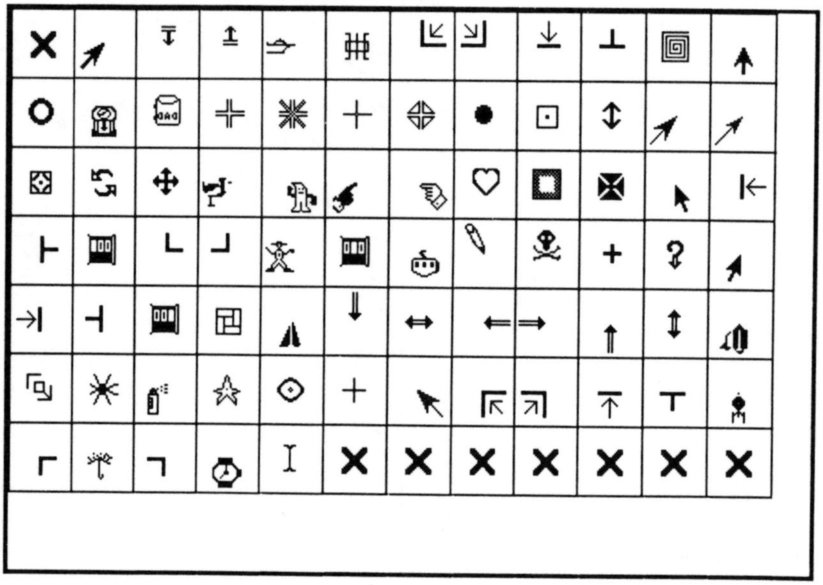

Figure B-1. The Standard Cursors

C
Standard Fonts

This appendix shows the standard display fonts available in the MIT X distribution. The images contained in this appendix are window dumps created with xwd *and* xpr, *showing the output of* xfd.

C
Standard Fonts

This appendix should tell you everything you need to know about the fonts in the X distribution. Not every font may be supported by particular server vendors, and some vendors may supplement the set. Also, a more descriptive naming scheme has been proposed, but it has not been accepted as part of the X standard at this writing.

Table C-1 lists the fonts provided in the standard X distribution. Fixed-width and variable-width fonts are listed in separated columns. After that, all or most of the characters in each font are shown actual size, as they would appear on a 900×1180 pixel, $10" \times 13.5"$ screen (Sun). On a screen with different pixel density, these fonts would appear a different size.

Table C-1. Fonts in the Standard Distribution

Fixed-width Fonts			Variable-width Fonts			
6x10	fgb1-25	oldera	apl-s25	hbr-s40	vg-25	vr-30
6x12	fgb1-30	rot-s16	arrow3	krivo	vg-31	vr-31
6x13	fgi-20	sans12	chp-s25	met25	vg-40	vr-40
8x13	fgi1-25	sansb12	chs-s50	mit	vgb-25	vrb-25
8x13bold	fgs-22	sansi12	cursor	plunk	vgb-31	vrb-30
9x15	fixed	serif10	cyr-s25	runlen	vgbc-25	vrb-31
crturz	fqxb-25	serif12	cyr-s30	stan	vgh-25	vrb-35
dancer	fr-25	serifb10	cyr-s38	sub	vgi-20	vrb-37
fg-13	fr-33	serifb12	ent	subsub	vgi-25	vri-25
fg-16	fr1-25	serifi10	fcor-20	sup	vgi-31	vri-30
fg-18	fr2-25	serifi12	fgb-13	supsup	vgl-40	vri-31
fg-20	fr3-25	stempl	fgb-25	sym-s25	vgvb-31	vri-40
fg-22	frb-32	swd-s30	fri-33	sym-s53	vmic-25	vsg-114
fg-25	ipa-s25	vtbold	fri1-25	variable	vply-36	vsgn-57
fg-30	lat-s30	vtsingle	ger-s35	vbee-36	vr-20	vshd-40
fg-40	micro	xif-s25	grk-s25	vctl-25	vr-25	vxms-37
fg1-25			grk-s30	vg-13	vr-27	vxms-43
			hbr-s25	vg-20		

The remaining pages of this appendix show the characters in each font, actual size, as they would appear on a 900 × 1180 pixel, 10" × 13.5" screen (Sun). On a screen with different pixel density, these fonts would appear a proportionally different size.

For most fonts, the entire character set is shown. For very large fonts, we have sometimes shown just a few characters to save space. Also, fonts that begin with many blank characters are shown with most leading blanks removed. Therefore, you can't always get the character number of each cell in the font by counting from the first cell we have shown. Use *xfd* to quickly determine the code for a particular cell.

6x10

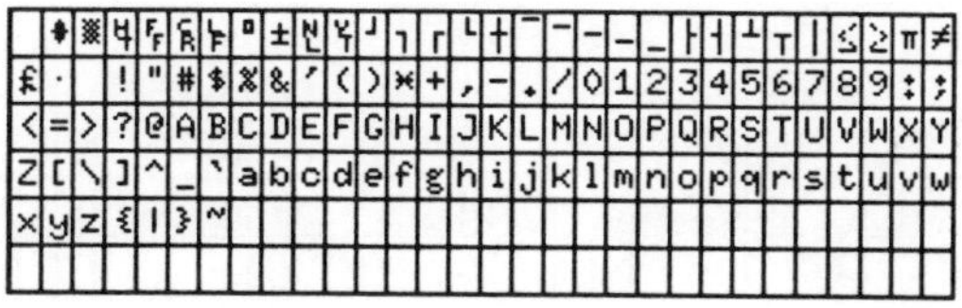

6x12

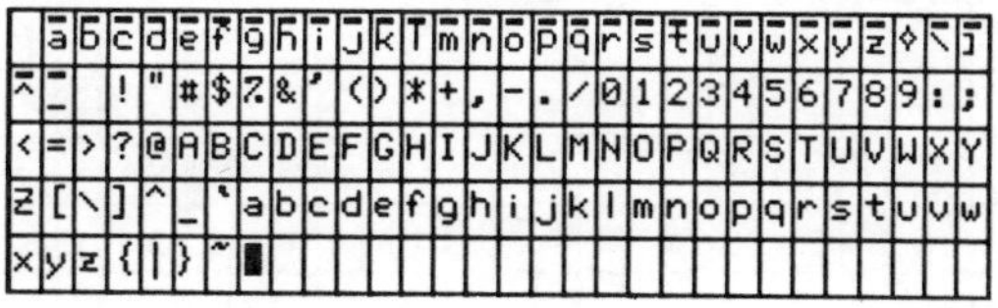

6x13

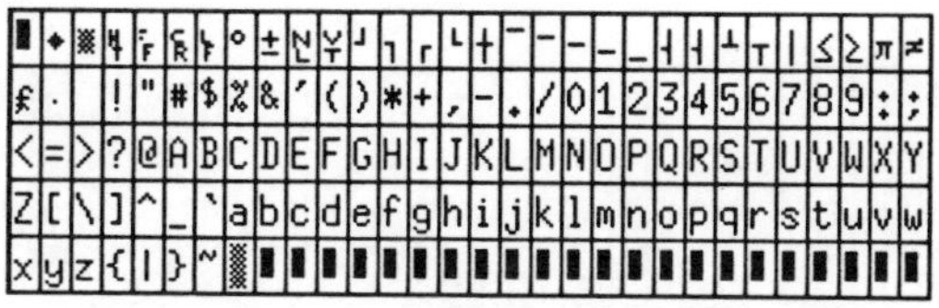

8x13

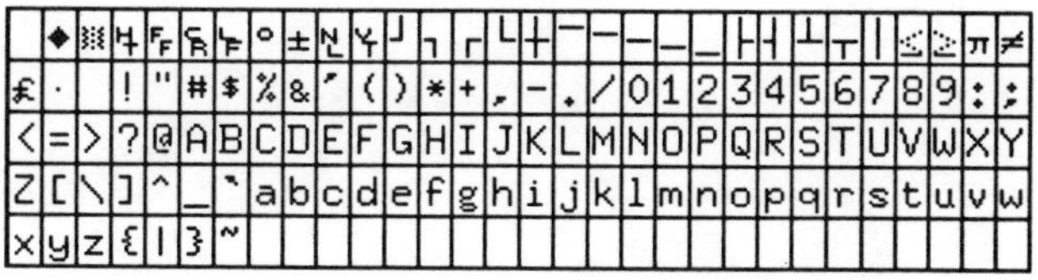

8x13bold

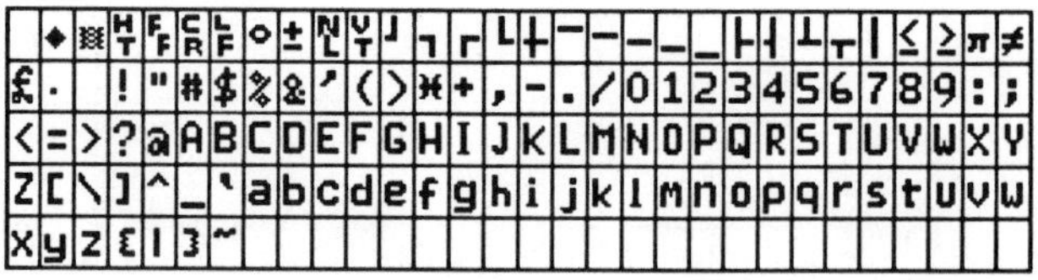

9x15

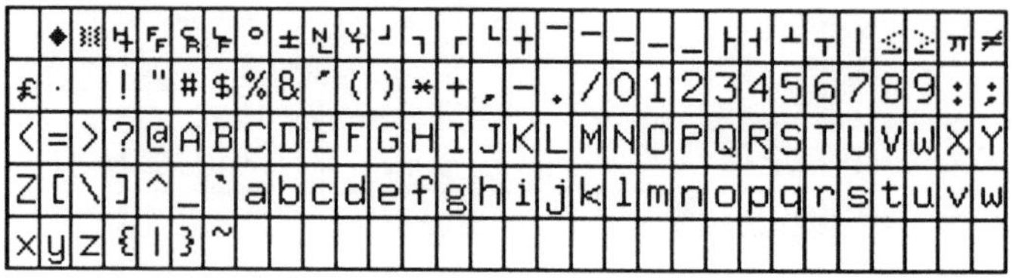

a14

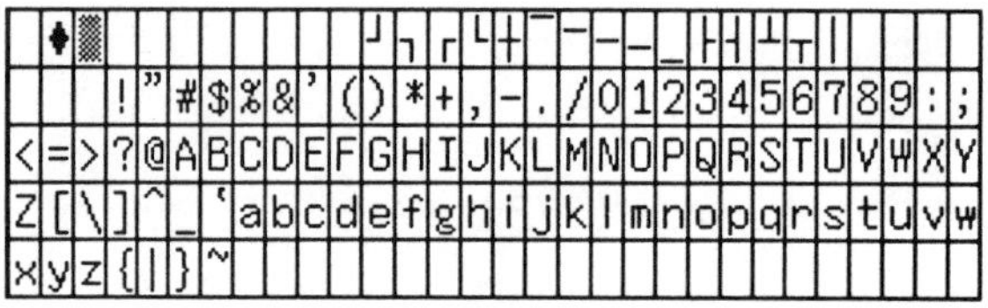

apl-s25

	;	:	[		!	φ	ϙ	I					
⌷	⊕	⋏	⋎	Ⴈ	⍋	⍒	⊖	⌿	⍀	⌾	⍢	⍫	⍇
⍈	⊟	$	Φ		(	)	]	$	=	×	≥	∨	∧
≠	÷	,	+	.	/	0	1	2	3	4	5	6	7
8	9	≤	<	‾	∙∙	>	\	←	∝	⊤	∩	⌊	∈
_	∇	∆	⍳	∘	'	□	∣	T	○	∗	?	ρ	⌈
~	↓	∪		⊃	↑	⊂	{		}		‒	→	A
B	C	D	E	F	G	H	I	J	K	L	M	N	O
P	Q	R	S	T	U	V	W	X	Y	Z	∀	∃	↔

arrow3

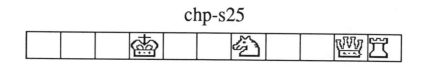

chp-s25

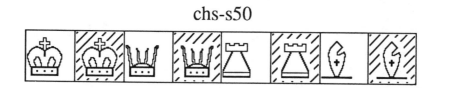

chs-s50

crturz

cursor

X Window System User's Guide

cursor2

cyr-s25

			ю	ы	я		Ш	А	Б			Д
Е	Ф	Г	Х	И		К	Л	М	Н	О	П	
Р	С	Т	У	В			Й	З				Ж
Ц	ъ	а	б		д	е	ф	г	х	и		к

cyr-s30

Ф	Г	Х	И		К	Л	М	Н	О
П		Р	С	Т	У	В			Й
З			Ж	Ц	ъ	а	б		
д	е	ф	г	х	и		к	л	м
Н	о	п		р	с	т	у	в	
	й	з							

cyr-s38

2	3	4	5	6	7	8	9	:	;
	=				А	В	С	Д	Е
Ф	Г	Н	И	Ж	К	Л	М	Ч	О
Р	Щ	Я	Ц	Т	Ю	Б	Ш	Х	У
З	[	\	]		ʿ	а	в	с	

dancer

H	I	J	K	L	M	N	O
P	Q	R	S	T	U	V	W
X	Y	Z					
	□	□	□	□			

ent

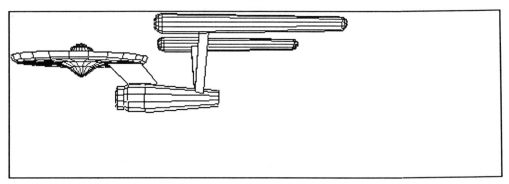

fg-13

↓ α β ⌐ ¬ ∈ π λ   ↑   ∞ ∂ ⊂ ⊃ ∩ ∪ ∀ ∃ ⊗ ↔ ← → ≠ ⌐ ∨ ⟨ ≥ ≡ ∨   ! "
$ % & ' ( ) * + , - . / 0 1 2 3 4 5 6 7 8 9 : ; < = > ? @ A B C D E
F G H I J K L M N O P Q R S T U V W X Y Z [\ ] ^ _ ' a b c d e f g h
i j k l m n o p q r s t u v w x y z { | } ~

fg-16

↑   ←
! " # $ % & ' ( ) * + , - . / 0 1 2 3 4 5 6 7 8 9 : ; < = > ?
@ A B C D E F G H I J K L M N O P Q R S T U V W X Y Z [ ]
a b c d e f g h i j k l m n o p q r s t u v w x y z { | } ~

fg-18

↑   ←   ◇
! " # $ % & ' ( ) * + , - . / 0 1 2 3 4 5 6 7
8 9 : ; < = > ? @ A B C D E F G H I J K L M N O P Q R S
T U V W X Y Z [\ ] ^ _ ` a b c d e f g h i j k l m n o
p q r s t u v w x y z { | } ~

fg-20

↓ α β ∧ ¬ ∈ π λ   ↑   ⇙ ∞ ∂ ⊂ ⊃ ∩ ∪ ∀ ∃ ⊗ ↔ ← → ≠ ◇
≤ ≥ ≡ ∨   ! " # $ % & ' ( ) * + , - . / 0 1 2 3 4 5 6 7
8 9 : ; < = > ? @ A B C D E F G H I J K L M N O P Q R S
T U V W X Y Z [\ ] ^ _ ` a b c d e f g h i j k l m n o
p q r s t u v w x y z { | } ~

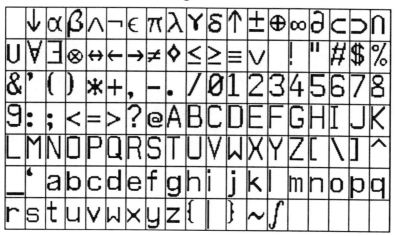

fg-22

fg-25

fg-30

fg-40

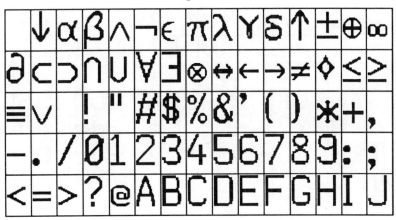

fg1-25

fgb-13

fgb-25

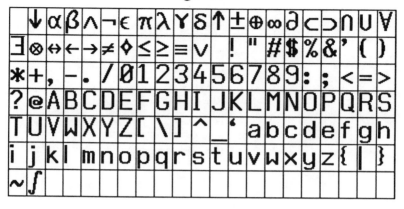

fgb1-25

fgb1-30

fgi-20

fgi1-25

fgs-22

fixed

fqxb-25

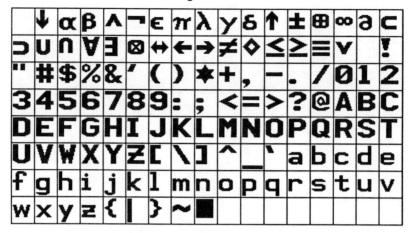

fr-25

fr-33

fr1-25

fr2-25

@	A	B	C	D	E	F	G	H	I	J	K	L	2	N	O	P	Q	R	S	T	U
V	W	X	Y	Z	$	\	]	↑	←		!	"	#	$	%	&	'	(	)	*	+
,	-	.	/	0	1	2	3	4	5	6	7	8	9	:	;	<	=	>	?	@	A
B	C	D	E	F	G	H	I	J	K	L	M	N	O	P	Q	R	S	T	U	V	W
X	Y	Z	[	\	]	^	_	`	a	b	c	d	e	f	g	h	i	j	k	l	m
n	o	p	q	r	s	t	u	v	w	x	y	z	{			}	~	?	@	@	@	@

ger-s35

grk-s25

grk-s30

B	X	Δ	E	Φ	Γ	H	I	φ	K	Λ
M	N	O	Π	Θ	P	Σ	T	Υ		Ω
Ξ	Ψ	Z							α	β
χ	δ	ε	φ	γ	η	ι	ϑ	κ	λ	μ
ν	ο	π	θ	ρ	σ	τ	υ	ς	ω	ξ
ψ	ζ									

hbr-s25

hbr-s40

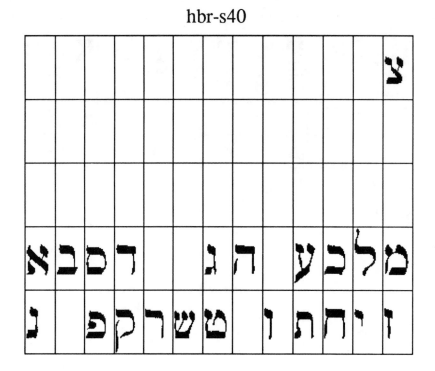

ipa-s25

↓	I	ε	∧	æ	ɔ	ʊ	λ				ə	ʒ	ŋ	θ	š	ʃ	ð	ž
ʒ	?	_	→	ɨ	≠	≤	≥	č	ǰ		!	"	#	$	%	&	'	()	✳	+
,	-	.	/	0	1	2	3	4	5	6	7	8	9	:	;	<	=	>	?	@	A
B	C	D	E	F	G	H	I	J	K	L	M	N	O	P	Q	R	S	T	U	V	W
X	Y	Z	[	\	]	↑	←	'	a	b	c	d	e	f	g	h	i	j	k	l	m
n	o	p	q	r	s	t	u	v	w	x	y	z	{			}	~

kana14

krivo

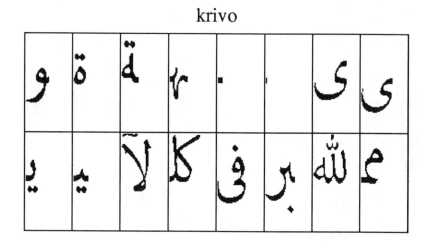

lat-s30

	↓	α	β	∧	¬	∈	π	λ		↑		∞	∂	⊂	⊃	∪	∩	∀	∃
⊗	↔	←	→	≠	◇	≤	≥	≡	∨		!	"	#	$	%	&	'	(	)	⁎	+
,	-	.	/	0	1	2	3	4	5	6	7	8	9	:	;	<	=	>	?	@	Ā
B	Č	D	Ē	F	Ğ	H	Ī	J	Ķ	Ļ	M	Ņ	O	P	Q	Ŗ	Š	T	Ū	V	W
X	Y	Ž	[	\	]	^	_	'	ā	b	č	d	ē	f	ğ	h	ī	j	ķ	ļ	m
ņ	o	p	q	ŗ	š	t	ū	v	w	x	y	ž	{			}	~	■				

met25

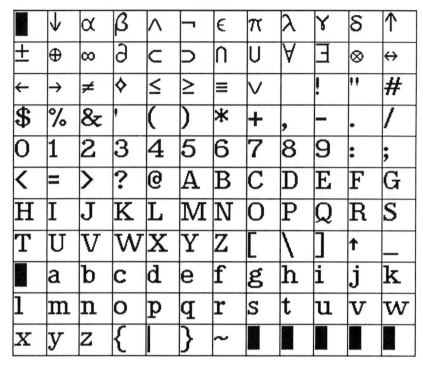

micro

mit

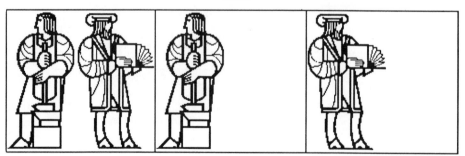

oldera

plunk

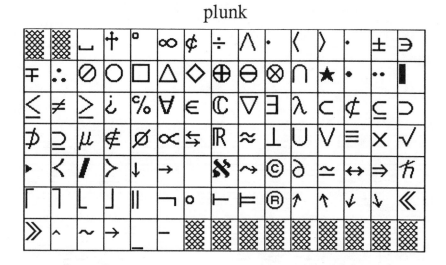

r14

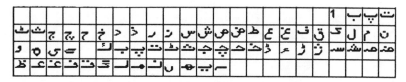

rot-s16

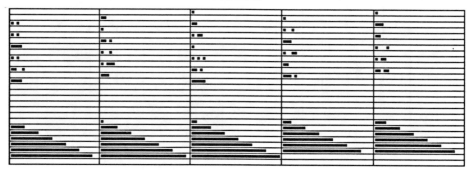

runlen

sans12

sansb12

	¿	ç	¨	`	ff	'	ı		´		¯		˜	ffi	ffl	—	fi	fl	–	˘	–		.
˜	°		!	"	#	$	%	&	'	(	)	*	+	,	-	.	/	0	1	2	3	4	5	6	7	8	9	:	;
<	=	>	?	@	A	B	C	D	E	F	G	H	I	J	K	L	M	N	O	P	Q	R	S	T	U	V	W	X	Y
Z	[	\	]	↑	←	'	a	b	c	d	e	f	g	h	i	j	k	l	m	n	o	p	q	r	s	t	u	v	w
x	y	z	{	|	}	~																							

sansi12

	¿	ç	¨	`	ff	'	ı		´		¯		˜	ffi	ffl	—	fi	fl	–	˘	–		.
˜	°		!	"	#	$	%	&	'	(	)	*	+	,	-		/	0	1	2	3	4	5	6	7	8	9	:	;
<	=	>	?	@	A	B	C	D	E	F	G	H	I	J	K	L	M	N	O	P	Q	R	S	T	U	V	W	X	Y
Z	[	\	]	↑	←	'	a	b	c	d	e	f	g	h	i	j	k	l	m	n	o	p	q	r	s	t	u	v	w
x	y	z	{	|	}	~																							

serif10

	¿	ç	¨	`	ff	'	ı		´		˜		˜	ffi	ffl	—	fi	fl	–	˘	–		~	°		!	"	#	$
%	&	'	(	)	*	+	,	-	.	/	0	1	2	3	4	5	6	7	8	9	:	;	<	=	>	?	@	A	B	C	D	E	F	G	H	I
J	K	L	M	N	O	P	Q	R	S	T	U	V	W	X	Y	Z	[	\	]	↑	←	'	a	b	c	d	e	f	g	h	i	j	k	l	m	n
o	p	q	r	s	t	u	v	w	x	y	z	{	|	}	~																					

serif12

	¿	ç	¨	`	ff	'	ı		´		˜		˜	ffi	ffl	—	fi	fl	–	˘	–		.
˜	°		!	"	#	$	%	&	'	(	)	*	+	,	-	.	/	0	1	2	3	4	5	6	7	8	9	:	;
<	=	>	?	@	A	B	C	D	E	F	G	H	I	J	K	L	M	N	O	P	Q	R	S	T	U	V	W	X	Y
Z	[	\	]	↑	←	'	a	b	c	d	e	f	g	h	i	j	k	l	m	n	o	p	q	r	s	t	u	v	w
x	y	z	{	|	}	~																							

serifb10

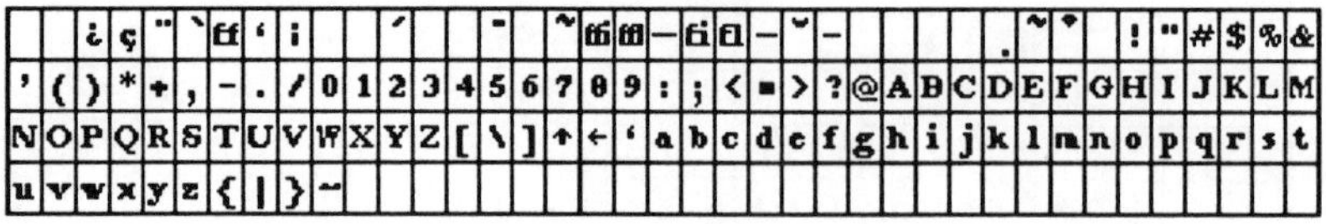

serifb12

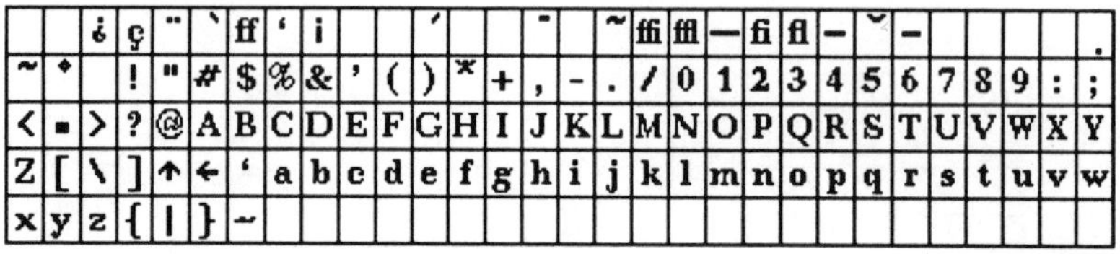

serifi10

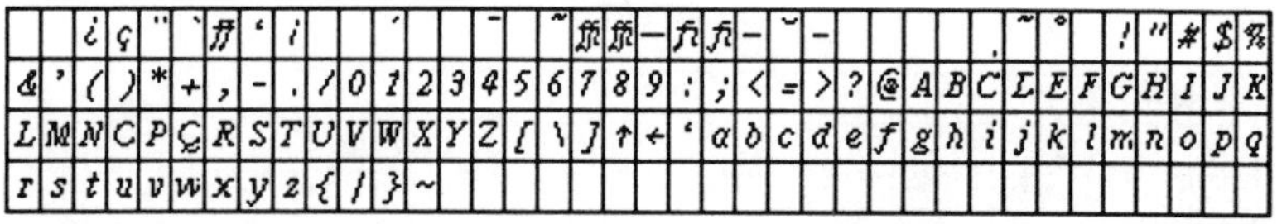

serifi12

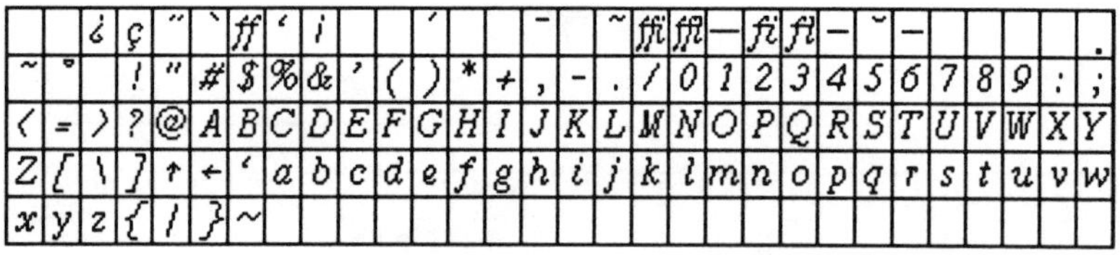

stan

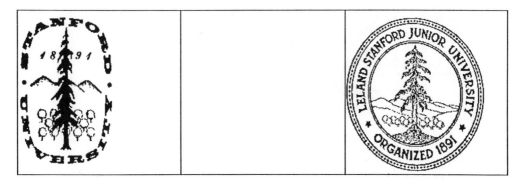

stempl

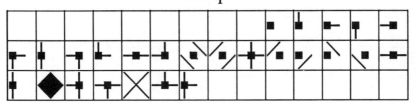

sub

	↓	α	β	∧	¬	∈	π	λ		↑			∞	∂	⊂	⊃
∩	∪	∀	∃	⊗	↔	←	→	≠	~	≤	≥	≡	∨		!	"	#
$	%	&	'	(	)	*	+	,	-	.	/	0	1	2	3	4	5
6	7	8	9	:	;	<	=	>	?	@	A	B	C	D	E	F	G
H	I	J	K	L	M	N	O	P	Q	R	S	T	U	V	W	X	Y
Z	[	\	]		_	'	a	b	c	d	e	f	g	h	i	j	k
l	m	n	o	p	q	r	s	t	u	v	w	x	y	z	{			}
~																	

subsub

	↓	α	β	∧	¬	∈	π	λ			↑			∞	∂	⊂	⊃	∪	∩	∀	∃	⊗	↔	←	→
≠	~	≤	≥	≡	∨		!	"	#	$	%	&	'	(	)	*	+	,	-	.	/	0	1	2	3
4	5	6	7	8	9	:	;	<	=	>	?	@	A	B	C	D	E	F	G	H	I	J	K	L	M
N	O	P	Q	R	S	T	U	V	W	X	Y	Z	[	\	]		_	'	a	b	c	d	e	f	g
h	i	j	k	l	m	n	o	p	q	r	s	t	u	v	w	x	y	z	{			}	~			

sup

	↓	α	β	∧	¬	∈	π	λ			↑			∞	∂	⊂	⊃	∪
∀	∃	⊗	↔	←	→	≠	~	≤	≥	≡	∨		!	"	#	$	%	
&	'	(	)	*	+	,	-	.	/	0	1	2	3	4	5	6	7	8
9	:	;	<	=	>	?	@	A	B	C	D	E	F	G	H	I	J	K
L	M	N	O	P	Q	R	S	T	U	V	W	X	Y	Z	[	\	]	
_	'	a	b	c	d	e	f	g	h	i	j	k	l	m	n	o	p	q
r	s	t	u	v	w	x	y	z	{			}	~						

supsup

												∩	∪	∀	∃	⊗	↔	_	→
~	≠	≤	≥	≡	∨		!	"	#	$	%	&	'	(	)	*	+	,	-	.	/	0	1	2	3
4	5	6	7	8	9	:	;	<	=	>	?	@	A	B	C	D	E	F	G	H	I	J	K	L	M
N	O	P	Q	R	S	T	U	V	W	X	Y	Z	[	\	]	↑	←	'	a	b	c	d	e	f	g
h	i	j	k	l	m	n	o	p	q	r	s	t	u	v	w	x	y	z	{			~	}			

swd-s30

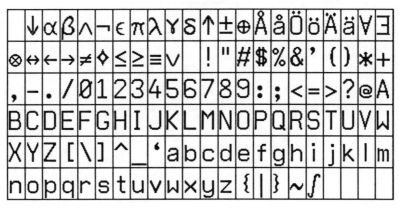

sym-s25

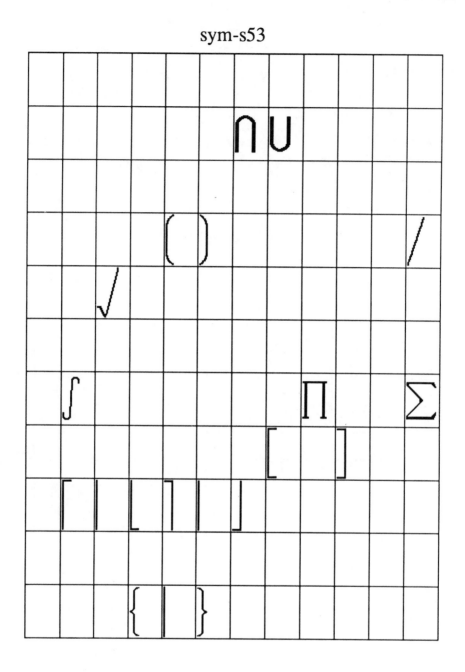

variable

	ˇ	¿	ç	¨	`	ff	'	ı			´			¯		~	ffi	ffl	—	fi	fl
–	˘	–						.		~	•		!	"	#	$	%	&	'	(	)	*	+
,	-	.	/	0	1	2	3	4	5	6	7	8	9	:	;	<	=	>	?	@	A
B	C	D	E	F	G	H	I	J	K	L	M	N	O	P	Q	R	S	T	U	V	W
X	Y	Z	[	\	]	↑	←	'	a	b	c	d	e	f	g	h	i	j	k	l	m
n	o	p	q	r	s	t	u	v	w	x	y	z	{			}	~			

vbee-36

!	''				?	(	)		
,	-	.	/	0	1	2	3	4	5	6
7	8	9	:	;		=		?		Æ
B	C	D	E	F	G	Ħ	Ï	Ĭ	K	L
M	N	O	P	Q	R	S	T	U	V	W
X	Y	Z	[		]			'	a	b
c	d	e	f	g	h	i	j	k	l	m
n	o	p	q	r	s	t	u	v	w	x
y	z									

vctl-25

vg-13

vg-20

vg-25

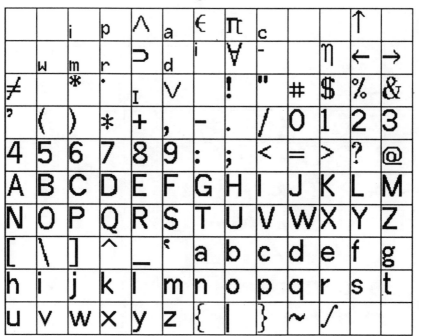

	↓	∝	ß	∧	¬	∈	π	λ	Υ	δ	↑	±	⊕	∞	∂
⊂	⊃	∩	∪	∀	∃	⊗	↔	←	→	≠	◇	≤	≥	≡	∨
	!	"	#	$	%	&	'	(	)	*	+	,	-	.	/
0	1	2	3	4	5	6	7	8	9	:	;	<	=	>	?
@	A	B	C	D	E	F	G	H	I	J	K	L	M	N	O
P	Q	R	S	T	U	V	W	X	Y	Z	[	\	]	^	_
`	a	b	c	d	e	f	g	h	i	j	k	l	m	n	o
p	q	r	s	t	u	v	w	x	y	z	{	|	}	~	∫

vg-31

		i	p	∧	a	∈	π	c			↑		
	ω	m	r	⊃	d	i	∀	⁻		η	←	→
≠		*	·	I	∨		!	"	#	$	%	&
'	(	)	*	+	,	-	.	/	0	1	2	3
4	5	6	7	8	9	:	;	<	=	>	?	@
A	B	C	D	E	F	G	H	I	J	K	L	M
N	O	P	Q	R	S	T	U	V	W	X	Y	Z
[	\	]	^	_	`	a	b	c	d	e	f	g
h	i	j	k	l	m	n	o	p	q	r	s	t
u	v	w	x	y	z	{	|	}	~	∫		

vgb-25

vgb-31

vgbc-25

```
⊃ ∩ ∪ ∀ ∃ ⊗ ↔ ← → ≠ ~ ≤ ≥ ≡ ∨   !
" # $ % & ' ( ) * + , - . / 0 1 2
3 4 5 6 7 8 9 : ; < = > ? @ A B C
D E F G H I J K L M N O P Q R S T
U V W X Y Z [ \ ] _ ' a b c d e
f g h i j k l m n o p q r s t u v
w x y z { | } ~
```

vgh-25

```
  á é   í ó ú ö           ő ű
    Í Ó Ú Ö Ü Ő Ű Á ≠ ~ É ≥ ü ∨
  ! " # $ % & ' ( ) * + , - . /
0 1 2 3 4 5 6 7 8 9 : ; < = > ?
@ A B C D E F G H I J K L M N O
P Q R S T U V W X Y Z [ \ ] _
' a b c d e f g h i j k l m n o
p q r s t u v w x y z { | } ~
```

vgi-20

				(	)						0	1	2	3	4	5
6	7	8	9								A	B	C	D	E	F	G
H	I	J	K	L	M	N	O	P	Q	R	S	T	U	V	W	X	Y
Z	[		]		_		a	b	c	d	e	f	g	h	i	j	k
l	m	n	o	p	q	r	s	t	u	v	w	x	y	z		

vgi-25

■	↓	∝	β	∧	¬	∈	π	λ	γ	δ	↑	±	⊕	∞	∂
⊂	⊃	∩	∪	∀	∃	⊗	↔	←	→	≠	◊	≤	≥	≡	∨
	!	"	#	$	%	&	'	(	)	*	+	,	-	.	/
0	1	2	3	4	5	6	7	8	9	:	;	<	=	>	?
@	A	B	C	D	E	F	G	H	I	J	K	L	M	N	O
P	Q	R	S	T	U	V	W	X	Y	Z	[	\	]	^	_
`	a	b	c	d	e	f	g	h	i	j	k	l	m	n	o
p	q	r	s	t	u	v	w	x	y	z	{	|	}	~	∫

		i	p	Λ	a	ε	π	c			↑
		w	m	r	⊃	d	i	∀	-		η
←	→	≠		*	·	I	∨		!	"	#
$	%	&	'	(	)	*	+	,	-	.	/
0	1	2	3	4	5	6	7	8	9	:	;
<	=	>	?	@	A	B	C	D	E	F	G
H	I	J	K	L	M	N	O	P	Q	R	S
T	U	V	W	X	Y	Z	[	\	j	^	_
`	a	b	c	d	e	f	g	h	i	j	k
l	m	n	o	p	q	r	s	t	u	v	w
x	y	z	{	|	}	~	√				

vgl-40

vgvb-31

vmic-25

Standard Fonts

Standard Fonts

291

vply-36

			≠		≤	≥			!	"		$	%	&	'	(	)	*	+
,	-	.	/	0	1	2	3				:	;	<	=	>	?		A
B	C	D	E	F	G	H	I	J	K	L	M	N	O	P	Q	R	S	T	U	V	W
X	Y	Z	[		]				a	b	c	d	e	f	g	h	i	j	k	l	m
n	o	p	q	r	s	t	u	v	w	x	y	z							

vr-20

	a	b	c	d	e	f	g	h	i	j	k	l	m	n
o	p	q	r	s	t	u	v	w	x	y	z			
			!	"	#	$	%		'	(	)		*	+	,
-	.		/	0	1	2	3	4	5	6	7	8	9	:	;
<	=	>	?		A	B	C	D	E	F	G	H	I	J
K	L	M	N	O	P	Q	R	S	T	U	V	W	X	Y
Z	[	\	]		_	`	a	b	c	d	e	f	g	h
i	j	k	l	m	n	o	p	q	r	s	t	u	v	w
x	y	z					~							

vr-25

↓	∝	β	∧	¬	∈	π	λ			↑	±		∞
∂	⊂	⊃	∩	∪	∀	∃	⊗	↔	←	→	≠	~	≤	≥
≡	∨		!	"	#	$	%	&	'	(	)	*	+	,
-	.		/	0	1	2	3	4	5	6	7	8	9	:	;
<	=	>	?	@	A	B	C	D	E	F	G	H	I	J
K	L	M	N	O	P	Q	R	S	T	U	V	W	X	Y
Z	[	\	]	^	_	`	a	b	c	d	e	f	g	h
i	j	k	l	m	n	o	p	q	r	s	t	u	v	w
x	y	z	{	|	}	~								

vr-27

	↓	α	β	∧	¬	∈	π	λ	*		↑	±	
∞	∂	⊂	⊃	∩	∪	∀	∃	⊗	↔	←	→	≠	~
≤	≥	≡	∨		!	"	#	$	%	&	'	(	)
*	+	,	-	.	/	0	1	2	3	4	5	6	7
8	9	:	;	<	=	>	?	@	A	B	C	D	E
F	G	H	I	J	K	L	M	N	O	P	Q	R	S
T	U	V	W	X	Y	Z	[	\	]		_	`	a
b	c	d	e	f	g	h	i	j	k	l	m	n	o
p	q	r	s	t	u	v	w	x	y	z	{	|	}
~	∫												

vr-30

vr-31

vrb-25

	↓	∝	β	∧	¬	∈	π	λ			↑			∞
∂	⊂	⊃	∩	∪	∀	∃	⊗	↔	←	→	≠	~	≤	≥
≡	∨		!	"	#	$	%	&	'	(	)	*	+	,
-	.	/	0	1	2	3	4	5	6	7	8	9	:	;
<	=	>	?	@	A	B	C	D	E	F	G	H	I	J
K	L	M	N	O	P	Q	R	S	T	U	V	W	X	Y
Z	[	\	]		_	`	a	b	c	d	e	f	g	h
i	j	k	l	m	n	o	p	q	r	s	t	u	v	w
x	y	z	{	|	}	~								

vrb-30

	↓	∝	β	∧	—	∈	π	λ			↑	
	ffl	∂	⊂	⊃	∩	∪	∀	∃	⊗	↔	←	→
ffi	~	≤	ff	fi	fl		!	"	#	$	%	&c
'	(	)	*	+	,	-	.	/	0	1	2	3
4	5	6	7	8	9	:	;	<	=	>	?	@
A	B	C	D	E	F	G	H	I	J	K	L	M
N	O	P	Q	R	S	T	U	V	W	X	Y	Z
[	\	]	^	_	`		a	b	c	d	e	f	g
h	i	j	k	l	m	n	o	p	q	r	s	t
u	v	w	x	y	z	{	|	}	~			

	↓	∝	ß	∧	¬	∈	π	λ		
↑		∞	∂	⊂	⊃	∩	∪	∀	∃	
⊗	↔	←	→	≠	~	≤	≥	≡	∨	
!	"	#	$	%	&c	'	(	)	*	+
,	-	.	/	0	1	2	3	4	5	6
7	8	9	:	;	<	=	>	?	@	A
B	C	D	E	F	G	H	I	J	K	L
M	N	O	P	Q	R	S	T	U	V	W
X	Y	Z	[	\	]	_	`		a	b
c	d	e	f	g	h	i	j	k	l	m
n	o	p	q	r	s	t	u	v	w	x
y	z	{	|	}	~					

							ffl
		ffi			**ff**	**fi**	**fl**
		''	#	$	%	×	'
(	)		+	,	-	.	/
0	1	2	3	4	5	6	7
8	9	:	;	<	=	>	?
	A	B	C	D	E	F	G
H	I	J	K	L	M	N	O
P	Q	R	S	T	U	V	W
X	Y	Z	[	\	]		_
'	a	b	c	d	e	f	g
h	i	j	k	l	m	n	o
p	q	r	s	t	u	v	w
x	y	z	{	|	}	~	∫

vri-25

	↓	∝	β	∧	¬	∈	π	λ			↑	ff	
∞	∂	⊂	⊃	∩	∪	∀	∃	⊗	↔	←	→	≠	~
≤	≥	≡	∨		!	"	#	$	%	&	'	(	)
*	+	,	−	.	/	0	1	2	3	4	5	6	7
8	9	:	;	<	=	>	?	@	A	B	C	D	E
F	G	H	I	J	K	L	M	N	O	P	Q	R	S
T	U	V	W	X	Y	Z	[	\	]		_	`	a
b	c	d	e	f	g	h	i	j	k	l	m	n	o
p	q	r	s	t	u	v	w	x	y	z	{	|	}
~													

vri-30

	↓	∝	β	∧	—	∈	π	λ			↑	±
	ffi	∂	⊂	⊃	∩	∪	∀	∃	⊗	↔	←	→
ffi		≤	ff	fi	fl		!	"	#	$	%	&
'	(	)	*	+	,	−	.	/	0	1	2	3
4	5	6	7	8	9	:	;	<	=	>	?	@
A	B	C	D	E	F	G	H	I	J	K	L	M
N	O	P	Q	R	S	T	U	V	W	X	Y	Z
[	\	]		_	`	a	b	c	d	e	j	g
h	i	j	k	l	m	n	o	p	q	r	s	t
u	v	w	x	y	z	{	|	}	~			

vsg-114

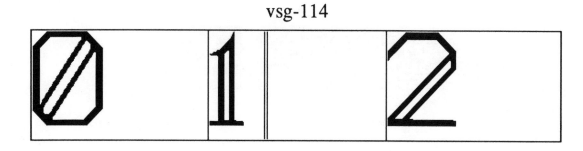

vsgn-57

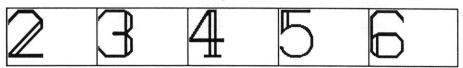

vshd-40

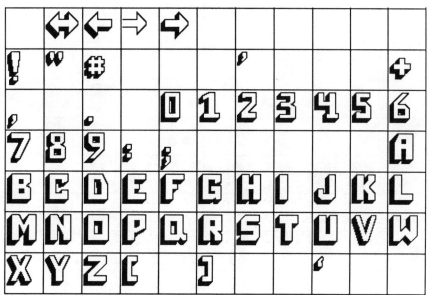

vtbold

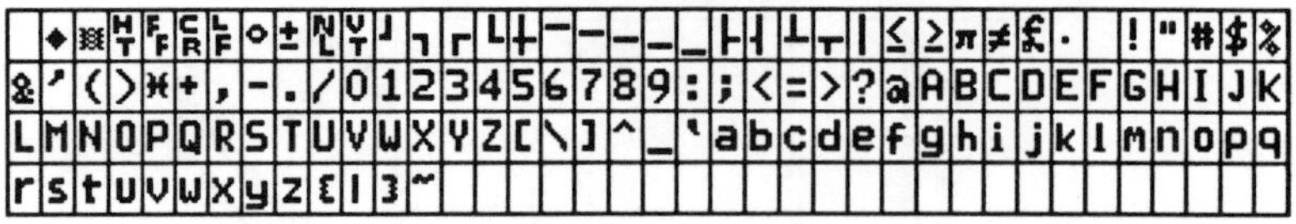

vtsingle

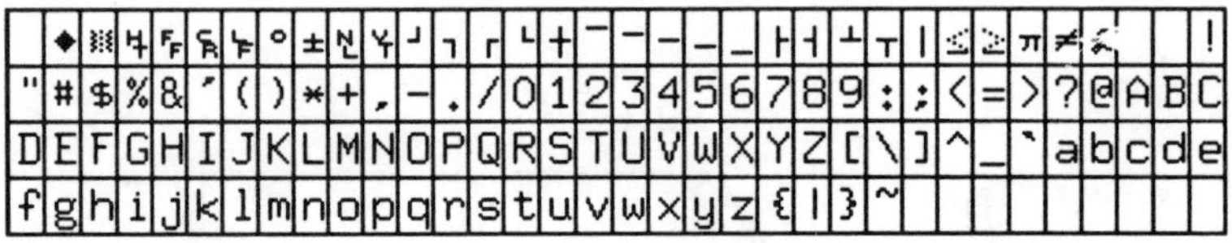

vxms-37

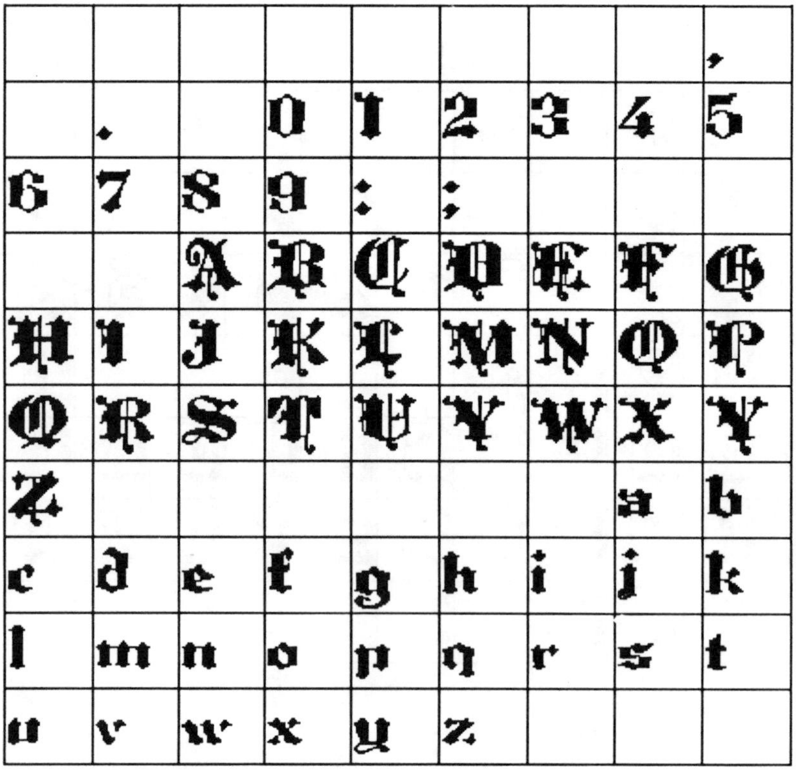

vxms-43

			†	(	)
		–	✕		0
1	2	3	4	5	6	7
8	9					
?		A	B	C	D	E
F	G	H	I	J	K	L
M	N	O	P	Q	R	S
T	U	V	W	X	Y	Z
						a
b	c	d	e	f	g	h
i	j	k	l	m	n	o
p	q	r	s	t	u	v
w	x	y	z			

xif-s25

D

xterm Control Sequences

This appendix lists the escape sequences that can be used from within a program to control features of xterm's window or its terminal emulations.

D
xterm Control Sequences

A standard terminal performs many operations in response to escape sequences sent out by a program. In emulating a terminal, *xterm* responds to those same terminal escape sequences. Under UNIX, programs use the *termcap* or *terminfo* database to determine which escape sequences to send out. For more information, see the standard UNIX man pages *termcap*(5) or *terminfo*(5), or the Nutshell Handbook *Termcap and Terminfo*, available from O'Reilly & Associates, Inc.

Xterm Control Sequences

Definitions

C A single (required) character.

P_s A single (usually optional) numeric parameter, composed of one of more digits.

P_m A multiple numeric parameter composed of any number of single numeric parameters, separated by ⌐;⌐ character(s).

P_t A text parameter composed of printable characters.

VT102 Mode

Most of these control sequences are standard VT102 control sequences. There are, however, additional ones to provide control of *xterm*-dependent functions, like the scrollbar or window size.

`BEL`	Bell (Ctrl-G)
`BS`	Backspace (Ctrl-H)
`TAB`	Horizontal Tab (Ctrl-I)
`LF`	Line Feed or New Line (Ctrl-J)
`VT`	Vertical Tab (Ctrl-K)
`FF`	Form Feed or New Page (Ctrl-L)
`CR`	Carriage Return (Ctrl-M)
`SO`	Shift Out (Ctrl-N) → Switch to Alternate Character Set
`SI`	Shift In (Ctrl-O) → Switch to Standard Character Set

`ESC` `#` `8`	DEC Screen Alignment Test (DECALN)
`ESC` `(` C	Select G0 Character Set (SCS)

$\quad$ $C =$ `0` $\rightarrow$ Special Character and Line Drawing Set

$\quad$ $C =$ `1` $\rightarrow$ Alternate Character ROM Standard Set

$\quad$ $C =$ `2` $\rightarrow$ Alternate Character ROM Special Set

$\quad$ $C =$ `A` $\rightarrow$ United Kingdom (UK)

$\quad$ $C =$ `B` $\rightarrow$ United States (USASCII)

`ESC` `)` C	Select G1 Character Set (SCS)

$\quad$ $C =$ `0` $\rightarrow$ Special Character and Line Drawing Set

$\quad$ $C =$ `1` $\rightarrow$ Alternate Character ROM Standard Set

$\quad$ $C =$ `2` $\rightarrow$ Alternate Character ROM Special Set

$\quad$ $C =$ `A` $\rightarrow$ United Kingdom (UK)

$\quad$ $C =$ `B` $\rightarrow$ United States (USASCII)

`ESC` `*` C	Select G2 Character Set (SCS)

$\quad$ $C =$ `0` $\rightarrow$ Special Character and Line Drawing Set

$\quad$ $C =$ `1` $\rightarrow$ Alternate Character ROM Standard Set

$\quad$ $C =$ `2` $\rightarrow$ Alternate Character ROM Special Set

$\quad$ $C =$ `A` $\rightarrow$ United Kingdom (UK)

$\quad$ $C =$ `B` $\rightarrow$ United States (USASCII)

`ESC` `+` C	Select G3 Character Set (SCS)

$\quad$ $C =$ `0` $\rightarrow$ Special Character and Line Drawing Set

$\quad$ $C =$ `1` $\rightarrow$ Alternate Character ROM Standard Set

$\quad$ $C =$ `2` $\rightarrow$ Alternate Character ROM Special Set

$\quad$ $C =$ `A` $\rightarrow$ United Kingdom (UK)

$\quad$ $C =$ `B` $\rightarrow$ United States (USASCII)

`ESC` `7`	Save Cursor (DECSC)
`ESC` `8`	Restore Cursor (DECRC)
`ESC` `=`	Application Keypad (DECPAM)
`ESC` `>`	Normal Keypad (DECPNM)
`ESC` `D`	Index (IND)
`ESC` `E`	Next Line (NEL)
`ESC` `H`	Tab Set (HTS)
`ESC` `M`	Reverse Index (RI)
`ESC` `N`	Single Shift Select of G2 Character Set (SS2)
`ESC` `O`	Single Shift Select of G3 Character Set (SS3)
`ESC` `T` P_s `LF`	Change Window Title to P_s

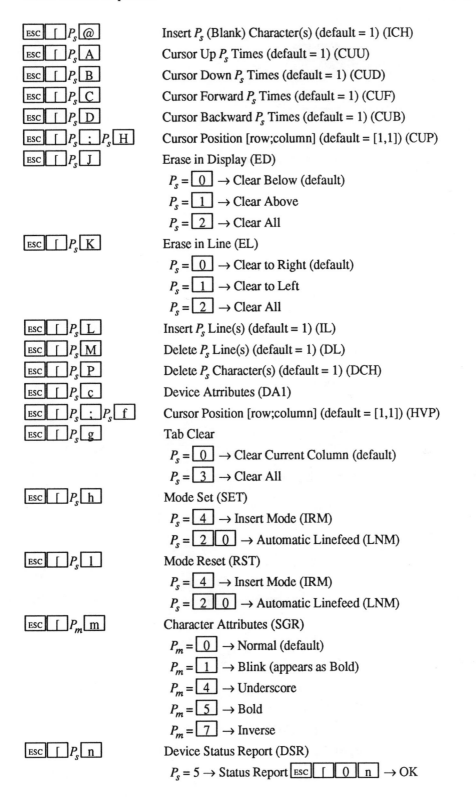

ESC [P_s @   Insert P_s (Blank) Character(s) (default = 1) (ICH)

ESC [P_s A   Cursor Up P_s Times (default = 1) (CUU)

ESC [P_s B   Cursor Down P_s Times (default = 1) (CUD)

ESC [P_s C   Cursor Forward P_s Times (default = 1) (CUF)

ESC [P_s D   Cursor Backward P_s Times (default = 1) (CUB)

ESC [P_s ; P_s H   Cursor Position [row;column] (default = [1,1]) (CUP)

ESC [P_s J   Erase in Display (ED)

    $P_s = \boxed{0}$ → Clear Below (default)

    $P_s = \boxed{1}$ → Clear Above

    $P_s = \boxed{2}$ → Clear All

ESC [P_s K   Erase in Line (EL)

    $P_s = \boxed{0}$ → Clear to Right (default)

    $P_s = \boxed{1}$ → Clear to Left

    $P_s = \boxed{2}$ → Clear All

ESC [P_s L   Insert P_s Line(s) (default = 1) (IL)

ESC [P_s M   Delete P_s Line(s) (default = 1) (DL)

ESC [P_s P   Delete P_s Character(s) (default = 1) (DCH)

ESC [P_s c   Device Atrributes (DA1)

ESC [P_s ; P_s f   Cursor Position [row;column] (default = [1,1]) (HVP)

ESC [P_s g   Tab Clear

    $P_s = \boxed{0}$ → Clear Current Column (default)

    $P_s = \boxed{3}$ → Clear All

ESC [P_s h   Mode Set (SET)

    $P_s = \boxed{4}$ → Insert Mode (IRM)

    $P_s = \boxed{2}\boxed{0}$ → Automatic Linefeed (LNM)

ESC [P_s l   Mode Reset (RST)

    $P_s = \boxed{4}$ → Insert Mode (IRM)

    $P_s = \boxed{2}\boxed{0}$ → Automatic Linefeed (LNM)

ESC [P_m m   Character Attributes (SGR)

    $P_m = \boxed{0}$ → Normal (default)

    $P_m = \boxed{1}$ → Blink (appears as Bold)

    $P_m = \boxed{4}$ → Underscore

    $P_m = \boxed{5}$ → Bold

    $P_m = \boxed{7}$ → Inverse

ESC [P_s n   Device Status Report (DSR)

    $P_s = 5$ → Status Report ESC [0 n → OK

xterm Control
Sequences

$P_s = 6 \rightarrow$ Report Cursor Position (CPR) [row;column] as `ESC` `[` r `;` c `R`

`ESC` `[` P_s `;` P_s `r`   Set Scrolling Region [top;bottom] (default = full size of window) (DECSTBM)

`ESC` `[` P_s `x`   Request Terminal Parameters (DECREQTPARM)

`ESC` `[` `?` `E`   Erase Status Line

`ESC` `[` `?` `F`   Return from Status Line

`ESC` `[` `?` `H`   Hide Status Line

`ESC` `[` `?` `S`   Show Status Line

`ESC` `[` `?` P_s `T`   Go To Column P_s of Status Line

`ESC` `[` `?` P_s `h`   DEC Private Mode Set (DECSET)

$P_s =$ `1` $\rightarrow$ Application Cursor Keys (DECCKM)

$P_s =$ `3` $\rightarrow$ 132 Column Mode (DECCOLM)

$P_s =$ `4` $\rightarrow$ Smooth (Slow) Scroll (DECSCLM)

$P_s =$ `5` $\rightarrow$ Reverse Video (DECSCNM)

$P_s =$ `6` $\rightarrow$ Origin Mode (DECOM)

$P_s =$ `7` $\rightarrow$ Wraparound Mode (DECAWM)

$P_s =$ `8` $\rightarrow$ Auto-repeat Keys (DECARM)

$P_s =$ `9` $\rightarrow$ Send MIT Mouse Row & Column on Button Press

$P_s =$ `3` `8` $\rightarrow$ Enter TekTronix Mode (DECTEK)

$P_s =$ `4` `0` $\rightarrow$ Allow 80 $\leftrightarrow$ 132 Mode

$P_s =$ `4` `1` $\rightarrow$ *curses*(5) fix

$P_s =$ `4` `4` $\rightarrow$ Turn On Margin Bell

$P_s =$ `4` `5` $\rightarrow$ Reverse-wraparound Mode

$P_s =$ `4` `6` $\rightarrow$ Start Logging

$P_s =$ `4` `7` $\rightarrow$ Use Alternate Screen Buffer

$P_s =$ `4` `8` $\rightarrow$ Reverse Status Line

`ESC` `[` `?` P_s `l`   DEC Private Mode Reset (DECRST)

$P_s =$ `1` $\rightarrow$ Normal Cursor Keys (DECCKM)

$P_s =$ `3` $\rightarrow$ 80 Column Mode (DECCOLM)

$P_s =$ `4` $\rightarrow$ Jump (Fast) Scroll (DECSCLM)

$P_s =$ `5` $\rightarrow$ Normal Video (DECSCNM)

$P_s =$ `6` $\rightarrow$ Normal Cursor Mode (DECOM)

$P_s =$ `7` $\rightarrow$ No Wraparound Mode (DECAWM)

$P_s =$ `8` $\rightarrow$ No Auto-repeat Keys (DECARM)

$P_s =$ `9` $\rightarrow$ Don't Send MIT Mouse Row & Column on Button

Press

$P_s = \boxed{4}\boxed{0}$ → Disallow 80 ↔ 132 Mode

$P_s = \boxed{4}\boxed{1}$ → No *curses*(5) fix

$P_s = \boxed{4}\boxed{4}$ → Turn Off Margin Bell

$P_s = \boxed{4}\boxed{5}$ → No Reverse-wraparound Mode

$P_s = \boxed{4}\boxed{6}$ → Stop Logging

$P_s = \boxed{4}\boxed{7}$ → Use Normal Screen Buffer

$P_s = \boxed{4}\boxed{8}$ → Un-reverse Status Line

$\boxed{\text{ESC}}\ \boxed{[}\ \boxed{?}\ P_s\ \boxed{r}$ Restore DEC Private Mode

$P_s = \boxed{1}$ → Normal/Application Cursor Keys (DECCKM)

$P_s = \boxed{3}$ → 80/132 Column Mode (DECCOLM)

$P_s = \boxed{4}$ → Jump (Fast)/Smooth (Slow) Scroll (DECSCLM)

$P_s = \boxed{5}$ → Normal/Reverse Video (DECSCNM)

$P_s = \boxed{6}$ → Normal/Origin Cursor Mode (DECOM)

$P_s = \boxed{7}$ → No Wraparound/Wraparound Mode (DECAWM)

$P_s = \boxed{8}$ → Auto-repeat/No Auto-repeat Keys (DECARM)

$P_s = \boxed{9}$ → Don't Send/Send MIT Mouse Row & Column on Button Press

$P_s = \boxed{4}\boxed{0}$ → Disallow/Allow 80 ↔ 132 Mode

$P_s = \boxed{4}\boxed{1}$ → Off/On *curses*(5) fix

$P_s = \boxed{4}\boxed{4}$ → Turn Off/On Margin Bell

$P_s = \boxed{4}\boxed{5}$ → No Reverse-wraparound/Reverse-wraparound Mode

$P_s = \boxed{4}\boxed{6}$ → Stop/Start Logging

$P_s = \boxed{4}\boxed{7}$ → Use Normal/Alternate Screen Buffer

$P_s = \boxed{4}\boxed{8}$ → Un-reverse/Reverse Status Line

$\boxed{\text{ESC}}\ \boxed{[}\ \boxed{?}\ P_s\ \boxed{s}$ Save DEC Private Mode

$P_s = \boxed{1}$ → Normal/Application Cursor Keys (DECCKM)

$P_s = \boxed{3}$ → 80/132 Column Mode (DECCOLM)

$P_s = \boxed{4}$ → Jump (Fast)/Smooth (Slow) Scroll (DECSCLM)

$P_s = \boxed{5}$ → Normal/Reverse Video (DECSCNM)

$P_s = \boxed{6}$ → Normal/Origin Cursor Mode (DECOM)

$P_s = \boxed{7}$ → No Wraparound/Wraparound Mode (DECAWM)

$P_s = \boxed{8}$ → Auto-repeat/No Auto-repeat Keys (DECARM)

$P_s = \boxed{9}$ → Don't Send/Send MIT Mouse Row & Column on Button Press

xterm Control Sequences

$P_s = \boxed{4}\ \boxed{0} \rightarrow$ Disallow/Allow 80 $\leftrightarrow$ 132 Mode

$P_s = \boxed{4}\ \boxed{1} \rightarrow$ Off/On *curses*(5) fix

$P_s = \boxed{4}\ \boxed{4} \rightarrow$ Turn Off/On Margin Bell

$P_s = \boxed{4}\ \boxed{5} \rightarrow$ No Reverse-wraparound/Reverse-wraparound Mode

$P_s = \boxed{4}\ \boxed{6} \rightarrow$ Stop/Start Logging

$P_s = \boxed{4}\ \boxed{7} \rightarrow$ Use Normal/Alternate Screen Buffer

$P_s = \boxed{4}\ \boxed{8} \rightarrow$ Un-reverse/Reverse Status Line

$\boxed{\text{ESC}}\ \boxed{]}\ P_s\ \boxed{;}\ P_t\ \boxed{\text{BEL}}$	Set Text Parameters

$P_s = \boxed{0} \rightarrow$ Change Window Name and Title to P_t

$P_s = \boxed{1} \rightarrow$ Change Window Name to P_t

$P_s = \boxed{0} \rightarrow$ Change Window Title to P_t

$P_s = \boxed{4}\ \boxed{6} \rightarrow$ Change Log File to P_t

$\boxed{\text{ESC}}\ \boxed{\text{c}}$	Full Reset (RIS)

Tektronix 4015 Mode

Most of these sequences are standard Tektronix 4015 control sequences. The major features missing are the alternate (APL) character set and the write-thru and defocused modes.

$\boxed{\text{BEL}}$	Bell (Ctrl-G)
$\boxed{\text{BS}}$	Backspace (Ctrl-H)
$\boxed{\text{TAB}}$	Horizontal Tab (Ctrl-I)
$\boxed{\text{LF}}$	Line Feed or New Line (Ctrl-J)
$\boxed{\text{VT}}$	Vertical Tab (Ctrl-K)
$\boxed{\text{FF}}$	Form Feed or New Page (Ctrl-L)
$\boxed{\text{CR}}$	Carriage Return (Ctrl-M)
$\boxed{\text{ESC}}\ \boxed{\text{ETX}}$	Switch to VT102 Mode
$\boxed{\text{ESC}}\ \boxed{\text{ENQ}}$	Return Terminal Status
$\boxed{\text{ESC}}\ \boxed{\text{LF}}$	PAGE (Clear Screen)
$\boxed{\text{ESC}}\ \boxed{\text{ETB}}$	COPY (Save Tektronix Codes to File)
$\boxed{\text{ESC}}\ \boxed{\text{CAN}}$	Bypass Condition
$\boxed{\text{ESC}}\ \boxed{\text{SUB}}$	GIN mode
$\boxed{\text{ESC}}\ \boxed{\text{FS}}$	Special Point Plot Mode
$\boxed{\text{ESC}}\ \boxed{\text{GS}}$	Graph Mode (same as $\boxed{\text{GS}}$)
$\boxed{\text{ESC}}\ \boxed{\text{RS}}$	Incremental Plot Mode (same as $\boxed{\text{RS}}$)
$\boxed{\text{ESC}}\ \boxed{\text{US}}$	Alpha Mode (same as $\boxed{\text{US}}$)
$\boxed{\text{ESC}}\ \boxed{8}$	Select Large Character Set

`ESC` `9`	Select #2 Character Set
`ESC` `:`	Select #3 Character Set
`ESC` `;`	Select Small Character Set
`ESC` `]` P_s `;` P_t `BEL`	Set Text Parameters

$P_s = \boxed{0} \rightarrow$ Change Window Name and Title to P_t

$P_s = \boxed{4}\ \boxed{6} \rightarrow$ Change Log File to P_t

`ESC` `` ` ``	Normal Z Axis and Normal (solid) Vectors
`ESC` `a`	Normal Z Axis and Dotted Line Vectors
`ESC` `b`	Normal Z Axis and Dot-Dashed Vectors
`ESC` `c`	Normal Z Axis and Short-Dashed Vectors
`ESC` `d`	Normal Z Axis and Long-Dashed Vectors
`ESC` `h`	Defocused Z Axis and Normal (solid) Vectors
`ESC` `i`	Defocused Z Axis and Dotted Line Vectors
`ESC` `j`	Defocused Z Axis and Dot-Dashed Vectors
`ESC` `k`	Defocused Z Axis and Short-Dashed Vectors
`ESC` `l`	Defocused Z Axis and Long-Dashed Vectors
`ESC` `p`	Write-Thru Mode and Normal (solid) Vectors
`ESC` `q`	Write-Thru Mode and Dotted Line Vectors
`ESC` `r`	Write-Thru Mode and Dot-Dashed Vectors
`ESC` `s`	Write-Thru Mode and Short-Dashed Vectors
`ESC` `t`	Write-Thru Mode and Long-Dashed Vectors
`FS`	Point Plot Mode
`GS`	Graph Mode
`RS`	Incremental Plot Mode
`US`	Alpha Mode

xterm Control
Sequences

E
Standard Bitmaps

A number of bitmaps are included with the standard distribution of the X Window System. These bitmaps can be used for setting window background, pixmaps, and possibly for application icon pixmaps.

E
Standard Bitmaps

A number of bitmaps are included with the standard distribution of the X Window System. These bitmaps can be used for setting window background pixmaps and possibly for application icon pixmaps.

By default, they are located in the *lusr/include/X11/bitmaps* directory. Each bitmap is in standard X11 bitmap format in its own file. The *bitmap* application can be used to view these bitmaps in larger scale and to edit them (though their permissions normally do not allow overwriting).

You can use these bitmaps to set the background of a window in any application that allows it. For example, if you wanted to change the root window background pixmap, you could do so using *xsetroot* as follows:

```
xsetroot -bitmap /usr/include/X11/bitmaps/wide_weave
```

Note that the bitmaps that come in pairs, such as `cntr_ptr` and `cntr_ptrmsk`, are intended for creating cursors. You won't find many uses for these unless you get involved in programming X applications.

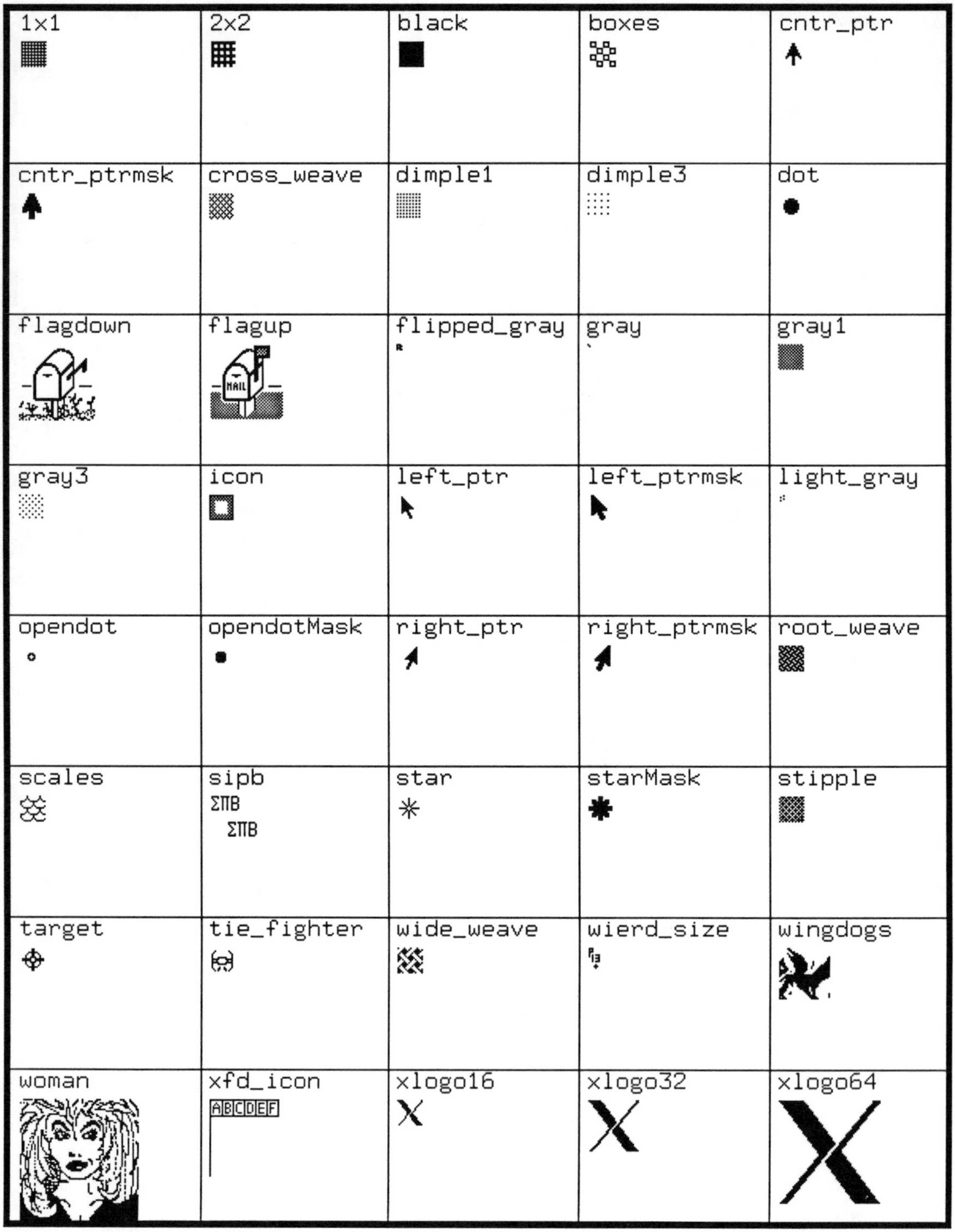
1x1
2x2
black
boxes
cntr_ptr
cntr_ptrmsk
cross_weave
dimple1
dimple3
dot
flagdown
flagup
MAIL
flipped_gray
gray
gray1
gray3
icon
left_ptr
left_ptrmsk
light_gray
opendot
opendotMask
right_ptr
right_ptrmsk
root_weave
scales
sipb
ΣΠΒ
ΣΠΒ
star
starMask
stipple
target
tie_fighter
wide_weave
wierd_size
wingdogs
woman
xfd_icon
ABCDEF
xlogo16
xlogo32
xlogo64

Figure E-1. The Standard Bitmaps

F

The xshowkey Program

This appendix lists the source code for the xshowkey *program described in Chapter 9.*

In This Appendix:

The xshowkey Program

This appendix lists the source code for the *xshowkey* program described in Chapter 9. Type in this program using your favorite editor, save it in the file *xshowkey.c*, and compile it with the command:

```
% cc -o xshowkey xshowkey.c -l X11
```

There are two versions of the program. The first is a very short one, which is not very robust, and doesn't follow some standard X programming conventions. The second, longer version works better, but is much longer. Choose either version depending on your whims.

The Short Version

```c
/*
 * This is a simple program to determine keycode and keysym names
 *
 * Compile and link with:
 *
 *              cc -o xshowkey xshowkey.c -lX11
 */

#include <stdio.h>
#include <X11/Xos.h>
#include <X11/Xlib.h>
#include <X11/Xutil.h>
#define XK_LATIN1
#include <X11/keysymdef.h>

typedef unsigned long Pixel;

char *ProgramName;
Display *display;
int screen;

main (argc, argv)
int argc;
char **argv;
{
    char *geom = NULL;
    char *displayname = NULL;
```

```
XSizeHints hints;
XFontStruct *font_info;
GC gc;
char *string = "Press any key with pointer in this window.";
int i;
Window w;
Pixel fore, back, border;

ProgramName = argv[0];

display = XOpenDisplay (displayname);
if (!display) {
    fprintf (stderr, "%s:  unable to open display '%s'\n",
            ProgramName, XDisplayName (displayname));
    exit (1);
}

load_font (&font_info);

screen = DefaultScreen (display);
fore = WhitePixel (display, screen);
back = BlackPixel (display, screen);
border = WhitePixel (display, screen);

hints.width = 400;
hints.height = 200;
hints.min_height = 10;
hints.min_width = 10;
hints.x = 0;
hints.y = 0;

w = XCreateSimpleWindow (display, RootWindow (display, screen),
        hints.x, hints.y, hints.width, hints.height, 2,
        border, back);

gc = XCreateGC(display, w, 0, NULL);
XSetForeground(display, gc, fore);
XSetBackground(display, gc, back);

XSetStandardProperties (display, w, "Keyboard Tester", NULL,
        (Pixmap) 0, argv, argc, &hints);

XSelectInput (display, w, (KeyPressMask | ExposureMask));
XMapWindow (display, w);

while (1) {
    XEvent event;
    XKeyEvent *kep;
    XButtonEvent *bep;
    XMappingEvent *mep;
    KeySym ks;
    char *ksname;
    char buffer[20];
    int buf_len = 20;
    XComposeStatus *status;

    XNextEvent (display, &event);
```

```
switch (event.type) {
    case KeyPress:
    case KeyRelease:
        kep = (XKeyEvent *) &event;
        XLookupString (kep, buffer, buf_len, &ks, status);
        ksname = XKeysymToString (ks);
        printf ("The key you just pressed is keysym %s, keycode %d (0x%x)\)
                (ksname ? ksname : "?"), kep->keycode, kep->keycode);
        if (ks == XK_q) {
            XCloseDisplay (display);
            exit (0);
        }
        break;
    case Expose:
        XDrawString(display, w, gc, 4, 15, string, strlen(string));
        break;
    default:
        printf ("Unhandled event type %d\n", event.type);
        break;

    }
    }
}

load_font(font_info)
XFontStruct **font_info;
{
    char *fontname = "9x15";

    /* Access font */
    if ((*font_info = XLoadQueryFont(display,fontname)) == NULL)
    {
        (void) fprintf( stderr, "Basic: Cannot open 9x15 font\n");
        exit( -1 );
    }
}
```

The Longer Version

```
/*
 * This is a simple program to determine keysym names and keycodes
 * It has two command-line arguments - for display and geometry.
 * It displays completely in a window.
 *
 * Compile and link with:
 *
 *                cc -o xshowkey xshowkey.c -lX
 */

#include <stdio.h>
#include <X11/Xos.h>
#include <X11/Xlib.h>
#include <X11/Xutil.h>
```

```
#define XK_LATIN1
#include <X11/keysymdef.h>

typedef unsigned long Pixel;

char *ProgramName;
Display *display;
int screen;

usage ()
{
    fprintf (stderr,
            "usage:  %s [-display host:server.screen] [-geometry geom]\n",
            ProgramName);
    exit (1);
}

main (argc, argv)
int argc;
char **argv;
{
    char *displayname = NULL;
    char *geom = NULL;
    int i;
    XSizeHints hints;
    XFontStruct *font_info;
    GC gc;
    char *string = "Press any key with pointer in this window.  \
            Press q to quit.";
    char *string2 = "The key you just pressed is:";
    char string3[40], string4[40];
    Window w, subw, subw2;
    Pixel fore, back, border;

    ProgramName = argv[0];
    for (i = 1; i < argc; i++) {
        char *arg = argv[i];

        if (arg[0] == '-') {
            switch (arg[1]) {
                case 'd':                   /* -display host:server.screen */
                    if (++i >= argc) usage ();
                    displayname = argv[i];
                    continue;
                case 'g':                   /* -geometry geom */
                    if (++i >= argc) usage ();
                    geom = argv[i];
                    continue;
                default:
                    usage ();
                    /* doesn't return */
            }
        } else
            usage ();
    }

    display = XOpenDisplay (displayname);
```

```
if (!display) {
    fprintf (stderr, "%s:  unable to open display '%s'\n",
             ProgramName, XDisplayName (displayname));
    exit (1);
}

set_sizehints (&hints, 10, 10, 400, 200, 100, 100, geom);

load_font(&font_info);

screen = DefaultScreen (display);
fore = WhitePixel (display, screen);
back = BlackPixel (display, screen);
border = WhitePixel (display, screen);

w = XCreateSimpleWindow (display, RootWindow (display, screen),
        hints.x, hints.y, hints.width, hints.height, 2,
        border, back);

subw = XCreateSimpleWindow (display, w, 100, 70, 150,
        font_info->max_bounds.ascent +
        font_info->max_bounds.descent + 4, 2, border, back);

subw2 = XCreateSimpleWindow (display, w, 100, 120, 150,
        font_info->max_bounds.ascent +
        font_info->max_bounds.descent + 4, 2, border, back);

gc = XCreateGC(display, w, 0, NULL);
XSetForeground(display, gc, fore);
XSetBackground(display, gc, back);

XSetStandardProperties (display, w, "Keyboard Tester", NULL,
        (Pixmap) 0, argv, argc, &hints);

XSelectInput (display, w, (KeyPressMask | ExposureMask));
XSelectInput (display, subw, ExposureMask);
XSelectInput (display, subw2, ExposureMask);

XMapWindow (display, subw);
XMapWindow (display, subw2);
XMapWindow (display, w);

while (1) {
    XEvent event;
    XKeyEvent *kep;
    XMappingEvent *mep;
    KeySym ks;
    char *ksname;
    char buffer[20];
    int buf_len = 20;
    XComposeStatus status;

    XNextEvent (display, &event);

    switch (event.type) {
        case KeyPress:
        case KeyRelease:
```

```
                kep = (XKeyEvent *) &event;
                XLookupString (kep, buffer, buf_len, &ks, &status);
                ksname = XKeysymToString (ks);
                sprintf(string3, "keysym: %s", (ksname ? ksname : "?"));
                XClearWindow(display, subw);
                XDrawString(display, subw, gc, 4, 15, string3, strlen(string3));
                sprintf(string4, "keycode: %d (0x%x)", kep->keycode, kep->keycod
                XClearWindow(display, subw2);
                XDrawString(display, subw2, gc, 4, 15, string4, strlen(string4))

                if (ks == XK_q) {
                    XCloseDisplay (display);
                    exit (0);
                }
                break;
            case MappingNotify:
                mep = (XMappingEvent *) &event;
                printf ("Someone changed the keyboard mapping: \n\trequest %d,
                        first_keycode %d, count %d\n",
                mep->request, mep->first_keycode, mep->count);
                XRefreshKeyboardMapping (&event);
                break;
            case Expose:
                /* redraw window here */
                if (event.xexpose.window == w) {
                    XDrawString(display, w, gc, 4, 15, string, strlen(string));
                    XDrawString(display, w, gc, 4, 40, string2, strlen(string2))
                }
                else if (event.xexpose.window == subw)
                    XDrawString(display, subw, gc, 4, 15, string3, strlen(string.
                else
                    XDrawString(display, subw2, gc, 4, 15, string3, strlen(strin
                break;
            default:
                printf ("Unhandled event type %d\n", event.type);
                break;
        }
    }
}

set_sizehints(hintp, min_width, min_height, defwidth, defheight,
        defx, defy, geom)
XSizeHints *hintp;
int min_width, min_height, defwidth, defheight, defx, defy;
char *geom;
{
    int geom_result;

    /* set the size hints, algorithm from xbiff */

    hintp->width = hintp->min_width = min_width;
    hintp->height = hintp->min_height = min_height;
    hintp->flags = PMinSize;
    hintp->x = hintp->y = 0;
    geom_result = NoValue;
    if (geom != NULL) {
```

```
        geom_result = XParseGeometry (geom, &hintp->x, &hintp->y,
                &hintp->width, &hintp->height);
        if ((geom_result & WidthValue) && (geom_result & HeightValue)) {
#define max(a,b) ((a) > (b) ? (a) : (b))
            hintp->width = max (hintp->width, hintp->min_width);
            hintp->height = max (hintp->height, hintp->min_height);
            hintp->flags |= USSize;
        }
        if ((geom_result & XValue) && (geom_result & YValue)) {
            hintp->flags += USPosition;
        }
    }
    if (!(hintp->flags & USSize)) {
        hintp->width = defwidth;
        hintp->height = defheight;
        hintp->flags |= PSize;
    }
    if (!(hintp->flags & USPosition)) {
        hintp->x = defx;
        hintp->y = defy;
        hintp->flags |= PPosition;
    }

    if (geom_result & XNegative) {
        hintp->x = DisplayWidth (display, DefaultScreen (display)) +
                hintp->x - hintp->width;
    }
    if (geom_result & YNegative) {
        hintp->y = DisplayHeight (display, DefaultScreen (display)) +
                hintp->y - hintp->height;
    }
    return;
}


load_font(font_info)
XFontStruct **font_info;
{
    char *fontname = "9x15";

    /* Access font */
    if ((*font_info = XLoadQueryFont(display,fontname)) == NULL) {
        (void) fprintf( stderr, "Basic: Cannot open 9x15 font\n");
        exit( -1 );
    }
}
```

G
Glossary

X uses many common terms in unique ways. A good example is "children." While most, if not all, of these terms are defined where they are first used in this book, you will undoubtedly find it easier to refresh your memory by looking for them here.

G
Glossary

access control list X maintains lists of hosts that are allowed access to each server controlling a display. By default, only the local host may use the display, plus any hosts specified in the *access control list* for that display. This access control list can be changed by clients on the local host. Some server implementations may implement other authorization mechanisms in addition or instead of this one. The list can currently be found in */etc/X#.hosts* where # is the number of the display. The access control list is also known as the host access list.

active window The window where the input is directed. To select a window as the active window, you must put the pointer in that window. The active window is sometimes called the *focus* window.

ASCII American Standard Code for Information Interchange. This standard for data transmission assigns individual 7-bit codes to represent each of a specific set of 128 numerals, letters, and control characters.

background Windows may have a *background*, consisting of either a solid color or a tile pattern. If a window has a background, it will be repainted automatically by the server whenever there is an Expose event on the window. If a window does not have a background, it will be transparent. See also **foreground**.

background color The color that determines the backdrop of a display, for example, on monochrome displays, the background color is gray.

background window A shaded area (also called the *root window*) that appears behind or to the side of the other windows.

binding An association between a function and a key and/or pointer button. *uwm* allows you to bind its functions to any key(s) on the keyboard, or to a combination of keys and pointer button (e.g., the control key and the middle button on a 3-button mouse.)

bitmap A grid of pixels or picture elements, each of which is white, black, or, in the case of color displays, some color. The *bitmap* client allows you to edit bitmaps, which you can use as pointers, icons, and background windows.

border	A window can have a border that is zero or more pixels wide. If a window has a border, the border can have a solid color or a tile pattern, and it will be repainted automatically by the server whenever its color or pattern is changed or an Expose event occurs on the windows.
clicking the mouse buttons	
	A click is defined as pressing the mouse button down. Multiple clicking is determined by the time from button up to button down. This allows you, for example, to change a selection of text in the middle of a selection.
client	A program that performs task such as terminal emulation or window management. Clients need not run on the same system as the display server program.
colorcell	An entry in a colormap is known as a *colorcell*. An entry contains three values specifying red, green and blue intensities. These values are always 16-bit unsigned numbers, with zero being minimum intensity. The values are truncated or scaled by the server to match the display hardware. See also **Colormap**.
colormap	A *colormap* consists of a set of colorcells. A pixel value indexes into the colormap to produce intensities of Red, Green, and Blue to be displayed. Depending on hardware limitations, one or more colormaps may be installed at one time, such that windows associated with those maps display with true colors. Regardless of the number of installable colormaps, any number of virtual colormaps can be created. When needed, a virtual colormap can be installed and the existing installed colormap might have to be deinstalled. The colormap on most systems is a limited resource that should be conserved by allocating read-only colorcells whenever possible, and selecting RGB values from the predefined color database. Read-only cells may be shared between clients.
console xterm window	
	A special type of *xterm* window that the X display server provides. This window is the first window to appear on your display. Exiting the console window kills the X server program and any associated applications.
containment	A window *contains* the pointer if the window is viewable and the hotspot of the cursor is within a visible region of the window or a visible region of one of its inferiors. The border of the window is included as part of the window for containment. The pointer is in a window if the window contains the pointer but no inferior contains the pointer.
default	A function-dependent value assigned when you do not specify a value e.g., the *xterm* option **-rv** reverses the foreground and background colors on the *xterm* window. If you do not specify this option, the default is normal.

depth	The *depth* of a window or pixmap is the number of bits per pixel.
device-dependent	Aspects of a system that vary depending on the hardware. For example, the number of colors available on the screen (or whether color is available at all) is a device-dependent feature of X.
display	A set of one or more screens driven by a single X server. The DISPLAY environment variable tells programs which servers to connect to, unless it is overridden by the *display* command line option. The default is always screen 0 of server 0 as the local mode.
event	Something that must happen before a task or process can occur.
focus window	The window to which keyboard input is directed. By default, the keyboard focus belongs to the root, which has the effect of sending input to whichever window is pointed to by the mouse. However, some clients may take the focus, which means that they may send input to a particular window regardless of the position of the pointer.
exposure	Window *exposure* occurs when a window is first mapped, or when another window that obscures it is unmapped, resized, or moved. Servers do not guarantee to preserve the contents of windows when windows are obscured or reconfigured. Expose events are sent to clients to inform them when contents of regions of windows have been lost and need to be regenerated.
font	A style and size of print for text output. Available fonts are listed in Appendix C.
font directory	By default, X11 fonts are stored in the directory */usr/lib/X11/fonts*. Some applications allow you to specify an alternate font directory on the command line.
foreground	The pixel value that will actually be used for drawing pictures or text is referred to as the *foreground*. The foreground is specified as a member of a graphics context.
foreground Color	The color in which the text in windows and menus, or graphics output are displayed.
geometry	The specification for the size and placement of a window. A window geometry specification has the form: $=width \times height \pm xoff \pm yoff$.
hexadecimal	A base-16 arithmetic system, which uses the digits A through F to represent the base-10 numbers 10 through 15. Hexadecimal notation (called hex for short) is frequently used with computers because a single hex digit can represent four binary digits (bits). The table below shows the equivalence between hex digits and binary numbers.

Hex	Binary	Hex	Binary	Hex	Binary	Hex	Binary
0	0000	4	0100	8	1000	C	1100
1	0001	5	0101	9	1001	D	1101
2	0010	6	0110	A	1010	E	1110
3	0011	7	0111	B	1011	F	1111

X clients accept a special hexadecimal notation (prefixed by a # character) in all command-line options relating to color. See Chapter 6 for more information.

highlighter The horizontal band of color that moves with the pointer within a menu.

hotspot The reference point of a pointer that corresponds to its specified position on the display. In the case of an arrow, an appropriate hotspot is its tip. In the case of a cross, an appropriate hotspot might be its center.

icon A small symbol that represents a window but uses little space on the display. Converting windows to icons allows you to keep your display uncluttered.

input device For a window-based system, a keyboard and the mouse are the most common input devices with which you send input to your system.

keyboard focus See **Focus Window**.

menu A list of commands or functions arranged in a small window which can be selected with the pointer.

modifier keys Keys on the keyboard such as **Control**, **Alt**, and **Shift**. X supports a set of "logical" modifier keys that can be mapped to physical keys. The most frequently used of these logical keys is called the "meta" key.

mouse An input device that, when moved across a flat surface, moves the pointer correspondingly across the display. The mouse usually has buttons that can be pressed to send signals that in turn accomplish certain functions.

occluding In a windowing system, windows may be stacked on top of each other much like a deck of cards. The window that overlays another window is said to occlude that window. A window need not completely conceal another window to be occluding it.

padding Bytes inserted to maintain alignment within the boundaries of windows and menus.

parameter A value required before a client can perform a function.

pixel The smallest element of a display surface that can be addressed.

pointer	A symbol on your display that tracks mouse movement on your desk. Pointers allow you to make selections in menus, size and position windows and icons, and select the window where you want to send the input. Some typical pointers you will encounter with the X are the target circle and the cross. Windows may have associated *properties*, each consisting of a name, a type, a data format, and some data. The protocol places no interpretation on properties; they are intended as a general-purpose data storage and intercommunication mechanism for clients. There is, however, a list of predefined properties and property types so that clients might share information such as resize hints, program names, and icon formats with a window manager via properties. In order to avoid passing arbitrary-length property-name strings, each property name is associated with a corresponding integer value known as an atom.
reverse video	The object appears in the color opposite its pre-selection color.
RGB	An additive method for defining color in which tenths of percentages of the primaries red, green, and blue are combined to form other colors.
root window	A shaded area (also called the *background window*) that appears behind or to the side of the other windows.
screen	A server may provide several independent *screens*, which may or may not have physically independent monitors. For instance, it is possible to treat a color monitor as if it were two screens, one color and the other black and white. There is only a single keyboard and pointer shared among the screens. A Screen structure contains the information about that screen and is a member of the Display structure.
scrollbar	A bar on the side of an *xterm* window that allows you to use the pointer to scroll up and down through the text saved in the window. The number of lines saved is usually greater than the number of lines displayed, and can be controlled by the **scrollBar** startup variable.
select	A process in which you move the pointer to the desired menu item or window and click or hold down a mouse button. Some action follows, e.g., the pointer might change from one shape to another or a function might be performed.
selection	*Selections* are a means of communication between clients using properties and events. From the user's perspective, a selection is an item of data which can be highlighted in one instance of an application and pasted into another instance of the same or a different application. The client that highlights the data is the owner, and the client into which the data is pasted is the requestor. Properties are used to store the selection data and the type of the data, while events are used to synchronize the transaction and to allow the requestor to indicate

the type it prefers for the data and to allow the owner to convert the data to the indicated type if possible.

server The combination of graphics display, hardware, and X server software that provides display services for clients. The display server also handles keyboard and mouse inputs.

terminate A signal sent which halts a process. Some programs may ignore this signal. Can be selected from the Xterm Menu.

text cursor The standard underscore or block cursor that appears on the command line or in a text editor running an *xterm* window. To make the distinction clearer, the cursor that tracks the movement of a mouse or other pointing device is referred to as the **pointer**. The pointer may be associated with any number of cursor shapes, and may change shape as it moves from window to window.

tile A pattern that is replicated (as if laying a tile) to form the background of a window or other area. This term is also used to refer to a style of window manager or application that places windows side by side instead of allowing them to overlap.

window A region on your display created by an client. For example, the *xterm* terminal emulator, the *xcalc* calculator, and the *bitmap* graphics editor are all windows. You can manipulate windows on your display using a window manager.

window manager Client that allows you to move, resize, and circulate windows on your display.

Index

Index

host control 245
hotspot (glossary definition) 336

I

icon
  definition of 9
  glossary definition 336
iconifying a window 34, 35
input device (glossary definition)
  336
instance (resource instance) 104

K

kernel console messages 245
key binding 37, 119
keyboard customization 131
keys
  modifier 131
kill
  xterm window 18

L

lock key 119
log file 245
Lower (WindowOps menu) 33
LowerIconify (WindowOps menu)
  34
lowering a window 33, 34

M

menu
  color menus 125
  glossary definition 336
  slip off 123
  submenu 122
meta key 119
Modes menu (*xterm*)
  description of menu items 46,
    49
modifier key mapping 131
modifier keys (glossary definition)
  336

mouse
  defining mouse button function
    120
  glossary definition 336
Move (WindowOps menu) 29
moving on-screen objects 29, 37

N

naming syntax
  for resources 102
New Window (WindowOps menu)
  27
NewIconify (WindowOps menu)
  34

O

occluded
  definition of 32
  glossary definition 336

P

padding (glossary definition) 336
parameter (glossary definition)
  336
paste (and copy) feature 54, 79,
  124
performance tuning 245
pipes
  and mouse interaction 67
pixel (glossary definition) 336
pointer (glossary definition) 337
pointing device
  defining context of 120
  definition of 9
  possible fonts 251
Postscript translation (*xpr*) 8, 66
Preferences menu 38
  example of 122
property 337

R

Raise (WindowOps menu) 32

V

VT102 (DEC) 7
Modes menu 46

W

widget
    binding (loose vs. tight) 103
    command button 77
    defining conventions 103
    definition of 76
    dialog box 76
    scrollbar 78
    text editing 81
    vertical panel 80
    VPane 80
    widget attributes 103
window
    circulating 34
    definition of 8
    glossary definition 338
    lowering 33, 34
    raising 32, 34
    size customization 27
    stacked 34
window manager
    customization file 8
    glossary definition 338
    restarting 37
    uwm 7, 16, 25
    .uwmrc 8, 26
WindowOps menu 26
    AutoIconify 34
    CircDn 33
    CircUp 33
    example of 121
    Focus 36
    Freeze 37
    Lower 33
    LowerIconify 34
    Move 29
    New Window 27
    NewIconify 34
    Raise 32
    Redraw 29
    RefreshScreen 28
    Resize 30
    Restart 37

windows
    circulating 33
    manipulating 25
    stacked 32

X

X 149 - 154
X Display Server 6
Xserver 155 - 158
xbiff 62, 172 - 173
xcalc 8, 60, 174 - 178
xclock 8, 20, 59, 179 - 182
    killing 59
.Xdefaults 8, 39, 43, 87
    sample *.XDefaults* file. 107
    vs. *xrdb* 101
xdpr 67, 183
xedit 81, 119, 184 - 186
XENVIRONMENT (shell environ-
    ment variable) 110
xfd 8, 64, 187 - 189
xhost 190 - 191, 245
xinit 14, 192 - 193
xload 63, 194 - 196
xlogo 197 - 198
xlsfonts 64, 199
xmodmap (modifier key customi-
    zation) 131, 200 - 203
xpr 8, 66, 204 - 206
xprop 207 - 211
xrdb 8, 87, 212 - 214
    using 109
    X resource database manager
    101
xrefresh 215 - 216
xset 8, 122, 217 - 219
xset (set display preferences) 135
xsetroot (set root window charac-
    teristics) 139, 220 - 221
xstart 14
xterm 7, 14, 27, 43, 222 - 231
    console *xterm* window 15
    default size 38
    killing 18
    multiple *xterms* 17, 27
    scrollbar 51
    temporary window 56
    terminal emulations 7
    terminating 18
    xterm and *termcap* 242

About the Authors

Tim O'Reilly is president of O'Reilly & Associates, Inc. Tim founded the company in 1978 to provide technical writing and consulting services. The company now has over 20 full-time employees providing a full range of services, including project management, writing, editing, graphics, and typesetting to clients in Massachusetts, New York, the Midwest and California. Clients include computer and software developers, as well as large corporate computer users such as banks and brokerage houses.

In 1985, O'Reilly & Associates launched a publishing division, which produces the bestselling series of Nutshell Handbooks on UNIX and the X Window System Series.

Tim is the author of many books and articles about UNIX and other computer topics.

Valerie Quercia is a technical writer at O'Reilly & Associates. She has written user guides for financial application packages and for networking software. Val has also written sales catalogs, customized UNIX documentation, and helped develop several Nutshell Handbooks.

Linda Lamb is a senior technical writer at O'Reilly & Associates. She has written user manuals for computer applications in various industries: automated stock exchanges, hospital intensive care units, sawmill management, alarm services. For O'Reilly & Associates, Linda wrote the Nutshell Handbook *Learning the vi Editor*, and designed marketing material and newsletters.